THE RESURRECTION AND THE ICON

THE RESURRECTION
AND
THE ICON

by
Michel Quenot

Translated from the French by
MICHAEL BRECK

ST VLADIMIR'S SEMINARY PRESS
CRESTWOOD, NY 10707
1997

Library of Congress Cataloging-in-Publication Data

Quenot, Michel, 1941
   [Résurrection et l'icône. English]
   the Resurrection and the icon / by Michel Quenot; translated from the
French by Michael Breck.
     p. cm.
   Includes bibliographical references and index.
   ISBN 0-88141-149-3
   1. Icons.   2. Jesus Christ—Resurrection.   3. Orthodox Eastern Church—
Doctrines.   4. Fasts and feasts—Orthodox Eastern Church.   I. Title.
   BX378.5.Q4713   1997
246'.53—dc21   97–5312
                                                                                    CIP

Translation © Copyright 1997
by

ST VLADIMIR'S SEMINARY PRESS
575 Scarsdale Rd., Crestwood, NY 10707
1-800-204-2665

ISBN 0-88141-149-3

PRINTED IN THE UNITED STATES OF AMERICA

The mystery of the Incarnation of the Word bears the power of all the hidden meanings and figures of Scripture as well as the knowledge of visible and intelligible creatures. The one who knows the mystery of the cross and the tomb knows the principles of these creatures. And the one who has been initiated into the ineffable power of the Resurrection knows the purpose for which God originally made all things.
(Maximus the Confessor, *Chapters on Knowledge*, I, 66; G. Berthold, trans., Paulist Press, N.Y., 1985, p. 139)

Cover: Descent into Hell, contemporary icon painted in Russia.

TABLE OF CONTENTS

Preface

"Man moves in images," wrote St Augustine. True indeed, but which man? And what image? It is these two fundamental questions which Michel Quenot raises through a three-faceted interior pilgrimage which is none other than a rereading of salvation history. It is first a pilgrimage through the fallen time and space of history in which emerge, by way of intuitions and prefigurations, both the notion of resurrection and the preparation for the incarnation of the Word of God. It is then a pilgrimage through an already transfigured space and time in the year of grace of the Lord, when the Church feasts not only commemorate the great moments of Christ's life, but make them present, fulfilling the mystery in an eternal present which achieves its fullness at Pascha, the Feast of feasts, the triumph of the Resurrection of the God-man and of every man in this world. Finally, it is a pilgrimage through the icon, the art *par excellence* of the Orthodox Church, which represents less than it renders present the mystery of the salvation effected by Christ and celebrated in these feasts.

At a time when the icon is losing its uniqueness due to a proliferation of images, when it is becoming more and more a piece of artwork for trade, it is imperative that its sacred and ecclesial dimensions be reaffirmed. By connecting it to the Resurrection, Michel Quenot reminds us that the icon is above all an element of faith, the fruit of a vision of God, of man and of the world. This is not a faith borne out of an impersonal meditation or a rational process but the revelation of God to man as the apostles and the saints received it, lived it and transmitted it, as the undivided Church calls us still to this day to live it as well. According to the Orthodox tradition, the icon is both theological and liturgical. It is theological because it is the expression, in colors and forms, of the divine revelation which culminates in the Truth of the resurrection. It is liturgical because it is the manifestation of this Truth here and now, an invitation to participate in it through prayer and repentance, both personally and communally. The point of an icon is not to be shown but to show, to serve as an open passageway toward God. This transparent quality presupposes certain dogmatic as well as formal conditions, a purifying ascesis and a humility without which the icon may become an obstacle to grace, may obscure one's vision thereby causing a false "mode of existence."

In an age of lukewarm consensus and endless relativism, such an insistence on the organic unity between faith, dogma, images and the world may very well seem "outdated." Michel Quenot does not bow to the current western mindset concerning death, the disenchanted state which has been brought about by a lapsarian culture that has turned (a disfigured) man, the (destroyed) cosmos and (shattered) images into "anti-icons." His resistance is truly revolutionary insofar as it stems from the only novelty of any consequence: the Incarnation-Resurrection of the Son of God through which we are brought henceforth into the "other time" of the Kingdom to come. The icon cannot be considered separately from the resurrection and remains both a potential means of access to and the indication of its reality. Christianity, claims Michel Quenot, is not a moral structure but a hope. It is a witness to the fact that "Christ, by his death, has conquered death," and that all are now able to participate in his eternal Life. This is possible to the extent that one is willing to welcome the Word of God into the very depths of one's being, to open one's heart to that which the eyes of flesh can no longer see and to fulfill one's true nature as created in the image of God. The Church Fathers teach us that man is called to become a mediator for all that became separated through sin and which Christ reunited in his person: the heart and the mind, the soul and the body, matter and spirit, heaven and earth. As an image of the Image of God, who is Christ, the icon is the manifestation of this unity. It is a place for awakening, for *metanoia,* for resurrection.

Such is the tremendous hope that is conveyed in this book. Bringing to mind the alpha and the omega of the icon—the Incarnation and Resurrection of Christ—also implies questioning the basis and end of all other images by which we are bombarded day and night as well as the way in which we live with them. At the heart of the frantic consumption of images that characterizes this age lies a profound lack of satisfaction, a nostalgic quest for a different, mysterious and whole image, a source of fulness and peace. The icon is the archetype of every image, just as Christ is that of every man; not only does it reveal the infection of images from which we are suffering, but it is its cure. As Christ raises man after the fall, so the icon frees him from the images to which he is bound; it purifies images of their deadly influence by rebaptizing them. It is another resurrection.

Connecting the resurrection to the icon is ultimately to evoke the profoundly mystical dimension of Christianity, together with its Eastern sources where action and contemplation are one. One must see to believe, yet it is true faith that enables one to see "God as He is," as Michel Quenot suggests. To see means to receive Christ in his Light. To believe is to know God, in the understanding that there is true knowledge only in His love. "And this is eternal life, that they know thee," says Jesus (Jn 17:3).

Maxime Egger
Geneva, Switzerland

1. The Visible and Invisible Church; 16th c. fresco, Church of the Resurrection;
Sucevitza Monastery, Moldavia, Romania.

Introduction

Christ is Risen!

Is He truly risen? If so, His is the premise for our own resurrection and concerns all of us, believers and non-believers alike, rich and poor, healthy and sick, every race and nation. Simply to ask the question, however tentative it may be, is to open the door to one's heart in an attempt to catch a glimpse of the luminous gaze of the Risen One. In any event, it enables us to avoid the reproach of the great spiritual master, Isaac the Syrian (seventh century), for whom "all sins are but dust before God; the only real sin is to be insensitive to the Risen One" (*Sayings,* 118).

At a time when faith in reincarnation is at its peak, when a substantial number of individuals of Christian origin are seeking their identity, and a growing element of society rejects the Resurrection, the finality of human existence cannot be disregarded. At a time when mankind is rejecting and disguising death, attempting by any means to push back the inevitable, the affirmation of Christ's Resurrection and of the resurrection of the dead, meaning our resurrection in the world to come, deserves the greatest attention.

So many among the baptized are now moving away from Christianity, unknowingly uprooting themselves, cutting off an essential part of their heritage. Certain rejections are understandable, as they are the result of psychological barriers which we cannot discuss here. But what does it mean to "be Christian," what is the cornerstone of this Christianity that is all too often perceived only as a caricature? The question itself is sufficient to reveal a deep misunderstanding. For the mere witness to the Resurrection, which stands at the very heart of the mystery of the Christian faith, never ceases to surprise us.

As the epicenter of Christianity, the Resurrection is of unparalleled importance within the Orthodox Church, where all liturgical life culminates in the paschal celebration, the Feast of feasts, the celebration beyond all celebrations, for "now all is filled with light: heaven, earth and the lower regions" (Paschal Matins, Ode 3). The icon of the Resurrection naturally represents the point where all things converge; it is the center from which radiate, and around which revolve, the Great Feasts and their own sacred images.

In an age where all things are becoming visual, it seems possible to rediscover—if not simply discover for the first time—the mystery of the Resurrection through the icon, which appeals to the senses and to the heart before it addresses reason. The mystery of mysteries can be perceived only through the heart, a pure heart to be sure, one that complements a pure vision. The light escapes those who live in the darkness of pride. He who hungers for God has already encountered Him, without even knowing it, for God is near to every man.

As a necessary preliminary to this study, we will attempt to show the subtle ties that exist between language and image, placing particular emphasis on the essential place of the image within the spiritual life. The Resurrection of Christ, the foundation of human destiny, is prefigured from the dawn of time in the great pagan myths, prior to and in parallel with its foreshadowing in the Old Testament. Before considering its proclamation in the New Testament, we will indicate the cosmic context in which it is inscribed, how evil is inextricably linked to the death which Christ came to conquer. We offer no proofs or "scientific" analyses. Science remains silent in the face of mystery. Before undertaking a detailed study of the icons of the Resurrection, as well as of the Festal icons in which it is reflected and through which its meaning is conveyed, some word about the essence of the icon seems necessary. There is a great deal of confusion in this area, due to ignorance as well as to more or less conscious distortion, because it concerns visualization of the faith. As the reflection and presence of the mystery of new creation brought about in Christ on the morning of Pascha, every icon directs one's gaze toward the essence of Christianity: toward Incarnation, Resurrection and Transfiguration in the Spirit. At the close of our analysis, we will specify how the "raised" person, ontologically recreated, moves in a new time and space, awaiting the final transfiguration of all of creation. Once resurrected, the human creature finally achieves the ultimate vocation of "becoming god."

A saying of the Fathers of the Egyptian desert recounts the story of Abba Agathon (fifth century), a pupil of the eminent Abba Poemen. Agathon was once visited by some monks who "came to find him, having heard tell of his great discernment. Wanting to see if he would lose his temper they said to him 'Aren't you that Agathon who is said to be a fornicator and a proud man?' 'Yes, it is very true,' he answered. They continued, 'Aren't you that Agathon who is always talking nonsense?' 'I am.' Again they said 'Aren't you Agathon the heretic?' But at that he replied, 'I am not a heretic!' So they asked him, 'Tell us why you accepted everything we cast at you, but repudiated this last insult.' He replied 'The first accusations I take to myself, for that is good for my soul. But heresy is separation from God. Now I have no wish to be separated from God'" (*Sayings of the Desert Fathers,* Benedicta Ward, SLG, trans., London; Mowbrays, 1975; p. 18).

When the faith is at stake, one must speak out and no longer remain silent. This said, however, how can we speak of the Resurrection without feeling the painful thorn of our own weakness, our own confusion and contradictions? Like the Publican, we make our own the prayer recited before communion at the Liturgy of St John Chrysostom: "I believe, O Lord, and I confess that Thou art truly the Christ, the Son of the living God, who camest into the world to save sinners of whom I am first."

Although an icon in the strict sense is a painting on wood, produced according to a clearly defined technique, we will also illustrate our study with frescoes borrowed from Orthodox churches. These murals are governed by the same canons as all iconography and were developed in deep harmony with the Church's liturgical life.

The joy of Pascha in the Eastern Church cannot be recounted, it must be lived. Over several days, paschal greetings, in the street and on private letter-heads, together with gifts of eggs marked with the sign of the victorious Christ and Hymns of the Resurrection, all contribute to quicken faith in the most remarkable event in history. It is this event that we seek to convey here through the *liturgical image* which is the icon.

1

On Words, Images and Meaning

Reinventing Language

For every noun there is a corresponding image or symbol. To each of the words "apple," "pastry," "lion," "war," "famine," there corresponds one or even several visual elements. Conversely, the sight of a town burned and bloodied by a slew of armed men evokes the word "war." Thus, a two way relation exists between the word and the image, between conceptualization and visualization. Within this dialectic one must avoid underestimating the one in favor of the other, even though the image possesses unimaginable power.

The use of a language with which Christians are traditionally familiar makes it possible to measure the extent of this dialectic in the contemporary world. What images do the words "hell," "paradise" and "Christmas" evoke for us? And what about the terms "Christ," "Virgin Mary" and "saints?" Let's assume that a profound dialectic exists between the word and the image, one that often goes unrecognized insofar as it is played out almost entirely on a subconscious level. Language is distorted when the corresponding image has lost its authenticity. The brilliant caricature of hell which, for example, Dante proposes in his *Divine Comedy,* contributes to this confusion. The same is true of Jerome Bosch in his famous work *The Garden of Delights,* where he gives free reign to his imagination and esoteric knowledge. We must not forget that certain theological writings of the period contributed to this view of things; hence the connection between such a conception and its artistic byproduct. Just like the image, although at a different level, language shapes and transforms reality. We cannot remain indifferent, then, when language becomes impoverished.

In asserting the necessity to reinvent language, we must consider all the determining factors which impose themselves upon it, all the pitfalls of the past which distort the meaning of particular words. The sacred texts refer to the Virgin Mary as the "All Pure One." What does "purity" mean? Though it is clear in the case of air or water, it is much less so when applied to a person. Conversely, the prostitute in the book of Revelation is the epitome of impurity. For prostitution entails a disintegration of the person, a loss of "integrity," which is the most precious quality of every human being. In the Church, the "All Pure One" is she who embodies this integrity to the highest degree.

Or what do we mean by the word "beauty"? Is it not beauty that permits and sustains the emergence of being? And goodness? Is it not love, of which God is the source: He who, in Christ, emptied Himself of His power and of His majesty in the Incarnation, in order to become in every way like man, whom He wants not only to raise up, but to deify? "Greater love has no man than this, that a man lay down his life for his friends." (Jn 15:13)

And what of the expressions "well-being," "joy" or "freedom"? We live in strange times in which a word can have two entirely different meanings depending on the speaker. Never before has freedom been so widely spoken of while being so misunderstood. Freedom is not debauchery. It implies responsibility, self-control, integrity and authenticity. Only a person freed from the passions and from evil is truly "free."

To speak of Christ implies, above all, to give an accurate depiction of Him, in conformity with the faith of the Church so succinctly expressed in the Nicene-Constantinopolitan Symbol of Faith (our "Creed"). The very same objections raised by the Arians, the Monophysites and the Nestorians have continually resurfaced over the centuries, even up to the present day. For such is the desire of the human mind to dissect, see, touch, and smell, however incapable it may be of accepting the mystery of an infinite God who reveals Himself to us within our very flesh through the Incarnation. Hence we find the recurring temptation to deny the divinity of Christ, to see in Him only a creature chosen by God to save the world: a view often conveyed by a religious art form in which only the human aspect is depicted.

How can we possibly know God without drawing near to Him, or rather, without undergoing the deification to which we are invited by the icon? For the icon is a constant reminder of the Incarnation of the Son of God, He who "became man that we might become god" (according to the formula of the Church Fathers, Irenaeus of Lyon [†202] and Athanasius of Alexandria [†373]). To speak this way amounts to recognition of the "apophatic" approach, which refuses to define God, but limits itself to a delineation of what He is not. Such an approach is only proper, in that it fully respects the divine mystery. There is, certainly, a continual risk of making out of God what He is not, to caricature Him, to create idols; hence the limitations of language and the importance of symbols. A god that alienates, fetters, belittles and suffocates us is a false god that we must rid ourselves of immediately, because he engenders death, anguish and suffering. In the icon of the Resurrection, God descends into the heart of darkness and abandonment to seek us out after having given up His own life for us. Such is the "boundless love" of God that Nicholas Cabasilas evoked back in the fourteenth century (*The Life in Christ,* C.J. deCatanzaro, trans., Crestwood, N.Y., SVS Press, 1974).

The Implications of Images

In his work *Images and Symbols,* Mircea Eliade writes: "The symbol, the myth and the image belong to the essence of the spiritual life...One may conceal them, maim them, debase them, but...they will not be done away with." And he emphasizes the extent to which symbolic thought proves to be "consubstantial with the human being: it precedes language and discursive reasoning. The symbol reveals certain aspects of reality—the deepest aspects—which defy any other means of knowledge" (Harvill Press, New York, 1961, p. 12). To admit that the symbol is a central element of a human culture in which visual precedes verbal communication implies that a visual symbol tends to take precedence over a verbal one. Thus, the image may prove to be more powerful than ideas and words when it conveys one or more symbols that provide a strong correlation between perception and meaning. Because our life is founded on images, that which comes forth from us and is expressed in some concrete form can play a cathartic role; it can lead to a partial release of our internal demons. That which enters us through our sight, on the other hand, penetrates to the uttermost depths of our being and directly influences our spiritual life.

Art is able to take over for words when words fail before the inexpressible. The language of ideas then gives way to that of images, which have a direct hold on the subconscious. The growing importance of images within the Church ever since the fifth century gave rise in the seventh century to a crisis of unprecedented violence. The implications of images were being emphatically brought to light. Consider, as well, the illuminations of the Middle Ages, the romanic frescos and sculptures, which served as open books for the so-called "illiterates" of the period who, unlike us, naturally deciphered this language because they had mastered its grammar.

If words and texts, as drawn from our thought, are addressed first and foremost to our intelligence, the image speaks to the senses, touching the heart above all. Although a text can also touch the heart, even quite powerfully, it must nonetheless pass through our intelligence, by which it is controlled to a certain degree. Conversely, due to its spontaneity, an image eludes the filter of reason when it is first beheld. Its impact varies in proportion to the viewer's cultural level. Thus the image may become the ideal means to condition people of minimal cultural background.

Gorged with images, modern man has created a veritable civilization of images. In large cities, they peer down on passers-by at every street corner, in every storefront and in the subway. The "audiovisual" is all-pervasive. Once accustomed to this constant stimulus, our eyes demand their daily dose. A temporary separation from this kind of sensory overload enables us to realize to what extent our minds are saturated and thereby prevented from enjoying a finer perception of life and the world around us.

Yet there are sounds and sounds, images and images. Everything depends on our ability to listen and on the quality of our visual perception. If their flow draws us out of ourselves and enslaves us, the superficiality is not merely in the images and sounds but also within us.

Who would deny that in less than twenty years television has not only modified a majority of people's way of life, but has even changed their perception of the world? Controlling images amounts to controlling at least a portion of the inner life of those who observe them.

Art can offer a pleasant alternative to this intoxication. But once again, this depends on the vision proposed by the artist, as it does on that of the observer who brings his own subjectivity to bear and "recreates" the work according to his own world-view.

Exposure to modern art rarely leaves us indifferent. Its deliberate attempt to lead us to new ground transforms us. In light of the power of art, the imagery which reflects the mystery of salvation takes on a primordial importance. As a travesty of reality, every distorted and decadent image bears the seeds of atheism. Are many of our contemporaries not atheists, victims of their ignorance of the true God manifested in Christ? There are multitudes of adulterated images of Christ and His mother which do not correspond to the truth of the faith because of their rationalistic coldness, or their sentimentality, their infantile character and sensuality, which are nothing but the direct product of the artist's imagination.

Throughout history, the Church has repeatedly and painfully experienced the true significance of images. The iconoclasts (destroyers of images) of the eighth and ninth centuries waged a fierce battle to suppress within the Church all use of icons of Christ, of the Virgin Mary and of the saints. Without question, the many elements which iconographers borrowed from secular art aggravated the debate. The debate itself, however, made possible a useful and precise reformulation of ideas that resulted, in 843, in the recognition of the legitimacy, and even the necessity of sacred images.

This dispute over images thus goes hand in hand with the fundamental formulations of the faith of the Church. The last of the great Ecumenical Councils was the seventh, held at Nicea in 787. This council sealed the four that preceded it by reaffirming the dual nature of Christ as "fully man and fully God, without mixture or confusion"; by upholding the divinity of the Holy Spirit, the third person of the Holy Trinity, "equal in power and majesty" with the Father and the Son; and by declaring the Virgin Mary to be "Mother of God" for having conceived by the power of the Holy Spirit and having borne Christ in the fullness of His two natures.

With the Reformation, in the beginning of the sixteenth century, the Church of Rome found itself caught up in tumultuous disputes over images. This experience translated into a massive and indiscriminate destruction of statues, images and frescoes in a radical reaction against the intrusion of profane elements in churches and monasteries under the guise of religious art. Is it any wonder that many felt threatened by "pious" scenes in which the artist inflicted his own view of the mysteries of salvation upon the faithful, giving free reign to his imagination in his ignorance of the Tradition of the undivided Church, the fruit of the teaching of the Fathers of the seven great councils?

Such a tangle of images is not easy to unravel because they are perceived differently from one person to the next according to their sensitivity, their religious education, and their artistic taste, as well as many other unrecognized factors. In the golden age of Byzantine art, St John of Damascus advised: "If a pagan comes asking you to explain your faith to him, take him to church and show him the holy icons." This truly reflects his conviction of the close connection between image and faith, even if it signals a certain deterioration in iconography. We are witnesses to several conversions that have followed a discovery of the icon, as it represents the royal door leading to "Orthodoxy" (right faith and worship), and expresses its essence.

How are we to distinguish what is true from what is false? Let us say that authentic sacred art communicates the truths of the faith. A well known catholic monk, Thomas Merton, rightly wrote that

> in a sacred image, the material elements recover a spiritual harmony that had been lost ever since the whole world fell with Adam; in other words, they become the means of transmitting the Holy Spirit, to whom they provide the opportunity to reach the soul by His hidden spiritual power...The work of art must be authentically spiritual, truly traditional and artistically alive...Without these fundamental qualities, the work of religious art remains spiritually dead. Contemplating and loving this type of work of art has a deplorable spiritual effect; it amounts to consuming spoiled food. (*Disputed Questions*)

Merton clearly distinguishes between sacred and religious art. We owe him a debt of gratitude insofar as this area causes the greatest amount of confusion. If the evolution in the representation of the truths of the faith is any indication, a progressive separation between the Church of Rome and the Oriental Church can be observed over the centuries preceding the official split of 1054. For the Byzantines, who ascribe to the image a central role in their spiritual life, the honor given to a particular image—that of Christ, for example—reverts back to the original, to His person. It is necessary, therefore, that sacred art be regulated by means of strict rules. The Roman Catholic Church, however, adheres to the educational and didactic aspect of the image, and does not take into consideration the sacramental character of the icon, venerated on the same level with the cross and the Gospel.

The end of the romanic period witnessed an increasing separation between the two Churches in their attitudes toward sacred images. This occurred in spite of the reprimand expressed in the solemn decree of the council of Trent, promulgated during its final session on December 3, 1563, which expressly recalled the conclusions of Nicea II (787). Yet this hasty decree does not reflect anything that was felt or lived out. It is undeniable that the excessive freedom granted the artist in the presentation of the truths of the faith leads, under the influence of militant humanism, to a progressive desacralization of sacred art.

The nature of a work of art is determined more by the form than by the subject. Thus, even if one's theme is religious, a painting using profane forms cannot be placed in the realm of sacred art, whose forms are derived from a spiritual vision. This art is autonomous and arises out of the artist's imagination as he presents, in his own way, the mystery of salvation.

Authentic sacred art, which always reveals a spiritual dimension, derives rather from the liturgical continuity of the Church and meets three fundamental criteria: the Tradition of the Church, the spiritual purity of the painter, and his or her artistic qualifications.

As the highest form of pictorial sacred art in the Christian tradition, the icon is an image which was developed over the centuries, and which little by little became codified through often turbulent debates. For St Theodore the Studite (759-826), Christ is not depicted "in the likeness of a corruptible man, which is reprehensible...but in the likeness of an incorruptible man...for Christ is not simply a man, but God become man" [*Seven Chapters Against the Iconoclasts,* ch. 1, *Patrologia Graecae* (*PG*) 99, 488C].

The Fathers of the seventh ecumenical council clearly demonstrated that the icon does not present a profane vision with a religious theme, but a spiritual vision. As a liturgical image, it reflects the truths expressed in the sacred texts. In other words, it is not human flesh in its corruptible state that is represented, but incorruptible, transfigured and deified flesh. For this reason the holy Fathers even claimed that the icon and the biblical account are "indications of one another and, without a doubt, explanations of one another" (Seventh Ecumenical Council, sixth session, *Mansi* 13, 269A).

The art of the icon, as the expression of the content of the faith in its purest form, does not belong to the painters. Nor could they possibly invent it, since it is a theological art which can only be claimed by the Church. As such, there is not only a rejection of what is artificial, but sentimentality, pseudo-religious emotion, imitation and false pretense are also absent.

In Russia, the icon was the subject of extensive debates during the sixteenth century. Once again, the foundations were examined and refined. The discussions bore above all on what is licit and illicit in Western influence which, after having weakened the faith, brought about a degradation of sacred art. The introduction into iconography of all that was acquired from the Renaissance, at the expense of canons that were being progressively abandoned, may be likened to a dredging tool that sweeps away everything in its path. This initial loss of doctrinal content in the icon led to a certain theological and spiritual decadence.

In a letter addressed to the Tsar on the occasion of the Great council of Moscow (1551), the iconographer Joseph Vladimirov

> blamed particularly the merchants, and rightly so: it is they who, in their own interest, suggested to buyers that "salvation cannot be gained by good painting."...Vladimirov recognized that miracles are not dependent on the images, just as He [God] "works through unworthy persons" and through the forces of nature. But if He acts this way, it is not because of the unworthiness of the icons but despite it. Thus "when a miracle occurs through one of these unsuitable images, this will not protect us before the just judge" (Quoted by L. Ouspensky, *The Theology of the Icon;* SVS Press, New York, 1992; p. 334).

Nonetheless, in his inability to distinguish between a religious painting and an icon, Vladimirov has the unfortunate tendency to make the aesthetic element a basic criterion. He confuses physical beauty and spiritual beauty, or rather, the corruptible body and the incorruptible body. In this new form of painting,

> the body of man and the world of his emotions do not seem to have the promise of sanctification. Man remains the main subject of the image, but in his current state, untransfigured. This image of man in all his internal meaninglessness becomes lost in the abundance of objects, animals and plants. He becomes simply a fragment of this large and boisterous world and is no longer capable of assuming a dominant role (*Ibid.,* p.343).

While the West is in need of direction, the East must become redirected, since there remains an excess of italianizing images in Orthodox churches that have not yet recovered from the shock of the Renaissance and its spiritual consequences. The main point is not whether a sacred image is ancient or modern but whether or not it expresses truth, which is always harmony. It must represent a revival of the Tradition that is lived out in the here and now of the Church, where the spiritual vision of the Fathers is transmitted and is always rejuvenated in the light of the life-giving Spirit.

Lex orandi, lex credendi (the rule of worship is the rule of faith), affirms a familiar theological formula. It underlines the essential interdependence between prayer and faith. What one believes determines one's attitude toward God, in the same way that attitude influences one's faith. We could even complement this by saying "lex videndi, lex credendi," thus joining St John of Damascus, who invited the pagans that had come to inquire about the faith simply to contemplate the icons.

"Your eye is the lamp of your body; when your eye is sound, your whole body is full of light; but when it is not sound, your body is full of darkness" (Lk 11:34). This is a conditional warning that emphasizes the close connection between the images one perceives and one's inner life. The great spiritual minds never separate sight from purity of heart.

The Search for Meaning

As a lucid observer of his time, the true artist is its conscience and expression. More so than a mirror or an echo reflecting the joys and tribulations of life, he gathers within himself the present and the future.

While the senses represented a fundamental source of knowledge in the Age of Enlightenment as well as for the Positivists of the nineteenth century, the creators of the impressionist movement, such as Monet, Renoire and Cézanne wanted to break through to the reality of things and of being itself, to venture beyond visual perception. This apparent attribution of a sacred quality to visible reality, along with the astounding progress of science, led to a new religion of matter—one then speaks of energies—which tended to ignore any openness toward a transcendent God. It corresponds to nothing other than a sort of pantheism. The fascinating beauty of impressionist painting must not make us forget this. Out of the new, even revolutionary path opened up by the impressionists would come the great currents of our century: expressionism, cubism, dadaism, surrealism, and all the metamorphoses of abstract art.

Modern art conveys the state of the world and, more specifically, of the human person. To shrug one's shoulders and remain aloof from these images amounts to depriving oneself of a privileged means of understanding our times. In its quest for the absolute (and Marc Chagall is a moving example) modern art often cries out humanity's rejection of suffering and death (consider Edward Munch's painting *The Scream*). Faced with many works of art that overwhelm us with wonder, how can we not perceive the anxiety, the risk, the alienation and especially the absurd in the works that reduce man to a composite of anomalous elements? Did Picasso himself, in his unrelenting quest for reality which he explored from a multitude of angles, not delve into all that is forbidden in his utter rejection of mystery? Does the dissolution of form itself, resulting in the hideous monsters of Goya, not reveal a demonic aspect? What becomes of the face in this flood of grimaces, of double-sided and robotic heads? The destruction of the face accompanies that of the person. It points to something infernal, because man is not an object among many. He is neither artificial nor an object of pure determinism, but a creature "in the image and likeness of God" (Gen 1:27).

Early in 1915, Paul Klee wrote in his diary: "The more horrifying the world becomes—as it is now—the more art becomes abstract; a peaceful world produces realistic art."

2. The Virgin of the Sign surrounded by angels and the righteous; fresco, 1535,
Church of the Dormition of the Mother of God, Humor Monastery
Moldavia, Romania.

"The world is overwhelmed, perturbed, unsettled and off course. We are bound in our infernal progress, closed into a vast pandemonium-like circus. And I am a teacher and a thinker of this destruction." Thus the bitter observation of artist Jean Tinguely on the disorder of the present world (In *Cooperation,* Basel, Switzerland, no. 39, 1989), an observation echoed by film director Bunuel: "The world is off-kilter and rotten... there is no way out." And the American writer Henry Miller, traveling through darkness and thirsting for freedom, continues:

> to be human seems like a poor, sorry, miserable affair, limited by the senses, restricted by moralities and codes, defined by platitudes and isms (*Tropic of Cancer,* Grove Press, New York, 1961; p. 256).

> It may be that we are doomed, that there is no hope for us, *any of us,* but if that is so then let us set up a last agonizing, bloodcurdling howl, a screeching cry of defiance, a war whoop! (*Ibid.,* p. 257).

This disillusioned expression, on the other hand, can in no way taint the silent quest of numerous artists who achieve an iconic beauty in their works. As Patriarch Athenagoras (†1972) plainly stated: "the more man's elemental longings are satisfied—and they must be, everywhere and for all—the more the longing for God will grow, overt or hidden, in adoration or in idolatry" (see O. Clément, *Dialogues avec le Patriarche Athénagoras,* Fayard, 1976; p.128).

Noise and the uninterrupted flow of images impede the inner life. Having lost a sense for divine omnipresence and forgotten that the Holy Spirit sustains the universe, man, deprived of his focus and with an abandoned heart, profanes the world that has turned away from its original destiny.

An investigation of the central element of Christian life reveals the magnitude of the crisis among those who are baptized. Few of them refer to the Resurrection, relegating it to the past, to being a mere accessory, although it is the cornerstone of the whole edifice. To forget this fact, or to minimize it, amounts to removing from the Church the Risen One whose beating heart must be perceived by each of the faithful in communion with Him, for He is the root of the vine that feeds every branch.

It is the supreme aspiration of man to become god. The first man, Adam, who gathers within himself all of humanity, had the bitter experience of self-deification. Against the will of God, he ate "the fruit of the tree that is in the middle of the garden" of Eden (Gen 3:2), succumbing to the temptations of the alluring serpent: "the day you eat of it your eyes will be opened and you will be as gods, knowing good and evil" (Gen 3:5). Adam's disobedience led to a loss of integrity, to a state of corruptibility, and ultimately to his death. Once his eyes were opened, he became aware of his infidelity toward his creator, having just tainted the image which he had received freely. Furthermore, he discovered his nakedness and that of his companion, for the loss of purity of heart which followed his error led to a sinful vision. The fall of the first man is thus summed up in an act of self-sufficiency as a preference for creatures over the creator. Self-worship and false gods of every kind supplant the worship of the true God.

Yet the "fall" is the result of this intense desire to become god, a desire that was never abandoned and has become even greater in our day. The Incarnation and Resurrection of the New Adam who is Christ, beckons to us and accomplishes within us that which had seemed impossible to us.

Our existence is played out in time. Yet it is only a lost and fragmented time, endured and lived out without the memory of the unique and unrenewable gift that it represents. How often we encounter the struggle against time, summed up in the familiar saying: "I don't have the time!" This is a situation which often leads us to live outside of ourselves, in an unrestrained race where all that is essential, beyond time, escapes us. Every plan implies time. Therefore time plays a major role for a Christian who, by his progressive union with the transfigured, dead and risen Christ, is in turn responsible for transfiguring space and time—indeed, the whole world.

In a disoriented society, deprived of meaning, a true Christian is the one who, in every instance, perceives the face of Christ present in this world. Strengthened by this presence, and with a peaceful heart, he opens himself to the Holy Spirit, who makes of him a sign of God to other people.

Faith: The Foundation of All Existence

The Chinese sage Confucius (†479 B.C.) wrote in Lun-yu: "A man without faith: I do not know what to make of him. A large chariot without a yoke, a small chariot without a collar, how can one make it move ahead?"

Ta aminu, ta amenu, says a Hebrew proverb: "If you do not believe you will not survive."

Far from being a luxury or something superfluous in human existence, faith is the very foundation of our life. Without it, we perish. The surrounding reality confirms this fact to a large degree, and the current success enjoyed by a multitude of sects supports it. Without faith man confronts interior conflicts unarmed. Given over to the tensions imposed by his social life, he returns defeated.

If God exists, those who squander their time, forgetting their creator, are like a flower that disregards the sun. The light determines its growth and the beauty of its colors.

3. Christ Pantocrator; 18th c. fresco, Church of the
Xeropotamou Monastery, Mount Athos, Greece.

Faith makes us more human. It enables us to delineate ourself, to define ourself and thus, to assume ourself fully. Every deep human encounter implies a reciprocal assessment of faith. Proceeding without it condemns one to superficiality and short-circuits the establishment of a real dialogue as the foundation of every friendship. Words take on different shades of meaning depending on the faith that moves us. Without an in-depth exchange with another person, those words lose their foundation and hence their meaning.

As the ancestor of the chosen people, Abraham "believed in God and it was reckoned to him as righteousness" (Rom 4:3). But true faith presupposes actions, for "if it has not works it is completely dead" (James 2:17). Thereby Abraham proves to be the father of believers, for he does not hesitate to sacrifice his only son, Isaac, at the time of the test imposed by God, who grants him an eternal reward.

The Gospels bear witness to the fact that faith can accomplish all things, even move mountains. Christ clearly states: "I am the Resurrection. Whosoever believes in me, though he were dead, yet shall he live" (Jn 11:25). St Paul's teaching centers on the confession of Christ, dead and risen: such faith grounds his very existence.

In a *Dialogue on Courage,* Plato cites Socrates, who explains the proper meaning of this term. He meticulously avoids any definition, subtly leading his hearers to conceive of courage in terms of knowledge: the courageous man draws his strength from his acquired convictions.

Christian faith is situated well beyond empirical knowledge. Recall the first Christians and the confessors of the Church, ready to bear witness (*martyria* in Greek) to their faith, even unto death. This indicates how much easier it is to doubt than to have faith, for faith requires effort and the involvement of the whole being.

Any reference to Christ's Resurrection implies a mystical approach that defies all rationalism and experimentation. Faith represents the only true attitude toward mystery. And yet, an authentic Christian enjoys a keen awareness of the truth of what he believes, because he experiences it, not in a tangible and measurable way, but as it wells up from the deepest part of his being. How can one speak of the presence of God within oneself without some perception of it? The greater this sense, the greater the feeling of deprivation in the event of a transgression of God's commandments; also greater is the awareness of one's limitations, of one's finality, of the manifold distortions of a nature marked by the "fall." Yet this cannot lead to despair, because a true knowledge of oneself in this case leads to putting all of one's hope in the resurrected Christ, who holds His hand out to us in the icon, beckoning us to become nothing more nor less than gods. Such is our vocation, as unbelievable and absurd as that may seem. Henceforth there is no place for a morose Christianity that spends its time castigating evil and imagines the whole world destined for utter annihilation.

The world, the entire cosmos will be transfigured. Since it has no substance proper to itself, evil will be destroyed. This miracle of a new world must be sought neither in the stars nor in distant space. A Christian often mechanically confesses: "I believe in the resurrection of the dead, and in the life of the world to come..." Christ is risen, this is the premise of the world to come.

Living in Him already opens us to a new dimension of solidarity with one another. For salvation is neither in the past, which is no longer, nor in the future, which is not ours, but in that which is lived out daily, at the heart of humanity, affected by the presence of God who assumed that humanity.

Nicholas Arseniev recounts an event that occurred in Russia, one that is quite characteristic of the faith of the Russian people. During a public conference held in Moscow at the Polytechnic Museum, during the fierce repression of believers, a Bolshevik commissioner in charge of education violently attacked the "out-dated faith" of the people, crying out that it bore the mark of capitalism and was not believable. At the conclusion of his brilliant presentation, the self-satisfied orator invited his hearers to engage in a brief dialogue. No one was to speak for more than five minutes and, of course, only after having identified himself. A young bearded priest from a rural background timidly stepped forward and was greeted by the orator with obvious contempt:

> "Remember, no more than five minutes!"

> "Yes, very well. I'll be brief," the priest replied.

Climbing to the podium, the priest turned toward the audience and declared:

> "Brothers and sisters, Christos voskresse!" ["Christ is risen!"]

They all answered with one voice:

> "Voistinu voskrese!" ["Truly, He is risen!"—This is the familiar greeting exchanged among Orthodox Christians during the Paschal or Easter season.]

> "I'm done," added the priest. "That's all I wanted to say."

The entire Christian faith is summed up in these words.

2

The Resurrection of Christ:
Myth, Reality or Mystery?

Pagan Myths

Anyone who delves deeply and without pre-conceptions into the study of myths begins to wonder if Christianity does not also represent a myth of sorts, a type of syncretism, an assimilation and adaptation of other earlier myths spread throughout the world. Amazing similarities do appear, and certain specialists do not hesitate to denounce the recovery by Christians of various elements that suit their own particular cosmological and anthropological outlook. Before we attempt to shed light on the subject, it would be appropriate to take a closer look at the nature of myth itself.

Derived from the Greek word *mythos,* which means legend, myths have existed since the dawn of time. They express the presence of unfathomable and presumably unlimited forces at the heart of the cosmos. Today, as then—in spite of the extraordinary means of investigation at our disposal in our quest for the infinitely large and the infinitely small—we have knowledge only of an infinitesimal part of the reality of the world in which we live and evolve.

In an attempt to respond to the great problems of existence, myths recount the story of the world's creation, the appearance of life and of man, and the connections between heaven and earth. They speak of love, of life and of death. In the face of a mystery for which there is neither language nor reason, symbols and images allow one to evoke the very essence of things (hence the importance of imagination). This explains the connection of such images with myths. The great myths of the world all revolve around the same themes: lost paradise, perfect humanity, the mystery of woman and of love, etc. So many symbols and images reflect the same desires: the dream of a life beyond time and corruptibility, an existence characterized by beauty, well-being and freedom, in which the human person might enjoy complete harmony.

The life of primitive man was marked by an incessant struggle against the forces of nature, against animals, and all too often against other men. As a result, his battles are recounted in myths, to which are added confrontations with the gods. Let us note as well the dichotomy of heaven and chaos, light and darkness, which sums up the antagonism

4. The Creation of the Heavens; 12th c. mosaic, Monreale Cathedral, Sicily.

of good and evil, knowledge and ignorance, those born of gods and those born of demons. Creation myths commonly stress the double nature of man: he proceeds from earth and from heaven. Furthermore, something divine dwells in him, possibly the heritage of a time in which he knew the gods. With this we are approaching the concept of "divino-humanity" so dear to Christian thought.

The widespread myths concerning the end of the world, or what one might call a stage in humanity, refer particularly to floods, but also to fires, epidemics, landslides and earthquakes. How can we not be struck by the fact that a flood generally corresponds to a punishment which the gods inflict upon man for his transgression? Every destruction leads, theoretically, to a new creation. A fact worth noting is that the Judeo-Christian tradition proposes a single end to the world, in which creation is restored to its original splendor for all eternity.

Together with Greece, and much more so than Palestine, Egypt provided the cultural foundation for Christianity. Here there originated the myth of Osiris, who died and was brought back to life by the breath of Isis before his final descent into the abode of the dead, whom he regenerates and revives. It is as significant as the myths of Orpheus, of Prometheus and especially, of Dionysius, the Greek version of Shiva. We may also note the lesser known ancient Chinese myth which takes place in the province of Yunan. The savior of the Mose tribe, Dto-Mbha Shi Lo, was assailed from his birth by a horde of three hundred and sixty cannibal devils. Dto disappeared into the center of the earth, from which it seemed he would never return. But then, as he reached the intersection of an infinite number of paths, the stalking devils took hold of him and cast him into a cauldron of boiling oil which they covered with an enormous lid. They stoked the fire for three days and three nights, impatiently waiting to devour their victim who, curiously, had not let out the slightest sound. When the fire went out, indicating that all was ready, Dto rose unscathed from the cauldron. Thereby he became the wise guide of all the departed who, from hell, make their way toward heaven. The devils had unwittingly made him incorruptible and immortal.

What should we learn from this? Must we conclude that Christ's "Descent into Hell," the most prized theme in the icons of the Resurrection, is a mere avatar of preexistent myths? Might Christianity itself derive from an earlier myth? Could it then have elaborated its own mythology which is nothing more than a fabrication, a vain attempt to explain the universe? Taken as a whole, myths express a convergence, an initiation precisely where language is lacking. Replete with symbols and images, such myths seem to prepare human thought for the notion of the divine Savior who becomes incarnate, the Word of God, the Second Person of the Holy Trinity, who is made flesh (Jn 1:14).

Whether it be Egyptian burial ceremonies or the Elysian mysteries, the hope of resurrection turns up in the mystery religions derived from the primitive rites based on the cycles of nature. An essential point is that these deities or heroes are totally lacking in substance and have no grounding in history.

The Scriptures bear witness to Christ and usher us out of the realm of myth. The entire Old Testament announces His coming, and the incarnate Christ, dead and resurrected, leaves behind a cloud of witnesses, who, of course, became Christians. How could it have been otherwise, since they were converted by what they themselves beheld?

The Spanish historian Garcilas records that shortly before his compatriots invaded Peru, the king of the Incas began to doubt the divinity of the sun. He had indeed noticed that the latter obeyed certain laws. Who had established these laws if not a greater power? Consequently, he ordered the erection of a completely empty temple which he dedicated to the "unknown God."

"We can say of an Image that it *is awaiting* the fulfilment of its meaning," wrote Mircea Eliade (*op. cit.,* p. 160). Could myth be a crystalized desire, a call that has sprung up from the collective unconscious toward an unknown God whom the prophets of the Old Testament announced, and whose Incarnation and Resurrection explain all that came before and all that comes after?

Chance has no place in the spiritual life. All things are imbued with meaning. From this perspective, myth takes on a still greater importance. In a majority of myths, man is a composite of earth and heaven. He spends his life between these two poles. Created in the *image* and *likeness* of God, he bears within himself the seed of the Logos (the *logos spermatikos* about whom St Justin writes) that quenches his thirst for the absolute, his sense for things beyond, his intuition regarding the end times.

The Old Testament

"In the beginning, God created the heavens and the earth" (Gen 1:1). There is a correlation between these first words of the Bible and the Prologue of the Gospel according to St John: "In the beginning was the Word and the Word was with God and the Word was God" (Jn 1:1).

Whether one is a creationist or an evolutionist is of little consequence. What is essential is to recognize that "all things were made by Him, and without Him was nothing made" (Jn 1:2). The saying is a perfect summary of the role of the Word, the "True Light," (Jn 1:9) who "became flesh and...dwelt among us" (Jn 1:14). The Old and New Testaments beckon and illumine one another. They comprise the whole of a progressive revelation. Therefore it is essential that we avoid any compartmentalization, even if the

Old Testament precedes and naturally announces the New. This conviction is well expressed by the famous frescos of the Saint-Savin church (11th century) in France, that represent Christ, already with a cruciform halo, as creator of the moon and the sun.

To say that "the Word was with God and the Word was God" (Jn 1:1) draws us immediately to the mystery of "Tri-Unity," so beautifully articulated by Gregory Nazianzen (†390):

> "No sooner do I conceive of the One than I am illumined by the splendor of the Three. No sooner do I distinguish them than I am carried back to the One. When I contemplate the Three together, I see but one living flame, and cannot divide or measure out the Undivided Light" (Sermon 40, *On Baptism*, *PG* 36, col. 417B).

Christ as Word of God, together with the Holy Spirit, are "the two hands of the Father," who acts and manifests Himself through them. All three are "equal in power and majesty." We proclaim in the Nicene-Constantinopolitan "Symbol of Faith" that the Spirit "spoke by the prophets." And the Fathers affirm that long before Christ's Incarnation, the many theophanies of the Old Testament referred to Him.

The biblical account of creation is rich with elements borrowed from earlier Sumerian myths. These are nevertheless reinterpreted by the inspired writers in the context of the history of man's relationship to God. "God created man according to His image!" (Gen 1:27). All Judeo-Christian anthropology rests on this assertion. The first man, Adam (from *adamah*: earth. *a*: breath, and *dam*: blood), is shown by his very name to participate equally in matter and in Spirit. In the same way that Christ, the Word of God, *is* the image of the Father (Jn 14:9), Adam, who sums up all of mankind within himself, *is in the image* of Christ. As Tertullian (†after 220) boldly wrote in his *Treatise on the Resurrection of the Dead* (VI):

> Imagine God entirely taken with it (the flesh), entirely dedicated to it, hands, thought, action, reflection, wisdom, providence, and especially with the love that inspired his plan. Because all that was expressed in this earthly mire was conceived with reference to Christ, who at that moment would be man, meaning also earth. For this was the Father's warning to the Son: "Let us make man in our image and likeness. And God made man," that is to say He fashioned him and "made him in the likeness of God" (Gen 1:26), meaning in the image of Christ.

Careful study of the Byzantine mosaics from the basilica of Monreale in Sicily reveals that the faces of the creator Word and of Christ, as well as that of the first man at the time of creation, are identical. This idea of Adam as a sort of replica of Christ appears as well

5. The Creation of Adam and the Animals; 12th c. mosaic, Monreale Cathedral, Sicily.

on the northern gate of the Chartres Cathedral. We can easily guess what the implications of this might be for icons.

It is difficult for us to imagine the state of total integrity enjoyed by the first human couple described in the book of Genesis. The term harmony is perfectly appropriate: harmony with God and with one another, harmony with nature, with the animals and all of creation. By choosing to eat of the only forbidden fruit, man challenged God, preferring the creature to the creator. He ignored the warning: "On the day you eat of it, you shall surely die" (Gen 2:17). The fall of man led to a loss of grace, or to a disintegration that means a loss of harmony, a blindness to God and to all of creation. For the first time, "they knew that they were naked" (Gen 3:7). Indeed, the "disintegrated" man discovers the passions. His heart becomes a battle field between good and evil, his spirit wavers between light and darkness. He knows death and corruptibility, the sources of further suffering. Death, in the Old Testament, implies a voyage "without return to the land of gloom and deep darkness, the land of gloom and chaos, where light is as darkness" (Job 10:21-22). This is because man sees no way out of the slavery of the spiritual death incurred by his disobedience. Yet, a few pious men in this age hope for deliverance: "Thy dead shall live, their bodies shall rise. O dwellers in the dust, awake and sing for joy!" (Isa 26:19). The story of the Maccabean brothers (2 Mac 7 and 14:46), condemned to death by the tyrant Antiochus, bears witness to an expectation of the resurrection in the end times. In fact, this means nothing more than a return to earthly life, where nothing is changed. As a unique instance in human history, the Resurrection of Christ followed upon a voluntary and genuine death that affected His whole being: body, soul and spirit.

The Church Fathers found the Old Testament to be replete with prefigurations or allusions to Christ and to His Death and Resurrection. St Irenaeus of Lyon (†ca. 202) saw in Christ the one "who sails with Noah, guides Abraham, journeys with Jacob; He is the Shepherd of those who are saved" (*Fragments* 13). Melitos of Sardis wrote around the same period (160-170): "Desolate lay the Father's image. This, then, is the reason why the mystery of the Pascha has been fulfilled in the body of the Lord" (*On Pascha*, no. 56. S. G. Hall, trans., Oxford at the Clarendon Press, 1979; p. 31).

> He is the Pascha of our salvation. It is He who in many endured many things:
> It is He that was in Abel murdered, and in Isaac bound, and in Jacob exiled,
> and in Joseph sold, and in Moses exposed, and in the lamb slain, and in
> David persecuted, and in the Prophets dishonoured (*Ibid*, no. 69; p. 37).

Of the many examples we could cite, we want to mention here only those that best suit our purpose. Chosen by God above all men, "the righteous" and "upright" man, Noah, saved mankind from the waters of the flood (Gen 6:9). The story of the sacrifice of Abraham (Gen 22:1-18) prefigures that of Christ with this difference, that while God spared Isaac in response to Abraham's faith, He gave His own Son, who offered Himself for the salvation of all. Taken from this perspective, the Resurrection fulfills the promise made to Abraham (Acts 13:32).

The Book of Exodus says that "the Angel of the Lord appeared to [Moses] in a flame of fire out of the midst of a bush... the bush was burning, yet it was not consumed" (Ex 3:2). The Lord declared, "I am the God of your fathers..." (Ex 3:6). When questioned by Moses as to His name, "God said to Moses, 'I AM who I AM'" (Ex 3:14). "Ὁ ὢν" ("He Who Is") is an inscription commonly found in the halo of the icon of Christ. This continuity with the Old Testament, or rather this relationship, is the result of the revelation of the Word of God, the Second Person of the Holy Trinity, as the following liturgical text affirms:

> To Moses Thou didst appear in the bush in the form of fire, O Word of God, and as the Angel of God, to show clearly Thy presence among us and to declare the triple reign of Thy unique divinity (Great Octoechos, tone 2, Saturday night, midnight service, Ode 5).

"Moses was very meek, more than all men that were on the face of the earth" (Num 12:3). Having been chosen to free the people from slavery and to lead them toward the Promised Land, he in turn announced and prefigured Christ whom he already bore in his heart. Pharaoh represents the Evil One, the one who keeps the people of God captive in Egypt, in a place of suffering and slavery. Just as Christ confronted the king of Hades, whom he conquered by the shedding of His blood, Moses delivered the people from the pharaonic yoke and brought them up through the Red Sea onto dry land. A similar prefiguration is found in the blood of the lamb, which spared the Hebrew people in Egypt during the devastation that took place on the night of the Passover (Ex 12:21-33).

The book of Exodus shows a people freed by the power of the hand of Yahweh (13:14)—that is, of Christ—who "went before them by day in a pillar of cloud to lead them along the way, and by night in a pillar of fire to give them light, that they might travel by day and by night" (Ex 13:21). The chosen people received manna (Ex 16) from the same Lord who would one day give them His flesh for food. Similarly, the water that sprang forth from the rock (Ex 17:6) prophetically announced the living water that flowed from Christ's side when He was pierced by a spear at the time of His crucifixion.

The Cross is linked to the Resurrection as the sign of victory and life, by which death and evil are conquered. Jacob blessed his grandchildren with crossed hands (Gen 48:14), just as Moses defeated Amalek with outstretched arms (Ex 17:8-16). Isaiah describes the Suffering Servant who offers his life as an expiation, and by whom that which is pleasing to Yahweh is accomplished (see Isa 53:2-10).

Ezekiel gives a forceful account of the way in which the Lord brought him "into a valley full of dry bones" (Ezek 37:1). Let us listen to the words of the prophet:

> As I prophesied there was a noise, and behold, a rattling; and the bones came together, bone to its bone. And as I looked, there were sinews on them, and flesh had come upon them, and skin had covered them; but there was no breath in them. Then he said to me, 'Prophesy to the breath, prophesy, son of man, and say to the breath, Thus says the Lord God: Come from the four winds, O breath, and breathe upon these slain, that they may live.' So I prophesied as he commanded me, and they lived, and stood upon their feet, an exceedingly great host (Ezek 37:7-10).

Along with Hosea who prophesied: "After two days he will revive us, on the third day he will raise us up, that we may live before him" (Hos 6:2), let us remember Jonah (Jon 2) as well, whom Christ himself gives as an example:

> For as Jonah was three days and three nights in the belly of the whale, so will the Son of Man be three days and three nights in the heart of the earth (Mt 12:40).

In the composite icon of the Resurrection there would emerge in later times the image of the whale spitting up, not Jonah, but all of mankind, freed by Christ.

Let us mention as well two accounts from the Book of Kings. The first recounts the way in which the prophet Elijah raised the son of the widow of Sarepta (1 Kgs 17:17-24), whom Jesus gave as an example of hospitality (Lk 4:24-26). The second shows the prophet Elisha, Elijah's disciple, who raised the son of the Shunamite woman (2 Kgs 4:8-37). These events directly foretell the raising of Lazarus and of all mankind.

The unknown author of "An anatolian homely on the date of Pascha in the year 387" attempts to demonstrate that Christ's choices concerning time are not haphazard. There may be a parallel between the week of creation and that of redemption (Holy Week). From this perspective, the first day of creation, Sunday, refers to the equinox during which day and night are of equal length. The fourth day (Wednesday) witnesses the creation of the moon and the sun, the sixth (Friday), the creation of man, the seventh (Saturday), God's rest, while the eighth harkens back to the first day that is "the Only Day": this is "the day which the Lord has made, let us rejoice and be glad in it!" (Ps 118:24).

Remembered symbolically as the day of the creation of man, but also as that of the fall, Friday is the day of Christ's death which raises up all of creation. God rested from His work on Saturday (Gen 2:2), which is none other than the day on which Christ rested in the tomb, once "all [was] finished" (Jn 19:30). The first day (Sunday) of the creation of visible light corresponds to the Resurrection, a new creation, a superabundant flow of spiritual light.

6. The Prophet Elijah; icon, first half of the 13th c., Church of St John Lampadistis Monastery, Kalopanayotis. Byzantine Museum of Nicosia, Cyprus.

Let us add that if the Annunciation, taking place at the Spring equinox, corresponds to the first day of creation, Christmas is then the fourth day, on which the light pierces the darkness. Just as the moon sheds its light, Christ is indeed the "other Sun" that surges out of the shadows. In the Byzantine liturgy, the first reading for vespers on Christmas day reviews the history of the creation of the world (Gen 1:1-13) only up to this point: "a third day." This is a clear indication that the Nativity is indeed on the fourth day, pointing to the eighth day that emerges from darkness, entirely bathed in the light of the Risen One.

Evil in the Cosmos

The spirit of our times is particularly dismal. A quick survey of oral and written media is enough to convince us of the disorders affecting the diverse areas of life. Powerless (when he does not indirectly cause them himself) in the face of cataclysms, droughts, typhoons, earthquakes and various epidemics, man also finds himself in the throws of other mischievous ills: abusive exploitation, unemployment, intolerance, envy, prostitution of all sorts, and wars with unfathomable consequences. Once exposed to illness, to a progressive degradation that inevitably leads to death, he finds himself subject to "necessity," perceived as blind fate.

Ancient Greek tragedy, as well as its poetry, reveals a sadness, a deep dismay in the face of human destiny and of death that relegates each of us to the subterranean realm of shadows. Hence the tension, the intense quest for immortality that led Plato to think that the human soul, being in part divine, achieves immortality only by freeing itself from matter through corruption and death. Thus freed, the soul returns to a place of beatitude, abandoning the body that is reduced to nothingness.

Many answers to this plight are provided by myths from around the world. The great traditions of Hinduism, Buddhism, Taoism, Islam, Judaism and Christianity each offer their own. Beyond the differences of approach, commonalities certainly exist among these various traditions, but the death and Resurrection of Christ remain absolutely unique.

Christianity speaks of "the fall." This amounts to affirming that man is born lame, with his mind and body inclined toward self-satisfaction, the consequence of disobedience toward God. But if Adam is disobedient and commits sin, preferring the forbidden tree to God, it is due to the fact that he is endowed with freedom of choice. Love, however, implies freedom; and the relationship of God with his creation bears the indelible mark of love. For those who base their atheism on the scandal of evil we must recall, along with St Macarius (†390), that our present condition proves superior to that of Adam, insofar as the Son of God has put on our flesh, becoming one of us and associating us with Himself (*Spiritual Homilies* 15-16).

Once tested by the tempter, who aimed at the spirit ("You will be like God;" Gen 3:5) and the senses ("The tree was good for food, and...a delight to the eyes;" Gen 3:6), the whole man—soul, body and spirit—chose autonomy, preferring the creature to the Creator. A point worthy of consideration is a certain parallelism with the fall of Lucifer ("The morning star"), who dared in his greed to compare himself to God and thereby became the Prince of darkness.

The Fathers of the Church considered sin to be an omission, leading to a sense of God's absence, rather than as the transgression of a legal code. The fault of Adam stems fundamentally from a lack of love, which destroys communion with God. His willful submission to the temptation to power and to envy turned him into a predator who could no longer see the value in a creation directed toward the praise of God. Rather, he could regard creation only as an object of consumption. Ingratitude toward God was thereby aggravated by a profaning of the cosmos that transformed creation into a mere material object. Accordingly, Adam missed his vocation as "priest" for the world, destined originally to make a "Eucharist" (from the Greek word *eucharisto*: "to give thanks") of all things as we are called to do by Christ, the new Adam: "What is Thine, having received it from Thee, we offer it unto Thee, in behalf of all and for all" (excerpt from the *Divine Liturgy* of St John Chrysostom).

In his work, *La Lumière sans déclin,* Fr. Sergius Bulgakov succinctly summarizes the meaning of the fall:

> Our first ancestors fell, succumbing to the temptation of lust. They allowed themselves to be overtaken by their lust for knowledge outside of the love or the knowledge of God; by the lust of the flesh, they sought corporeal pleasures beyond the spirit; by the lust for power they sought gain beyond spiritual growth. All equilibrium in man's spiritual powers was lost. He became powerless over creation because of the magical action to which he was tempted: he had counted on wielding power over the world through exterior, non-spiritual means, symbolically represented by eating of the forbidden fruit (L'Age d'Homme, Lausanne 1990, 320-321).

Through his idolatry, Adam cut himself off from God, the only true source of life. Having become corruptible, alienated, his heart and spirit darkened by the passions, he dragged into captivity the whole of creation that was subject to him (Gen 1:28-29). And while the "fall" is the result of submission to the passions, of a consumptive and predatory attitude toward the world, the re-establishment of communion with God requires the opposite movement. It is through dispassion, through fasting and by opening himself entirely to God, that man puts on Christ (Gal 3:27) in order to regain his original purity and to bring creation back to the Creator.

Death is nothingness. It proceeds from evil which is, ontologically speaking, "non-being." The expression "kingdom of Satan" is a misnomer, since the supreme impostor is the incarnation of evil, the source of death, meaning nothingness. We are forced to use words in order to express the reality of hell, a place of darkness and, consequently, of death. Life, on the other hand, together with any authentic personal encounter, requires light.

We would have to be blind not to recognize the countless bruises and wounds that mar the flesh of the world as a result of the divisions, injustice and fraud that infect the human body, from the family unit all the way to the sphere of international relations. How many men and women today deny God, either by word or by action? The self-worship so rampant today has culminated in technological advances and wonderful inventions that nevertheless increasingly betray us, making of us victims of our lack of discernment concerning the true meaning and ultimate end of life.

As depth psychology has clearly demonstrated, man is a fundamentally divided being. Denying this fact may lead to serious consequences. Thus, for example, by ignoring man's divine vocation and his "fall," and by concerning itself strictly with the level of his fallen nature, psychoanalysis runs the risk of leading astray the patient it claims to heal by representing as harmonious, stable and good what is in fact a mere illusion, a parody of the integrity to which every man is called, as one created "in the image of God!"

All of life is carried out under the sign of death. We experience this through a multitude of small, daily deaths: personal set-backs, betrayed friendships, separation from loved ones, together with sickness and cruelty in inexpressible forms. What about the "death homes" where, alone and in anguish, today's elderly await who knows what? How many people are there in the world who are crippled, abnormal, incurable, mutilated or tortured by suffering? The answer is given to us, in fact, in the message of the icons of the Crucifixion and of the Descent into Hell.

If we persist in denying the source of life, it can only lead to a perversion of our spirit and our heart. While not ignoring the alienating effects of the demonic rhythms of modern life, we must acknowledge that the majority of nervous disorders—which are currently on the rise—are the price we are paying for our spiritual emptiness.

Finally, how can we justify the ugliness, so often set forth as normative, produced by those who consider themselves to be "creative"? Isn't this proof of a profound imbalance in those "artists" who create nothing more than an illusion of beauty?

Cast out of Paradise on account of a "tree" charged with symbolism, humanity reenters its gates, regenerated by the tree of the Cross. By the Resurrection of Christ, death is no longer a merely negative factor. It has in fact become a means of access to the spiritual world.

In conclusion let us quote the philosopher Nicholas Berdiayev:

> Modern psychology of the subconscious mind reveals within man a terrifying depth of darkness, and makes evident the inferior character of his most elevated states of being. Thus it humiliates him and tramples him to the ground. The doctrine of the fall, however, sheds a completely different light on the deepest regions discovered within man and on the criminal instincts of his subconscious. It sees in the fact that he is fallen a proof that he is a superior being, a free spirit. If he fell from a high place, he can once again rise up to it. (*On the Destiny of Man*)

In the early Church, we should remember, a Christian was referred to as *aphoberos thanatou* (one who does not fear death).

The New Testament

The Resurrection marks the pages of the New Testament with an ever increasing intensity.

> "Destroy this Temple and in three days I will raise it up again... He was speaking of the temple of his body" (Jn 2:19, 21).

Before enumerating various miracles, Saint Gregory of Nyssa (†394) spoke of the divine pedagogy:

> Since by its greatness the Resurrection surpasses any expression of faith, the Lord begins with lesser miracles, in order slowly to accustom our faith to greater wonders...

> Before revealing His power of Resurrection, He begins by treating an incurable illness; though this healing is a great miracle, it is not one that leaves us in disbelief. Simon's mother-in-law was burning with fever: at the Lord's command, it left her, so that she who had been expected to die regained sufficient strength to serve those present (Lk 4:38ff).

The events that follow include the healing of the hemorrhaging woman and the raising of Jairus' daughter (Mk 5:21-43). Even more marvelous is the raising of the son of the widow of Nain, where the conciseness of the account emphasizes the power of the event. Walking with his disciples and a large crowd, Jesus reached the doors of the town of Nain.

> "Behold, a man who had died was being carried out, the only son of his mother, and she was a widow; and a large crowd from the city was with her. And when the Lord saw her, he had compassion on her and said to her, 'Do not weep.' And he came and touched the bier, and the bearers stood still. And he said, 'Young man, I say to you, arise.' And the dead man sat up, and began to speak. And he gave him to his mother. Fear seized them all; and

they glorified God, saying, 'A prophet has arisen among us!' and 'God has visited his people!'" (Lk 7: 12-16).

In the account of the raising of Lazarus (Jn 11:1-44), every element contributes to the manifestation of Christ's power of Resurrection. When addressed by Martha: "Lord, if you had been here, my brother would not have died," Jesus answers: "I am the resurrection and the life; he who believes in me, though he die, yet shall he live, and whoever lives and believes in me shall never die" (Jn 11: 21, 25-26).

Having been dead for four days, Lazarus would undoubtedly have given off an unbearable smell because of his advanced state of decomposition. It is at that very moment that Jesus, having dried his tears, called his friend back to life, so that those present might believe that He was the Son of God (Jn 11:42). At the same time He announced the universal resurrection.

Jesus declared to the Sadducees who had come to question Him: "As for the resurrection of the dead, have you not read what was said to you by God, 'I am the God of Abraham, and the God of Isaac, and the God of Jacob?' He is not God of the dead, but of the living" (Mt 22:31-32). Then: "All who are in the tombs will hear his voice and come forth" (that is, the voice of the Son, Jn 5:28). For if the Word of God created the world through His own Word, that same Word also heals the sick and the lepers, just as it makes the paralytics walk, the deaf hear and the blind see. By His word Christ raised not only the daughter of Jairus, the son of the widow of Nain and Lazarus, but He shall raise us all at the end of the age.

Miracle of all miracles, Christ's Resurrection no longer affects merely a select number of individuals, as in the Gospel stories, but everyone that has come into this world. The account of the Resurrection proves to be fundamental in this respect; it embraces the entire Scripture as the fulfillment of all that came before.

Death and Resurrection form a single reality through the death of Jesus, since the New Adam vanquished the death that the first Adam had brought upon himself. As "true God and true man," Christ fully assumes and refashions our human condition.

> "He made Himself man, He who made man; He nursed at His mother's breast, He who rules the stars. As the bread, He hungers; as the fountain, He thirsts; as the light, He sleeps; as the way, He tires of his journey; as truth, He is accused by false witnesses; as judge of the living and the dead, He is judged by a mortal; as justice, He is condemned by unjust men" (*Christmas Sermon* of St Augustine of Hippo in 411 or 412).

In a text following the same line of thought, Gregory Nazianzen (†390) confesses:

> He hungered; yet He fed thousands, He is "the living bread," "the heavenly bread." He was thirsty, yet he said: "if anyone thirst, let him come to me and

7. The Raising of the Son of the Widow of Nain; 14th c. fresco,
Church of the Pantocrator, Decani Monastery, Serbia.

drink!"...He prayed, yet He hears our prayers. He wept, yet He dries our
tears...He was given vinegar to drink, and offered gall, but who is He? He
who changed water into wine...He gave his life, yet He has "the power to
take it back" (Jn 10:18)...He died, yet He bestows life and destroys death by
His own death. He was buried, yet He rose; He descended to hell, but
brought back souls; He went up to heaven and shall return to judge the living
and the dead (*Oration* 29).

In his work *The Mystical Theology of the Eastern Church,* Vladimir Lossky writes:

In Him, "each nature acts according to its own properties: the human hand
raises the young girl, the divine restores her to life; the human feet walk on
the surface of the water, because the divinity has made it firm. 'It is not the
human nature that raises Lazarus, it is not the divine power which sheds tears
before his tomb,' said St John the Damascene" (SVS Press, Crestwood, NY,
1976; p. 146).

Before going on to the accounts of the Resurrection, it would be useful to familiarize
ourselves with the prologue to the Gospel according to St John, read only once in the
liturgy of the Byzantine rite, during the night of Pascha. This passage makes especially
clear how closely connected to one another Incarnation and Resurrection really are.

8. The Raising of Lazarus; late 15th c.-early16th c. icon, two-sided tablet, from the Cathedral of St Sophia of Novgorod. History and Architecture Museum, Novgorod.

In spite of the discrepancies that appear in the testimonies of the four evangelists (differences that, far from minimizing their authenticity, indicate a desire on the part of each sacred author to transmit an unaltered oral tradition of the Church), each one recounts the event of the Empty Tomb (Mt 28:1-8; Mk 16:1-8; Lk 24:1-8; Jn 20:1-9). They all agree on the fact that "on the first day of the week," Mary Magdalen (Jn) and other women (Mt, Mk and Lk) were the first to go to the tomb at the break of day and discover, to their astonishment, that the stone had been rolled away. Disconcerted and overwhelmed with sorrow, they were addressed by one (Mt, Mk) or two (Lk, Jn) angels: "Why do you seek the living among the dead? He is not here, he has risen!" (Lk 24:5-6).

Matthew recounts the deceit of the Jewish leaders (Mt 28:11-15), baffled by the account of the guards who had witnessed the intervention of the angels who came to roll away the stone from the tomb. The religious leaders gave the guards a large sum of money, charging them to spread the rumor that Jesus' body had been stolen by His disciples. An element of special importance is that the apostles, Peter and John, trembled at the sight of the linen cloth on the ground (Jn 20:5; Lk 24:12) and the napkin "rolled up in a place by itself" (Jn 20:7). The evangelist John declares simply that they "saw and believed" (Jn 20:8).

All reason having been overwhelmed in the presence of the mystery of mysteries, only faith remains possible. And yet, it would be false to conclude that the apostles spontaneously accepted the notion of their master's Resurrection. The words of the women returning from the tomb were dismissed as idle tales. Likewise, they refused to believe the testimony of the disciples from Emmaus, which led to Jesus' reproach for "their unbelief and their hardness of heart" (Mk 16:11-14). Luke's concise, factual account (Lk 24:11-43) leaves little doubt as to the skeptical state of mind of the apostles and disciples regarding the event, be it fabrication or miracle. Far from being duped, as their words and demeanor clearly show, they soon confess not only to having seen and heard this Jesus who was put to death by the Jews, but to having touched Him and eaten with Him, something they could hardly have done with a ghost!

Why were the disciples so slow in recognizing their resurrected master? Full of tears, before the empty tomb, Mary Magdalen turned around, saw Jesus whom she mistook for the gardener and said to Him: "Sir, if you have carried him away, tell me where you have laid him, and I will take him away.' Jesus said to her, 'Mary.' She turned and said to him in Hebrew '*Rab-boni!*' (which means Teacher). Jesus said to her, 'Do not hold me, for I have not yet ascended to the Father'" (Jn 20:15-17).

The same day, two disciples on their way to the village of Emmaus were "talking with one another about all these things that had happened....Jesus himself drew near and went with them. But their eyes kept them from recognizing him" (Lk 24:14-16). Invited to stay with them that evening, Jesus sat at table with them. "He took the bread and blessed, and broke it, and gave it to them. And their eyes were opened and they recognized him; and he vanished out of their sight. They said to each other, 'Did not our hearts burn within us while he talked to us on the road, while he opened to us the scripture?'" (Lk 24:30-32).

Another time, the disciples had been fishing all night with no results. At dawn Jesus stood on the shore of lake Tiberias, but they did not recognize Him. He invited them to cast their nets "to the right of the boat." The net was filled with one hundred and fifty-three large fish and yet was not torn. John then said to Peter: "It is the Lord!" When they got out on land, they saw a charcoal fire there, with fish lying on it, and bread. Jesus asked them to bring some of their fish and invited them to have breakfast. "Now none of the disciples dared ask him 'who are you?' They knew it was the Lord" (Jn 21:7-12).

What is striking in these accounts is the change that has taken place in Jesus' physical body. Freed from the laws of gravity, from space and time, His transfigured body is filled with the Holy Spirit; thus He inaugurates within His flesh the "spiritualization" of the flesh of the world.

Recognition of the Risen Lord is made from within, by what is most fundamental in man, namely his heart. The disciples also recognize Jesus through a personal relationship in which their whole being is engaged, past and present eventually merging into one insofar as the Resurrection marks the fulfillment of Scripture.

It may be impossible to elaborate on Christ's appearing "to more than five hundred brethren at one time" (1 Cor 15:6). That event, nonetheless, is recounted in passing by the apostle Paul, whereas the evangelists John (20:19-24) and Luke (24:36-43) rival one another in the precision of their accounts of the appearance of the Risen One to the eleven and to their companions on the evening of Pascha.

The very night after their encounter with their master, the travelers on the road to Emmaus returned in haste to Jerusalem, where they joined the other disciples who confirmed their story:

> "'The lord has risen indeed, and has appeared to Simon!' Then they told what had happened on the road, and how he was known to them in the breaking of the bread. As they were speaking, Jesus Himself stood among them. But they were startled and frightened, and supposed that they saw a spirit. And He said to them, 'Why are you troubled, and why do questionings rise in your hearts?' See my hands and my feet, that it is I myself; handle me, and see; for a spirit has not flesh and bones as you see that I have.' And while they still disbelieved for joy, and wondered, He said to them, 'Have you anything to eat?' They gave Him a piece of broiled fish, and He took it and ate before them" (Lk 24, 34-43).

9. The Apostle Paul; late 13th c. icon, Panagia Chrisaliniotissas Church.
Byzantine Museum of Nicosia, Cyprus.

10. The Decent into Hell; 1191 fresco (detail), St George Church, Kurbinovo, Macedonia.

And this took place on "the first day of the week, all the doors being shut where the disciples were for fear of the Jews" (Jn 20:19). Initially dumbfounded and disbelieving, the disciples were soon convinced. No one has ever seen a spirit of flesh and blood, and certainly not one that eats what it is given.

Having been absent that evening and refusing to believe the account of the eleven, the apostle Thomas finds himself being challenged "eight days later" (Jn 20:26) under similar circumstances:

> "Put your finger here, and see my hands; and put out your hand and place
> it in my side; do not be faithless, but believing" (Jn 20:27).

While speaking through him to every person throughout the ages who wishes to see and touch, Jesus again says to Thomas:

> "Have you believed because you have seen me? Blessed are those who have
> not seen and yet believe" (Jn 20:29).

At the end of the forty days during which he appeared to the disciples, telling them about the Kingdom of God (Acts 1:3), Jesus leaves them in Galilee on a mountain near Bethany. He promises them the Spirit, the power that would allow them to announce the Resurrection unto the ends of the earth (Mt 28:16-29; Lk 24:49-53).

"Taken up to heaven" and seated "at the right hand of God" (Mk 16:19), He simultaneously deifies the whole of human nature, of which He Himself is the most perfect representative. Thereby He fulfills His Word to His disciples: "And I am with you until the close of the age" (Mt 28:20).

The central Gospel message of the Resurrection fills not only the Acts of the Apostles but also the Pauline Epistles. The fifteenth chapter of First Corinthians—verses 3 to 8 in particular—offer a sober summary of the Christian teaching.

The Apostle Paul confronts us with an irrefutable logic: "If Christ has not been raised, then our preaching is in vain and your faith is in vain" (1 Cor 15:14).

Yet with the apostle we exclaim: "In fact Christ has been raised from the dead, the first fruits of those who have fallen asleep. For as by a man death came, by a man has come also the resurrection of the dead. For as in Adam all die, so also in Christ shall all be made alive" (1 Cor 15:20-22).

To Socrates' question, "What is courage?", we may answer with the example of Christ's disciples. Cowards during their master's Passion, they are transformed at the sight of the Risen One. Henceforth, nothing could hinder them in their witness: neither the temptations of the world, nor suffering, nor death. Their courage flows from their faith, the deep conviction of a reality that embraces them completely.

Mystery Replaces Science

We need to state unequivocally that the Resurrection cannot be subjected to any scientific analysis or any historical criterion. Moreover, it provides us with the only answer to the fundamental question that faces everyone: that of death.

Men of science have at their disposal extraordinary means by which to explore the mysteries of the universe. Still, science falters in a number of areas. Although filled with objective knowledge, a great many modern graduates, technicians and scientists, limit reality strictly to the field of scientific observation, the empirically verifiable. This automatically excludes any possibility for miracle and, *a fortiori,* for "Resurrection," which is labeled a myth, a fable or even an hallucination. The deepest reality eludes the man of this world, insofar as he does not know the God who alone gives meaning to all things. Thus, "the reason why man remains and will remain a mystery to science is the fact that what lies at his core by reason of his very structure, is a *theological being*" (Panayiotis Nellas, *Deification in Christ;* SVS Press, New York, 1987; p. 30). St Paul spoke of the false wisdom of the world (1 Cor 1:19-20), while the eminent Church father, Gregory Palamas (†1359), wrote that "those who have acquired an exterior and profane culture more than need be...cannot understand the things of the Spirit" (*PG* 151, 445B).

The Greek word *logos* includes "word" and "reason," both of which were lost in the fall. As the *Logos* of God, Christ restores human integrity. As "the power of God and the wisdom of God" (1 Cor 1:24), He alone is the true wisdom granted to those who receive Him and clothe themselves with Him. Far from being the fruit of intellectual activity, knowledge of God is the result of a union with Christ in and by the Holy Spirit, who engenders such knowledge within Christ's disciples. The essential point is not to "believe in the Resurrection," but to have faith in the Risen One.

As we are faced with the need for a personal experience of the Resurrection, the icon can be of precious help. The great Russian spiritual thinker Alexander Elchaninoff wrote in his *Diary*: "Faith originates in love; love in contemplation. It is impossible not to love Christ" (*Diary of a Russian Priest*, SVS Press, New York, 1982; p. 36).

Contemplating the icon of the "Descent into Hell" with the eyes of the heart slowly brings forth the love that grounds one's faith. It is necessary, however, for the icon to provide an image that corresponds to the *kerygma* (or proclamation of salvation), for which it serves as a powerful visual representation. It is equally necessary for those that venerate the icon to have received, if not an inspiration by the Holy Spirit, at least an "education," a religious formation that is more necessary today than ever before to an understanding of its foundation and its meaning. The icon often enables a person to grasp in an instant what the richest texts are unable fully to express. Hence the importance of creating icons with respect for the Tradition—the fruit of ages-old theological reflection—because every deviation inevitably leads to a compromise of the truth. Thus, even if they do not provoke any particularly negative reaction because they are so familiar, the images representing Christ coming out of the tomb offer a poor example of "sacred art." Such examples stem from the imagination of the artist and from a misdirected sentimentality that deliberately ignores the mystery expressed in the liturgical texts of the paschal season:

> O Lord, despite the seals affixed by the lawless ones, Thou camest forth from the tomb even as Thou wast born of the Theotokos. Thy bodiless Angels knew not how Thou becamest incarnate; the soldiers who guarded Thee did not perceive when Thou didst arise: for both these things were kept from those that inquired, but the wonders were made manifest unto those who worship the mystery with faith (Thursday Orthros, bright week).

Both a man of science and a theologian, Pavel Florensky labels the choice of a rationalizing faith as the worst form of atheism. An atheist is not merely one who rejects the existence of God. He is rather one who, while affirming his belief in God, declares his autonomy from Him, and deifies himself in an exclusivist humanism. As the image of Christ, and thereby called to be His "Icon," a Christian moves and grows within the sphere of mystery. Suspended between this world and the next, living in both time and eternity, he perceives within the depths of every one and every thing an ineffable divine presence.

3

The Essence of the Icon

The meaning of the icon of the Resurrection, and of those that most clearly derive from it, is truly accessible only to those who have already gained a significant familiarity with iconography. Every icon is rooted in the Incarnation, finding its fulfillment in the paschal light, and must henceforth be read from a resurrectional perspective. This indicates the importance of this chapter which will allow us, among other things, to emphasize the pressing need for an iconography of high quality, that is faithful to the Church's Tradition.

The Icon: A Liturgical Image

Having long been disregarded in the West, in spite of a past marked by its presence, the icon is now beginning to penetrate the various layers of our society. Many works broach the subject from a purely archeological and artistic perspective, offering only a few words concerning its original objective which was, among other things, to convey a Christian vision. Though they are generally scholarly, these studies are nonetheless minimalistic insofar as they ignore what is essential about the icon: precisely that which makes up its essence.

Because the icon originated at the heart of the undivided Church, it belongs to every Christian. However, since the separation of the Eastern and Western Churches, only the Orthodox Church has been able to keep iconography alive to this day. In fact, the icon stands at the very heart of Orthodoxy. It constitutes an integral part of the faith of Orthodox faithful and is accepted by them as second nature. One can grasp its fullness, therefore, only by entering without reservation into the spirituality of this Church that is the guardian and birthplace of the sacred image.

The Church of the first centuries experienced animated and even fierce debates concerning the legitimacy of representing Christ and the saints. The icon found its defenders among monks, faithful laypeople, persecuted bishops, and others in exile, who were brutally killed by the iconoclasts. As unconditional partisans of the Old Testament prohibition: "You shall not make for yourself any graven image" (Ex 20:4), these iconoclasts destroyed and burned thousands of icons. The seventh and final great ecumenical council—held in the year 787 at Nicea, near Constantinople—cut right to the heart of this quarrel. It declared the importance of the icon and of its veneration, anathematizing "those who accept in word the coming of the Word of God in the Flesh, but refuse to contemplate him through icons, thus receiving only in theory—but in fact denying—our salvation" (*Synodikon* of Nicea II).

The historical victory of the iconodules (those who defended veneration of sacred images) was followed by violent clashes with unyielding iconoclasts until the time when the veneration of icons was generally reestablished, giving rise to a solemn feast celebrated on March 11, 843, known as the "Triumph of Orthodoxy." This feast, proclaiming "right faith" and "right worship," has been commemorated within the Orthodox Church ever since, on the first Sunday of Great Lent.

Numerous Christians in our day continue to adhere to the iconoclastic tenets of the Reformation. Their mistrust reveals a certain lucidity with regard to the image, to its powers, its utter ambiguity and occasional negative influences. We understand what provoked their rejection of images, but the real debate for or against icons is of a theological nature.

Although the Church of Rome received and fully recognized the council of Nicea II, it never did assimilate it. The proof is that after having solemnly subscribed to the veneration of images in 787, the legates of the iconodule Pope, Adrian II, recommended the rejection of this same veneration seven years later at the Council of Frankfurt: the essential connection between the icon and the faith was not perceived the same way in Rome as it was in Byzantium. It is enough to recall the famous *Libri Carolini,* a pamphlet of the Frankish Church drawn up as its response to what was in fact a defective translation of the *Acts of Constantinople* that had been addressed by the Pope to the Carolingian theologians. The latter, in turn, falsely accused the Nicenes of "worshipping" icons, in spite of the original Greek text that referred explicitly to "veneration." Nor did the Franks understand the ancient Byzantine practice of bowing before the emperor or his portrait, incensing him and kissing his feet. Those same gestures that were carried over to icons were labeled idolatrous by the Franks. For them and the Council of Frankfurt (794), as well as those that followed in its wake, images were acceptable only within the limits of their didactic usage, as memorials and decorations. In their view, far from spiritually uplifting believers, the icon rather confined them to earthly things. As an organic connection to liturgy, the icon is nevertheless its realization, according to the Eastern Fathers of the Councils, and the constant reminder of the Incarnation and the economy of salvation.

To deny any sacramental value to the images of Christ, His Mother and the Saints, is not only to deny their ability to make the depicted person mystically present. It also gives too great a freedom to the artist, with disastrous and long-term effects of which the iconoclasm of the Reformation is only one example.

The "Caroline Books" (*Libri Carolini*) undermined the extraordinary effort toward clarification, initiated by Nicea II, which declared that only the artistic dimension of the icon ought to be left up to the painter, since it was the fruit of the Tradition of the Church and sealed by the Holy Spirit. Freely interpreted by the artist, the sacred mysteries become subject to the arbitrary perspective of imagination and emotion, turning the image into a mere ornament, disconnected from liturgical life. This is an open door for idolatrous images, caricatures of the Truth who is Christ, the head of the one Church that alone knows His true face.

The first iconoclastic crisis was provoked in part by the introduction of heterodox elements into iconography. Christian faith originally inspired the works of art that adorn Christian temples in an effort to crystallize religious thought. The catacombs, the meeting place of the first Christian communities, are replete with frescos of Christ, of the Virgin Mary, and of the martyrs. These images were present on sacred vessels and were engraved on metal; and they also decorated the pectoral crosses that Christians risked their lives to wear.

The history of the sacred image in the Church abounds with teachings that are indispensable for those who wish to understand the current state of the various Christian confessions. After a lengthy common progress with the Orthodox beyond the schism of 1054, the Western Church adopted naturalism in its religious art. To be sure, the famous council of Trent (1545-1563) encouraged the veneration of images. But the freedom granted the artist at a time when the ideas of the Renaissance prevailed, led to painting Christ, His Mother and the Saints according to human categories (anthropomorphism). The artist became too readily disposed to celebrating physical beauty without any connection to a spiritual vision rooted in the Tradition of the Church. An identical trend developed, beginning in the seventeenth century, in the decadent icons that invaded the Orthodox churches under the influence of an undiscerning westernization. Such an insertion of foreign elements into the Tradition inevitably leads to a falsification of the *kerygma* (proclamation of the Good News).

The icon is a vision of God and of a transfigured world. It is a language that cannot be properly spoken without faith and a close connection to the Church. It leads one, initially, to distinguish between sacred and religious art, then to situate the icon relative to an ill-defined sacred art. (We are admittedly touching on a sensitive area here, one in which a poorly expressed thought can inadvertently be harmful. This is because authentic images are grasped by the heart and are rooted deep within us.)

In religious art that obeys the rules of secular painting, the religious theme serves primarily as an excuse for the painter. It becomes a means of displaying his talent, together with his personal concept of man and the world. Decorative images that serve only as illustrations inhibit true prayer, suppressing the mystery for the sake of sentimental imagination. Faith, which moves mountains, can also use such images to touch the heart. But this does not change the fact that this art fails to capture the spiritual beauty of Christ, of His Mother and of the Saints and all too often merely distorts it. Instead of promoting the concentration that is necessary for prayer, as does the realistic symbolism of the icon, these images scatter one's attention; they are deceptive and distracting. Such a judgment has validity, of course, only in light of faith; secular artists necessarily limit themselves to purely artistic criteria.

It is insufficient to consider the icon strictly from the perspective of "sacred art," without seeing its profound connections with faith and "doxology" (praise). The current use of the expression "sacred art" is too broad, insofar as it gives the artist complete freedom of interpretation. Consequently, it now encompasses works depicting everything from the ineffable reality which is God, to products of artists imbued with an agnostic or atheistic concept of creation.

Liturgy reaches its zenith in the eucharistic celebration, the recapitulation of the two poles of salvation: the Incarnation and the Transfiguration. As an image of the Eucharist, the icon bears witness to the penetration of divinity into man and into creation, which it sanctifies. In this sense, it is not only a sacred art but a liturgical art as well.

Orthodoxy does not dissect, it does not analyze; it contemplates the mystery. The liturgical texts are unparalleled in expressing this contemplation. The icon is at the heart of the liturgical celebration that presupposes its presence. We can say that it is to one's sight what the texts are to one's ears. Word and image are united, revealing the hidden face of Scripture. If the Eucharist enables each baptized individual to become "one flesh" with Christ, the icon brings one face to face with Him. We have here two forms of mystical union that are essential in the Orthodox Church. For Orthodoxy, an image that cannot be used liturgically is simply not an icon.

Together, the liturgy and the icon express what is primordial in an Orthodoxy that, instead of formulas, offers the words of Christ recorded by the evangelist John: "Come and see" (1:39). More than by formulas or concepts, the great truths of the faith (dogmas) are expressed in doxologies and in prayers, for which the icons of the great feasts provide a visual counterpart.

We may be thankful to the Byzantine tradition for integrating beauty into its faith, a beauty that is none other than the fruit of harmony and balance, of an integrity that is rediscovered in all things. Incorporating the icon, bathed in light and radiant with every color of the rainbow, the liturgy as a whole expresses a beauty that is perceptible only through the eyes of faith.

11. Christ Pantocrator together with the Mother of God and John the Baptist, with the twelve apostles on either side. Byzantine icon, 1545. Bishopric Museum of Roman, Romania.

Because it is organically connected to the liturgy, the icon is fully decipherable only within Orthodox Tradition and practice; hence the difficulty facing the non-orthodox who have not received an initiation to this particular language. Unlike modern religious art—which, however beautiful it may be, fragments more often than it unites because of the innumerable interpretations it may be given—the icon serves as an important unifying principle. But of course a similar contradiction can be found in Orthodoxy as well, when an iconographer, unfaithful to his eminent ministry, follows his own inspiration and disregards the canons that serve precisely to guarantee the purity of the evangelical message and the transmission of the faith.

As a liturgical image that we incense, kiss, carry in procession and venerate in different ways, the icon draws its legitimacy from the incarnation of the Second Person of the Holy Trinity:

> The uncircumscribed Word of the Father became circumscribed, taking flesh from thee, O Theotokos, and He has restored the sullied image to its ancient glory, filling it with divine beauty. This our salvation we confess in deed and word (Sunday of Orthodoxy kontakion, tone 8).

"To be circumscribed," in this case means that He takes human form, assumes human flesh, enters into time and space. He "restores the image of old" because He is the New Adam, the Christ of Mount Tabor, streaming with light, the Risen One who liberates those held in bondage. Having been grafted onto Christ, who has deified humanity by assuming human nature, the human creature can in turn be clothed with light. Hence the gold of the icons that symbolizes the kingdom of the never-setting sun. The liturgy and the icon are complementary elements, the one moving in time, the other evolving in space.

As for knowing to what extent a painting can become iconic, let us say that all true art must be purified. It requires a *metanoia* that is a conversion of the heart. Only thus can it become a transfiguring, prophetic and revelatory reflection of the beauty of the creator. Only the acquisition of the Holy Spirit—which, according to the Fathers is the aim of the Christian life—can effect this miracle. Fra Angelico understood this when he humbly acknowledged: "One cannot paint Christ without loving Him."

Components of the Icon

As the finest product of a spiritually rich era in Russia, the icons of the second half of the fourteenth century and of the fifteenth century bear a striking "pneumatophoric" (Spirit-bearing) quality. They no longer depict bodies draped in vestments that are "billowing" with the breath of the Spirit. These, rather, are souls that bear witness to the victory which the saints have achieved over the flesh, using the weapons of asceticism and perpetual prayer. It is not that these beings are "disincarnate,"—the icon is always rooted in Christ's

Incarnation—but their thin bodies and emaciated faces suggest a "dematerialization" that expresses the "spiritualization" of matter.

The three realms, animal, vegetable and mineral (the chalky base, pigments, wood, rabbit-pelt glue and egg yolk) coexist within the icon, which prefigures the new earth where the Risen One will be all in all, where everything will be permeated with the Holy Spirit. From this perspective, the icon brings us back to an awareness of a divine presence in creation, along with what that implies for our relation to nature. Hence the rejection of artificial materials, such as acrylic paints, that disrupt the union with the natural world which is called to "spiritualization."

The mark of Christian culture on the Serbian language was such that the words for "holy" and "holiness" came to be closely linked to the word for "light." Under similar influence, the great fourteenth century iconographer, Theophanes the Greek (Andrei Rublev's teacher), painted a spiritual portrait of the father of monks, St Macarius, rendering him "all light," out of his concern for extreme "dematerialization."

"God is light," the apostle affirms (1 Jn 1:5); and everything in the icon must be bathed in this light, since it is itself a theophany. Yet far from representing divinity as such, the icon renders visible "the participation of beings and of objects in divine life" (Nicea II). According to the image of the Transfiguration of Christ—which reveals to our blind eyes of flesh the fullness of divinity within the human face of God—the icon depicts the world as already transfigured, illumined by the "divine energies." Already evil and nothingness have been vanquished. The background filled with light, the golden radiance of Christ's vestments, together with the halos, are all expressive of this "solar mysticism" that casts out every shadow, because God fills all things.

In the same way that the rays of the sun produce the rainbow, the colors live through the light which the iconographer lays down in white touches. These dabs of light create a movement that animates faces, vestments and landscapes in what is once again an ultimate expression of dematerialization.

Long before the advent of writing, at the dawn of civilization, color was a preferred means for transmitting and memorizing thoughts and ideas. Because it precedes and is independent of form, color itself is the living medium for a message perceived by the soul. Aware of this phenomenon, Byzantine art made use of "mystical" colors that convey the purity of the faith. Nothing is left to chance. Oil paint is rejected as being too voluptuous and carnal, primarily because it is opaque, incapable of expressing the transparency obtained through the technique of egg-tempera. The latter, consequently, is reserved for the icon.

In continuity with the language of the liturgy (which in the Orthodox Church is most commonly the vernacular), the icon reflects the particular culture of each people without

12. St Macarius the Egyptian; fresco painted in 1378 by Theophan the Greek.
Church of the Transfiguration of Ilina Street, Novgorod, Russia.

in any way allowing stylistic differences to alter the unity of the message. The canons, or iconographic rules formulated at the second council of Nicea, show signs of rare wisdom: "Only the artistic side of the icon is left up to the painter, the spiritual content depends on the holy Fathers" (*Mansi,* col. 252 a). It is they who, through contemplation, perceive what the icon must depict. This requirement is explained by the fact that the uprightness of one's life is inseparable from the correctness of one's faith. The icon is not an art to which faith is added, but an art that flows out of a vision of faith. It becomes one with that faith, as an ontological, spiritual vision which perceives the world as reflecting the transfiguring beauty of Mount Tabor. Far from being hindered by these canons, the iconographer can quickly raise the level of his composition to the spiritual level that mankind has attained. His creativity remains intact within the abundance of forms, rhythms, color schemes and compositions that are equally signs of the icon's incomparable boldness.

Religious paintings and icons belong to different worlds, each of which is characterized by a very specific vision. The one plays on the emotions, on the ephemeral, on pure humanism. It is the representation of a material world in which the angels themselves are carnal, subject to passion. The other bursts out of the closed structures of the fallen world through a revelation of the supreme reality, through the uninterrupted flow of praise and the proclamation of faith. In reality, things are certainly not as clear cut. Yet we must define our terms, since it is undeniable that a great fervor is present in many religious paintings, even if the essential, ontological element gives way to secondary considerations. Because its purpose is to concentrate one's thought, an authentic icon neither caters to one's sensitivity nor does it stimulate one's imagination. It does away with every superfluous element, rejecting sentimentality, sensuality and illusion. In contrast, baroque art plays on illusion, thereby legitimizing its place in the theater as opposed to a church, particularly when it goes unchecked. As an image of the spiritual world, though never an abstract one, the icon never represents biological or physical life, but an already transfigured body. Unlike a photo—which generally reproduces exterior aspects, the surface of a being—an icon reveals the deepest reality of the person and of the world, beyond the physical exterior. The absence of naturalism is most evident in the hands, the feet and the "atrophied" bodies that it represents. Such characteristics are an obvious sign of abandoning the flesh for the sake of the "glorious body" (Phil 3:21) promised to the elect, a "spiritual body" characterized by its transparency, subtlety and light.

The face alone provides a focus for the spiritual life in all its fullness. The gaze reflects the soul that beckons us. The eyes, illumined by the vision of God, reveal total openness, welcome, communion, transparency and contemplation. The other sensory organs are reduced to a minimum and are turned inward. In spite of varying positions and clothing, the similarity of the faces of the saints in the icons reverts back to the face of Christ whom

13. St John the Baptist; 15th c. icon, element of a Deisis,
Novgorod School. National Gallery, Oslo.

they have "put on." Because the transformation of the world to come has already been accomplished, the human figure is often seen in the company of wild beasts. The predatory reign of flesh has ended. As light, the icon emphasizes the break in the cycle of day and night, the evolution beyond time and space. Freedom is manifested within it through the unlimited inversion of perspective. In accordance with a disconcerting type of architecture that situates doors and windows without any regard for logic, it overthrows every law of reason and illusion in order to obey the law of the Gospel and of the Beatitudes. Thus it represents a reversal of the wisdom of this world. The proclamation of truth cannot accommodate techniques of artifice and illusion such as chiaroscuro and trompe-l'oeil painting. As for scenes that take place in front of structures, the notion of time is disregarded and the characters in the foreground are smaller than those behind them. By being a-temporal, it seeks to be realistic in transmitting the faith of the Church of which Christ is the head, "the truth and the life" (Jn 14:6).

If the Gospel constitutes a verbal icon of Christ, the image of the painted icon must correspond to the Truth expressed by the Word. Hence the invitation made to the iconographer to withdraw himself and thereby remove his subjectivity in order faithfully to follow the Tradition of the Church. As a painter of what is invisible and inexpressible, he is not a creator in the usual sense. It becomes his responsibility to seek the integrity derived from the unification of his being, by emptying himself through his perpetual conversion. Bound to Christ, and thus to the Church, he must engender the icon from within himself, lest he be relegated to painting cold images, devoid of the warmth of the Holy Spirit. If the asceticism of the faces in the icons is to allow the spiritual aspect to emerge, such a breakthrough toward light can be achieved only through the intense spiritual life of the iconographer. Asceticism and joy coexist, a fact borne out by the vitality of the colors used. Indeed, the Resurrection presupposes the cross and sacrifice—in a word, purification.

In the icon, the face of Christ, the New Adam, resembles the color of clay. Appropriately, the word clay translates into Hebrew as *Adamah*: a reminder that His image belongs to every race, to every people, and that the Son of David, born of the Virgin Mary, was a Jew, fully rooted in history. To give Him a black, white or yellow face, as has been done by some pseudo-iconographers in the United States, transgresses the historical truth of the Incarnation.

A correct interpretation of the icon requires a substantial knowledge of the liturgical texts that are themselves imbued with the Apocrypha [or Deutero-canonical writings—ed.] by which the Fathers were inspired. As for the indispensable inscription of the name of the person who is re-presented, the name is recognized as a true "presence" in the Orthodox tradition, which "mystically" realizes that presence. Thus, as in the Old

Testament where the name alone signifies the presence of the Most High, the icon of Christ, inscribed with his name, becomes the new Temple, a place of encounter: "If evil comes upon us, the sword, judgment, or pestilence, or famine, we will stand before this house, and before Thee, for Thy name is in this house, and cry to Thee in our affliction, and Thou wilt hear and save" (2 Chr 20:9).

Built up from a geometric structure and defined space in which colors and light play a fundamental role, the icon is a theophanic art whose harmony derives from the unity of composition, graphics, colors and light. As for the artist-iconographer, he must master the technique in order to surpass it, allowing himself or herself to be guided by a correct vision of the faith and a profound respect for the Tradition.

The Icon, Theology in Color

The icon proclaims God and reveals Him. Accordingly, we have a theology of the icon as well as through the icon. Because this theology exists in fact only within the Orthodox Church, its absence elsewhere explains the different perceptions, the deep divergence and even outright iconoclasm often found today in other Christian confessions.

But if the icon constitutes a theological language, this language must be purified. It needs to be freed from the distortions represented in all-too-common decadent images. In turn, theology cannot be reduced to an autonomous field of knowledge. In the Orthodox tradition, the theologian is one whose search for God is accomplished through asceticism, prayer, and praise, which together lead to an intimate union with God. Orthodoxy has adopted the definition of Evagrius (†399), the holy monk of Egypt: "If you are a theologian, you will truly pray. And if you truly pray, you are a theologian" (*On Prayer*, no. 61).

As a counterbalance to "cataphatic" theology, which seeks a definition of God within the limits of human language and states what He is, there is another theology known as "apophatic," which expresses what God is not. It is to this apophatic approach that the iconophiles fervently adhered. Yet images often lead one deeper into the mystery of God than any theological treatise, however beautiful the latter may be. The icon is able to convey profound truths of the faith that are awkwardly represented by concepts.

As it does today, and has done repeatedly in the past, the iconoclasm of the eighth century insisted on the impossibility of circumscribing God. The opposition between this perspective and that of the iconodules led to a theology of the icon that was produced only through bloodshed and tears.

The entire Old Testament echoes with Moses' call to God: "What is your Name?" (Ex 3:13), "Show me your glory" (Ex 33:18). The image of God, therefore, could only be the product of one's imagination, since He remained invisible. Understandably, the resulting

14. Praying Theotokos (Virgin of the Sign); 18th c. icon, Russia.
Private collection, France (Photo: Victor Bakchine).

injunction against any representation of the divinity had only one aim: to avoid the idolatry to which people so easily succumb.

The New Testament is founded on the Incarnation of Christ, the Word (*Logos*), "the Everlasting God" (Gen 21:33), who made man in His image and likeness. It is a response to the supplication of the Old Testament that asks to see the face of God and to know His name. As we sing in the liturgy on the day of the Lord's Nativity: "The middle wall of partition has been destroyed...For the express image of the Father, the imprint of His eternity, takes the form of a servant, and without undergoing change He comes forth from a Mother who knew not wedlock" (Vespers, Lord I Call, tone 2). [Therefore] "The deception of idols has come to an end" (Litia, tone 6).

Christ is the visible "image (*eikon*) of the invisible God" (Col 1:15). With this notion we come to the Gospel account in which Philip asks Jesus: "Show us the Father;" to which Jesus responds: "Whoever has seen me has seen the Father" (Jn 14:8-9). The Father is known only through the incarnate Son, the express image of the Father. This is a powerful reminder that the only true image of God has its source in Christ.

Rejecting the icon amounts to denying the reality of the Incarnation. This in turn denies the possibility for us to return to God who, according to the patristic affirmation, is said to have clothed Himself with flesh in order that man might be clothed in divinity. The icon is the foundation of Christian anthropology, which serves to refute the great heresies of Arius and Nestorius that constantly threaten to reappear.

The icon of the "Virgin of the Sign" was named after the prophecy of Isaiah (Isa 7:14; Mt 1:23) and recalls that fundamental truth of the faith expressed as the Incarnation. The human body serves as a receptacle for the divine, allowing it to enter into the world. Yet much like Moses' burning bush, that body is not consumed. In the Nicene-Constantinopolitan Symbol of Faith, we confess that as "true God and true man," Christ "took flesh from the Virgin Mary." The council of Ephesus proclaimed that she was *Theotokos* ("Mother of God"). She is first among human creatures, and the eight-pointed stars of her *mopharion* (veil) point to the fact that the eighth day is fulfilled within her. Just as the icon of Christ represents His person, a union "without confusion" or "separation" of the human and the divine natures, so the Virgin Mary gives birth to Christ, the Second Person of the Holy Trinity. Mary and her incarnate Son belong together in the most intimate union. One can not be accepted or rejected without the other.

As an "acheiropoieic" image (meaning one "not made with human hands," in the sense that it is marked by the seal of the Holy Spirit), the icon of Christ justifies the icons of the saints whom we venerate. Having become through grace what Christ is by nature, they are henceforth heirs (Jn 1:12), adopted sons of God (Gal 4:7), by whom they have been glorified. As the new creation, the face of all faces, the face of Christ stands behind the faces of the saints, since He has assumed and thereby recapitulated the fullness of human nature.

Although all persons participate in one and the same nature, fashioned as they are out of flesh and blood, each one is distinct by virtue of his name and his diverse characteristics. This nature that is common to all men cannot be separated from the singularity of personhood, which makes each one a different being, a unique model, a hypostasis. Thus the icon of Christ is not identified with God because the painted board does not participate in the divine nature. However it does participate in the person of Christ, Son of God, in His hypostasis, since it is His image and it bears His name. The great iconophile, Theodore the Studite, once said: "It is not the nature but the depicted person that is manifested in the icon." He adds:

> Engrave Christ, wherever it is appropriate, as the one who lives within your heart, that reading about Him or seeing Him in an icon, you may know Him by the two means of knowledge...and that you learn to see with your eyes that which you learned through words (*PG* 99, col. 1213C).

To his indomitable opponents, St John of Damascus responds: "I do not venerate matter but the creator of matter, who became matter for my sake and who deigned to inhabit matter and, through it, to effect its salvation" (*Imag.* 1:16, *PG* 94, col. 1245 AC). If the Fathers of the second Nicene council affirmed that the icon and the Gospel accounts "point to one another and certainly explain one another" (*Acts, Mansi* 12), it is because the icon, as a liturgical image, reflects the truths expressed in the sacred texts and because the human flesh that is represented does not appear as corruptible, but as incorruptible, transfigured and deified.

The image reflects the actual condition of theology and of the Church. This was obvious to the counselor of the Caliph of Damascus, St John the Damascene, who lived in the midst of an iconoclastic Islam and, ironically—or rather by divine Providence—became one of the greatest iconographic theologians: "Show me the images you venerate and I will tell you what you believe."

We can never adequately emphasize this key aspect of the icon. Because of it, the iconographer takes on a grave responsibility. The sacred ministry with which he or she is entrusted cannot be improvised. The icon of the Lord's Nativity, for example, expresses a mystical vision which is that of the Gospels. What value is there in a representation of the Incarnation that removes the figurative elements in favor of abstract art? Or to take another example, the significance of the theological tradition is manifest in the icon of the Resurrection, which requires a purely mystical reading of the event.

Far from reflecting the conflicts of a given period or of existence in general, the art of the icon renders the meaning of life, it conveys the apostolic tradition and opens us to the Holy Spirit.

In a world of chaos, of dissolution and only apparent, short term progress, the icon anticipates our coming face to face with God. It conveys the essence of beings and of things, and it transmits grace by serving as a ladder raised up to encounter the divine mystery.

As the *Alter ego* of the Word, a venerated icon resonates with the mystical presence of Christ to the same degree as the proclaimed Word. Just as the Jews of the Exodus reached the Promised Land at the time of "Pascha" (passage/Passover), the icon enables one to "pass" from mere sight to spiritual vision, from the visible to the invisible, from the material to the immaterial. This is what makes necessary a dematerialization, though not a disincarnation. Although the icon does not depict a fallen world, but a world penetrated on every side by divine energies, faith is necessary in order to open the eyes of the heart and the intellect, in order to apprehend the kingdom where all is in harmony and where interior beauty eludes any superficial consideration.

Through His Incarnation, God entered time and space, becoming subject to them and assuming their laws. The icon is a depiction of the incarnate Christ that represents the coincidence of His two natures as a single reality, inviting those who are nourished by it to avoid opposing the divine and the human, heaven and earth. The icons of the great feasts cause the depicted mystery to be present. More than others, they lead the worshipper into another "aeon." The result is an absence of chronological order and a total freedom relative to history.

Christian anthropology is founded on the idea that "God created man in his own image" (Gen 1:27). Christ is the image of the Father, fully God and fully man. In Him and through Him the tarnished image of man recovers its initial beauty. Because God became one flesh with man by nature through the Incarnation of Christ, we are now able to become one with God by grace, through communion in the death and Resurrection of Christ. This is why the icon reveals the New Man and the New Creation, what "today" we are called to be "tomorrow." Embracing man in his entirety, revealing him as *microtheos,* the icon thus concerns every one of us as it confers new meaning upon history.

The Fathers often insisted that, unlike darkness that engenders death, all that is real and true can evolve in the light. Life and being presuppose light. As we have already noted, the icon is light, the locus of an acting presence; for "if one claims that Christ is the wisdom and power of God, the same must be true of his depiction" (Theodore the Studite).

The existence of numerous icons said to be miraculous, due to the wonders that God has effected through them, requires that we consider every icon to be miraculous insofar as it is venerated by faith and in the mystical presence of Christ, of His Mother or of the depicted saint. Consider the hemorrhaging woman of the Gospel (Lk 8:43-48), impatiently trying to touch Jesus' garment. She was healed because of her faith. Thus the icon lives through the faith of those that contemplate it. Physical reality merges with spiritual reality as the wood becomes a medium of grace.

In accordance with the Gospels where Christ says to His followers: "You are the light of the world" (Mt 5:14), the transfigured figure of the icon does not reflect back divine light as the angels do, but becomes radiant with light. This point is powerfully brought out by the halo.

The inscription "Ὁ ὤν," "I Am" (Ex 3:14) on the halo of every icon of Christ, along with the letters IC XC (*Isous Kristos,* Jesus Christ), reminds us with certainty that the God revealed to Moses in the Burning Bush, and the Son of God born of the Virgin Mary, are one and the same person. Just as the Eucharist "commemorates" the Risen One by manifesting His bodily presence among us, the icon actualizes salvation. It makes us live, by way of texts and images, in the "remembrance of God" which is fundamental for spiritual growth. In accordance with, and as an extension of Liturgy, the icon of Christ invites us to "lay aside all earthly cares," as indicated by the frequent inscription: "Come to me all ye that are heavy laden."

In Christ, who came to restore the human countenance, God assumed a face that was struck and spat upon. He who was transfigured before the apostles was willing to be disfigured out of His love for man, so that, once dead to sin, we might discover in Him the face of the Risen One.

The icon is the tangible sign of His presence and of those who have already entered into the eternal light. It turns each place that shelters it into an *ekklesia domestica,* the

15. Mandylion ("acheiropoieic image," that is not made with human hands); scenes around the border of the icon: 1) King Abgar sends a messenger to Christ, 2) who makes an impression of his face on a napkin 3) before offering it to the messenger, 4) who takes it to the king. 16th c. icon, Sts Cosmos and Damien Church of Lokov-Venecia. National Slovenian Gallery, Bratislava.

point of contact with, and concentration on, "the one thing needful." When contemplated with the eyes of the heart for a sufficient length of time, the depicted faces are slowly inscribed upon that heart. Thereby they accompany those who pray and progressively transform them into pure prayer.

The Icon, an Art of Depth

"Color provokes a psychic vibration. Its superficial effect is, therefore, only the means by which it reaches the soul," Kandinsky wrote (*Du Spirituel dans l'art et dans la peinture en particulier,* Denoël-Gonthier, Paris, 1979). A prolonged observation is necessary in order to perceive the language of the medium in a painting by Klee, Mondrian or by Kandinsky himself. The importance of color for these painters is such that one's perception must become imbued with them in order to allow for a sort of dialogue in which the questions outweigh the answers. Modern abstract painters have helped us to understand the extent of the autonomy of color relative to form; here color precedes form. The same does not apply to the icon, however, as it is subject to certain canons. If the colors themselves do in fact convey a message perceived by the soul, it remains subordinate to the drawing. As in all authentic sacred art of an ontological and universal nature, content determines form.

The icon is an art of depth that touches the subconscious by way of the powerful symbols it employs. The symbol takes on its full power when concepts are lacking to express a particular reality. It provokes a reaction, it activates latent mental "structures," it crystallizes a given reality which is perceived primarily by the subconscious. In this sense, the icon exerts a largely unrecognized influence on those that contemplate it, as it escapes the filter of reason and directly touches the heart.

Several visually powerful biblical symbols are recurrent elements in the icon: "light," which accompanies every theophany; "the tree" of life and of the knowledge of good and evil; "the mountain," the center of the world and the sign of proximity to the divinity; "the temple," the point of contact between man and God; and "the door," a figure used as a self-reference by Christ.

The archetype (original model), exemplified by Christ who is "Light," "Temple," "Door," "Truth" and the "Way," provides us with a symbol of first importance in iconography. As the vanquisher of evil and darkness, He is the New Adam, a microcosm, the cosmic man from whom every human person derives their reason for living and in whom each is fulfilled.

Water, fire, birth, growth, and death are all references to the rhythm of nature and life present in the icons of the great feasts. These natural symbols are complemented by other cultural symbols as the result of a long, conscious gestation. The symbol "mother," for example, is common to all civilizations and is related to the notions of fertility, tenderness, and protection. But insofar as the symbol escapes rational thought, any rationalistic society that is insensitive to mystery and thereby materialistic, no longer perceives these vivifying symbols that touch the depth of our being.

As a spiritual vision translated by forms and colors, the icon conveys symbols whose value depends on an interior perception that alone enables one to grasp the reality of salvation which they mediate. It is important, however, that these symbols be sustained by a pure faith, so as not to slip into allegory. The dialogue that exists between image and word, the reciprocal contributions they make and control they exercise toward each other, help significantly in this regard, even if the word is the foundation of the image.

An Armenian monk and defender of icons wrote in the seventh century:

> We behold images with our eyes, we hear them with our ears, we understand
> them with our hearts, and we believe (Sirarpie Narsessian).

Sight, hearing, heart! While "faith comes from what is heard," (Rom 10:17) so also every authentic vision is one of faith or of what is proclaimed. The Gospels cannot be contradicted by the image. Before touching the spirit that is highly receptive to symbols, the image touches the heart, the battleground of good and evil, of darkness and light. Furthermore, guarding the heart, a subject continually referred to by great spiritual minds, requires an ascesis of one's sight, a flight from fantasies and sensual images. The ascetic quality of the icon reveals an image that has been starkly simplified and does not allow the mind to wander or feelings and sensuality to be projected onto it. Hence its penetrating power and the extreme level of concentration it allows. The Fathers strongly cautioned against the inherent idolatry of sensory images. They are idolatrous insofar as they transgress the truth, remain on the level of un-spiritualized flesh, and are foreign to the kingdom.

"Blessed are the pure in heart for they shall see God!" (Mt 5:8). The heart plays a fundamental role in one's spiritual life. It refers to our spiritual center, the noetic center. Therefore the "prayer of the heart," so highly regarded in the Orthodox tradition, means the prayer of one's entire being. The heart in this case has nothing to do with emotions; icons depicting ascetic faces should suffice to recall this fact. Indeed, the warmth of the Holy Spirit is not sentimental; it means rather abnegation, receptivity, acceptance and openness in the sense of the Beatitudes. The purity of our heart determines the purity of our mind. The hesychasts' recommendation to "make one's mind descend into the heart," and their precepts concerning "guarding the heart," were prompted by this truth. As doors to the heart, one's eyes and ears are purified by the sound of the Word and the sight of the icons. When contemplated in faith and love, the image gradually becomes engraved on one's heart.

"To put on Christ" entails assimilating His image presented by the icon which, in a continually renewed Pentecost, transforms us into His likeness. No doubt the "old Adam"

16. Christ Enthroned; early 17th c. icon, from an iconostasis of Petesti, region of Arges, Valachia, Romania. National Art Museum, Bucharest (Museum photo).

retains his weaknesses, his limitations and his conditionings of every kind. Yet the heart changes. It is permeated with new life. This does not lead to some clamorous joy such as the world imagines, but to serenity, peace and assurance that we are with the Risen One who, because of our faith, forgives us and continually raises us up with Himself.

The Incarnation solicits our attention through hearing and sight, two fundamental senses that subtly include that of touch. On an unconscious level, rejecting the visual amounts to preferring absence to presence, the unarticulated Word of the Old Testament to the manifested Word "made flesh" (Jn 1:14), who is the living Word, who died and was resurrected, and is seated in His glorified body—our deified humanity—at the right hand of God the Father.

As a testimony to and justification of the Incarnation, the icon keeps alive the memory of Christ while avoiding the creation of an image that is strictly the product of our imagination. Where words fail, it speaks to the heart, to the spirit, and is capable of inspiring a multitude of reflections:

> There was a time when the Church fought for icons. Today, icons fight for the Church (see L. Ouspensky, *Vers l'Unité,* Y.M.C.A. Press, Paris; p. 26).

The icon is an image composed of an inverted perspective. More precisely, it provides a threshold that enables one to enter and engage in a life-giving dialogue from person to Person. This silent presence imposes nothing, not even itself.

Lights and Shadows in the Current Renewal

We must not be lured by contemporary sensibilities. Apart from Christians who are rediscovering connections to an authentic spiritual vision through the long-forgotten theological language of the icon, there are many others who are more or less innocent victims of a commercial and religious "renewal." These people perceive in the icon only the faintest glimmer of substance. Once it has been reduced to a simple decorative element—appreciated only for its beauty, a commodity subject to speculation and trivialized in a number of other ways—the icon no longer fulfills the "epiphanic" function of sanctifying space.

During the second international meeting of Orthodox theologians held in Athens in 1976, Constantine Kolokyros brought out one of the reasons for the current "success" of the icon: "Modern art has drawn the majority of its characteristic traits from Orthodox iconography. It has effectively eliminated the third dimension, the scientific perspective. Rather, it represents objects according to an axiological order, avoiding anatomical precision by resorting to an impressionistic style, precisely as in the icon."

If the rediscovery of the icon by many Christians promises an intense spiritual renewal, it is important that this renewal be made with discernment. Only by taking into account the icon's every dimension, particularly the liturgical environment to which it belongs, can one grasp its essence.

We suggested earlier that a distinction should be made between the icon and other forms of sacred art presently found in the Roman Catholic Church. Yet we would certainly not consider the icon to be the only legitimate model of sacred painting. Still, everyone can and must ask certain questions. With what images are we nourished? Do they reflect our faith, the *Creed* which we confess? Are they of sacramental value? Do they prefigure the kingdom to come through a purely "mystical" approach rather than a sentimental and imaginative one?

The veneration of icons, often misunderstood by heterodox groups, is in no way magical. The painted board is merely a medium that gives access to the prototype, who alone is venerated. Likewise, the icon must not be specifically Greek or Slavic, but must portray the entirety of the *kerygma*.

Parallel to the account of the conversion of a great sinner, a woman who was touched by an icon, Gregory Nazianzen, known as the Theologian (†390), refers to the iconographer as the greatest teacher of Christianity (*PG* 37, 591ff and 737). Before being a painter, he is a theologian in every sense of the word. His true attitude is inspired by St John the Forerunner, who withdrew in favor of the master (Lk 3:16). This "theology in color" is not a domain for personal expression, but must represent a true answer ("I am the way, the truth and the life," Jn 14:6) to the current thirst for images.

Far too many Orthodox churches are still being invaded by decadent images, sometimes caricatures, which are the sign of a loss of purity in faith as well as of the powerful influence of Western art dating back to the seventeenth century. How can we possibly defeat conceptual heresies while we remain unaware of the visual heresies that are so often conveyed through images?

Many icons painted by non-Orthodox have made us sensitive to the dilemma of the iconographer who is rooted in a tradition that is more or less foreign to that in which the icon was developed. The question is whether it is possible to live in one form of spirituality and to evolve in another. An individual's personal integrity would seem to make this impossible. Hence the pressing need to return to the sources of authentic iconography in order to fully master this foreign language.

Be they intentional falsehoods or the product of indifference, icons that are foreign to the liturgy which underlies them must be rejected. In the current, abundant production of images, multitudes of pseudo-icons rely on "art for art's sake." They are moving away from the Tradition, only to be disfigured by the impulses of the imagination. Even if the correct forms are present, the bodies remain naturalistic, molded of flesh and blood, without any real dynamic of spiritualization. All the latent sensuality of so many church images remains imperceptible to eyes accustomed to this sort of representation. What is the use of strictly respecting the canons, the purity of forms, of lines and of colors, if the essential components of the spiritual vision and the striving of one's soul toward God are defective? Having only just been rediscovered, the icon is liable already to be reduced to a pious image, emptied of its transfiguring substance and of the presence of the Risen One.

The Icon, Locus and Source of Unity

The discovery or authentic rediscovery of the icon leads inevitably to renewing connections with the undivided Church of the first centuries. In particular, it leads to assimilating the achievements of the seven great Ecumenical Councils, especially those of Nicea II (787) that were dedicated to Christology and Pneumatology and laid down the dogmatic basis for icons. Though we do not claim that time came to a standstill with these fundamental debates, it is necessary, under the guidance of the Spirit, to integrate them into our current experience. It is only under these conditions that the icon can become a source of unity.

Through both his painting and his writing, Leonid Ouspensky is a theologian who has contributed more than any other of our contemporaries to the rediscovery of the icon. His words, which some will find severe, are those of a deep and discerning man, whose testimony is of the utmost importance:

> In the image we find the most convincing manifestation, not only of truth but also of every distortion of the truth, by virtue of its visual character. While the words may remain the same, the image emphatically denounces every violation of the patristic Tradition, every instance in which it is betrayed. It is precisely in the image that we observe most clearly the discrepancies between Orthodox doctrine and spiritual life on the one hand, and those of Western confessions on the other...
>
> Since [the icon] is the common heritage of the millennium which preceded the separation of the West, one may claim that it can still serve as a common heritage for all Christian confessions, independantly from canonical and confessional presuppositions. Once removed from its proper context, however, the icon is arbitrarily included in another in which it has no doctrinal foundation nor any organic connection with the liturgy, the sacraments and canonical order. One may say that the icon loses its sacred character just as the Church itself does (see *Vers L'Unité;* pp. 9, 27).

Once it had been cut off from the Church's Greek, Slavic, Germanic and Anglo-Saxon branches, Rome came to consider the pagan and naturalistic art produced by the Renaissance

17. Christ separating the wheat from the tares (parable); 19th c. fresco, Church of the
Pantocrator, Decani Monastery, Serbia.

as the model for Christian art. This was a death sentence, no doubt with a reprieve for sacred art. But while detours outside the apostolic Tradition had repercussions in Western religious art and in the decadent icons it inspired, a rediscovery of the most pure Tradition has brought many back to the true faith, to right praise and worship. Purified by a centuries-old theological development, Christian faith becomes crystallized in the icon according to the previously stated maxim: *lex credendi, lex orandi, lex videndi!* The icon reflects the faith and evokes it to such an extent that a return to the sources, the reactivation of the "Christian memory," today can take that path in reverse: *lex videndi, lex credendi, lex orandi!*

As a witness to the reality of Christ's Incarnation, the icon is an integral part of the Christian legacy. Although the Orthodox have been able to preserve and transmit the iconographic tradition to this day, it does not belong to them. Yet although it is clearly a gift for our time, its full rediscovery cannot occur without the Orthodox. It is incumbent upon them, with great discernment, to purify their own iconography, to get rid of decadent influences that have been tolerated for too long, and to be, by way of example, at the forefront of the "defense of holy images."

In today's world, assaulted and saturated as it is with empty and all too often harmful images, the life-bearing icon traces a luminous pathway, as a silent and faithful guide toward the kingdom of God.

4

The Icons of the Resurrection

Initial Comments

The Resurrection constitutes the world's center of gravity and its axis, since, having assumed humanity through His Incarnation, Christ restored it by His death and Resurrection. Today, as in the time of nascent Christianity, the world refuses to take the message of the Gospels seriously; it is nonsense and folly to some, narrow-mindedness and scandal to others. Twenty centuries later, the reactions to Paul's discourse at the Areopagus in Athens are as familiar as ever: "Now when they heard of the resurrection of the dead, some mocked; but others said, 'We will hear you again about this'" (Acts 17:32).

Who indeed is able to hear such words? Is it possible for a God, the One and only God, to be born of a woman, to live the life of men, to allow Himself to be crucified out of love for them and to be resurrected, henceforth leading them up with Himself to the right hand of the Father? The wisdom of the world stands opposed to this and regards authentic Christians as an infection that needs to be eradicated. According to Christ's own words: "If you were of the world, the world would love its own; [but] you are not of the world" (Jn 15:19).

With its one-sided insistence on the role of the Cross, "the tree of salvation" through which Christ triumphed over death, the West has created an imbalance at the expense of the Resurrection, which tends to be relegated to a secondary position. Although Jesus' death was attested to by many witnesses and may be historically verified, His Resurrection cannot be. This is because it derives from a mystery, one that illumines the history of mankind from the very first day of creation.

During the paschal vigil, the priest raises the cross and sings: "Christ is risen! For by the cross Christ has vanquished death and sin which held us captive."

The body of the Risen One is a constant reminder of the cross. As an echo of the Paschal Matins, the Orthros of every Sunday morning celebrates the slaying of death, the despoiling of hell by the cross, and the light of the Resurrection. At every eucharistic liturgy, the priest reads this prayer after the communion of the faithful:

> Having beheld the Resurrection of Christ, let us worship the holy Lord Jesus, the only sinless One. We venerate Thy Cross, O Christ, and we praise and

glorify Thy holy Resurrection; for Thou art our God, and we know no other than Thee; we call on Thy name. Come all you faithful, let us venerate Christ's holy Resurrection! For, behold, through the Cross joy has come into all the world. Let us ever bless the Lord, praising His Resurrection, for by enduring the Cross for us, He has destroyed death by death....

To claim, as some do however, that the Orthodox Church focuses solely on the Transfiguration and the Resurrection, reveals a profound misconception that ignores its firm insistence on preaching salvation precisely through the Cross. Nevertheless, it may be necessary to reflect further on the fact that the Resurrection escapes reason, and that reason can approach this mystery only through its own crucifixion.

Dead once for all on the Cross, outside the walls of Jerusalem, and resurrected on the third day after His burial, Christ continues to die and to rise, mystically, mysteriously, until the end of the age, in each person whose nature He has assumed. Before the scandal and the horror of death—of all the daily deaths such as sickness, hatred, injustice, the destruction of our natural environment, physical and psychic disorders—the Resurrection of Christ traces a path of light. It produces an abundant flow of life in the midst of death, it transforms death into a "passage" (Pascha). The Paschal mystery is an invitation to keep our lamps lit (Lk 12:35). It introduces us to another aeon, which is a new dimension, the anticipation of the world to come, the Kingdom already secretly present among us.

As a liturgical image that expresses the essence of Orthodoxy, the icon also provides a visual representation of the faith proclaimed in the texts of a liturgy of unutterable depth. Therefore we are naturally led to draw abundantly from such a source. It would benefit the reader to begin listening to the liturgy of Holy Saturday, followed by the paschal vigil, while fixing his gaze on the icon of the Descent into Hell. The height of Orthodox liturgy is truly attained on the night of Pascha. At the close of a long and fervent vigil, around midnight, the priest proclaims the Good News to the world: "Christ is risen from the dead, trampling down death by death, and upon those in the tombs bestowing life!" (Paschal Matins, Troparion, tone 5). The verses of the Paschal Canon, composed by St John of Damascus, flow like majestic waves over the faithful. The paschal candles held by the faithful become like quivering flames of life that proclaim in unison: "Let us celebrate the slaying of death, the destruction of hell, the beginning of a new life...for all things are filled with light: heaven, earth and hell. Let all Creation rejoice in the Resurrection of Christ!"

Everything is suffused with light and bathed in incense, a symbol of the prayers that rise toward God, which by its sweet aroma announces the Kingdom to come. The ceaselessly chanted refrain: "Christ is risen from the dead," is intended to convince each and every one of us of that an unfathomable mystery is unfolding in our midst. "This is

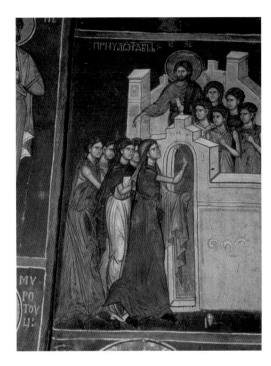

18. The Parable of the Wise and Foolish Virgins;
fresco, 1335-50, Church of the Decani
Monastery, Serbia.

the day of Resurrection, let us be illumined by the feast, let us embrace one another; let us call brothers even those that hate us, let us forgive all by the Resurrection" (Paschal stichera, tone 5). By His death, Christ freed us all from our bonds, transforming death into a "passage" to everlasting life.

As disciples of Christ, how can we not rejoice on the morning of Pascha when we hear the Risen One declare: "you are my beloved!" (Jn 15:14)? To be Christian means first and foremost to have an experience of Christ at the heart of one's life. In his homily, read on the morning of Pascha, St John Chrysostom (†407) declares that the Lord welcomes everyone who turns toward Him: "And he showeth mercy upon the last, and careth for the first...Let no one weep for his iniquities, for pardon has shone forth from the grave. Let no one fear death, for the Savior's death has set us free."

Following in the way of thousands of witnesses from the past, both known and unknown, Dostoyevski, the inimitable voice of the Russian soul, offers a vision marked by the primordial reality of the Resurrection. From his profoundly Christian perspective, even those below ground, "in [their] great sorrow...shall rise again to joy, without which man cannot live nor God exist: for God gives joy" (*The Brothers Karamazov,* book 11, chap. 4; C. Garnett, trans., Random House, 1950; p. 720).

The desire to penetrate the Christian mystery, which our veiled eyes cannot fathom, can only increase our blindness. Rather than sounding a retreat, we must seek an interior perception, through the eyes of the heart (the νους). Given the silence and omissions of the Gospels, the only fitting attitude is that of the doubting Thomas, our perfect representative who, confronted with the Risen One, exclaimed: "My Lord and my God" (Jn 20:28). Thereby he confessed both His humanity and His divinity without division.

"No one can say: 'Jesus is Lord,' except by the Holy Spirit" (1 Cor 12:3). Without the Spirit it is impossible to believe in Christ and in His Resurrection. The example of the apostles—their disbelief, followed by their faith suddenly revived by the resurrected Christ, who sends them the Spirit in order to make them steadfast in their witness—proves that it is the Spirit Himself who resurrects. Underestimating the power of the Spirit amounts to depriving the Resurrection of Christ of its vital dynamism. Without the Spirit, one inevitably objectifies the Resurrection and makes of it a mere abstraction.

The development of iconography occured at the same time as the great ecumenical councils of the fourth, fifth and sixth centuries that were dedicated especially to Christology (the doctrine concerning Christ). Among the first images that bear witness to the ineffable event of the Resurrection we encounter that of the Myrrhbearing Women at the tomb, then progressively, illustrations of other scenes about the Risen One.

Like the icon, which is a theology expressed through forms and colors, the liturgy fulfills theology. Rooted in time, the Resurrection nevertheless eludes both time and space through its presence in the divine eternity. The liturgy cannot be more explicit concerning the mystery of Holy Week and Pascha; any addition would be a mere gloss. A full understanding of the paschal iconography implies a great familiarity with the liturgical texts of the Orthodox Church and with its eucharistic liturgy. As clever as they may be, the all too common deviations and fantastic interpretations of the paschal event result from a lack of faithfulness to the "canons" and from ignorance of the Tradition. In obedience to the laws of spiritual life, iconography simply testifies to the liturgical life in which, in the mystery of the eighth day and beyond the flow of time, all things commune within a vast Trinitarian gathering.

Compared with myths of death and revival referred to earlier, the Resurrection of Christ includes not only the soul but also the body, as does the resurrection in which we are called to follow Him. Man is a microcosm who bears within himself the "flesh of the world." Through him and by the power of Christ who bestows the Spirit, that flesh is destined to a total transfiguration. Resurrected with Christ, living a new existence in which death leads to eternal life, man recovers his original harmony with creation. He changes from being a predator to receiving creation as a gift from God. Accordingly, he is called to perceive in every speck of dust the life-giving breath of the Spirit.

The two primary icons of the Resurrection are those of the Descent into Hell and the Myrrhbearing Women at the Tomb, each of which represents one aspect of a single reality. Though they are not interchangeable, they point to one another and complement one another, as they reflect both symbol and history, mystery and vision, the event of Holy Saturday and that of the morning of Pascha. This complementarity is apparent in Orthodox churches that naturally place these two icons side by side. Because it is never described as such in the Gospels, the moment of the Resurrection cannot be reproduced. Such is possible only for related events: Peter at the tomb, the appearance of the Risen One to Mary Magdalen, to the apostles, to Thomas, on the shore of the Sea of Tiberias, and to the Myrrhbearing women. It is a striking fact that the first icon of Pascha is that of Holy Saturday, which reveals the true spiritual meaning of the feast.

The Descent Into Hell

> Christ is risen from the dead, trampling down death by death, and upon those in the tombs bestowing life...This is the day of resurrection!...Pascha, the Pascha of the Lord! For from death to life and from earth to heaven has Christ our God led us...Now all is filled with light: heaven, earth and the lower regions. Let all creation celebrate the rising of Christ. In Him we are established! (Paschal Matins).

This proclamation, ceaselessly uttered throughout the paschal liturgy of the Orthodox Church, gradually penetrates every fiber of one's being. It is during this spiritual ascent—with an unparalleled if often unrecognized richness—that the icon of the Descent into Hell attains its most powerful expression and fully introduces us into the heart of the mystery of salvation.

Origins and sources

The highly symbolic icon of the Descent into Hell shows Christ opening a pathway through the earth, trampling the gates of Hell, illuminating all things with His radiance, and raising Adam from the slumber of death. Although it appears on a column of St Mark's Cathedral in Venice (sixth century), this composition was common especially at Sinai and in Cappadocia between the eighth and tenth centuries. André Grabar believes this image dates back to the seventh or eighth century, from a fresco of Sainte-Marie-Antique, on the Roman Forum. It was presumably "a response to the allegorical images of the victorious Roman emperor, drawing toward himself the kneeling or prostrated personifi-

19. The Descent into Hell; 12th c. (?) fresco, Karanlik Kilise, Cappadocia.

cations of conquered provinces or towns, or their representatives. The official language of the Empire described them as images of the 'liberation' of the defeated peoples, wrenched from the 'tyranny' of their leaders by the Roman emperor. This interpretation enabled Christians to use the same iconographic scheme for Christ descending into Hell: vanquisher of the tyrannical prince of death, he frees and draws to Himself those inhabiting that kingdom against their will, beginning with Adam and Eve" (from *Les voies de la création en iconographie chrétienne*, Flammarion, Paris, 1979, p. 114). The ancient texts, from which we will draw some examples, establish an obvious parallelism with the development of this iconography.

The images of the Descent into Hell and of the Myrrhbearing Women became closely associated with one another in the West from the thirteenth century onward. Beginning with the sixteenth century, the Eastern Church borrowed from the Latins the image of Christ rising from the tomb, a motif that had been firmly rooted in Western tradition since the eleventh century. Here we find clear indication of two very diffrent perceptions of the very event of the Resurrection.

The illustrated text of the *Acts of Pilate*, which appears to date back to the fourth century, represents an interesting source for the later elaboration of the icon of the Descent into Hell. Syrian liturgical texts of the same period, however—which later became a powerful inspiration for St Romanos the Melode (†after 556), as well as for numerous sermons—constitute an earlier and richer source. Suffice it to mention the sermon On Pascha of St Melito of Sardis, who lived in Asia Minor in the middle of the second century:

> I have freed those condemned and given life to the dead.
> I awoke those who were buried,
> vanquished death and triumphed over the enemy.
> I descended into hell, where I bound the mighty one
> and raised men up to heaven (*PG* 101-102, 775-785).

During the same period, St Irenaeus of Lyon wrote: "The Lord, the Holy One of Israel, remembered His departed ones asleep in their tombs, and He descended to them to bring the news of salvation...to raise them up and save them" (*Adv. Haer.* III, 20, 4).

The *Odes of Solomon* were composed in the first half of the second century. Intended as liturgical prayers, they provide a remarkable witness to the importance attributed by the early Church to Christ's victory over death and hell:

> I opened the barred gates,
> I broke the iron locks,
> and the iron became red and turned to liquid before me;
> and nothing more was shut up,
> because I am the door for every being.
> I went to free the captives,
> they are mine and I abandon no one.
> (Ode 17)

> Hell saw me and it was defeated,
> death released me and many with me.
> I was its gall and vinegar.
> I descended through death into hell,
> into its very depths.
> Death...was unable to behold my countenance.
> Of the dead I made a living assembly...
> The dead ran towards me.
> They cried out: Have mercy on us, son of God...
> Remove us from the darkness that binds us!
> Open the door for us, that we may go out with you.
> (Ode 42)

Everything is present already in the second century. This fact tends to relativize the importance often attributed to the *Acts of Pilate* (the Gospel of Nicodemus) and frees us from reservations we might have in using it since it is apocryphal. Besides, St Hippolytus of Rome, at the beginning of the third century, offers this explanation of the way in which Christ abased Himself:

> All those whom Satan had bound in his lakes, the Lord came to deliver from death...(He came) to bind the one who, more than all others, was the "Strong One," and to free humanity (*Commentary on Daniel,* IV, 33).

Nicknamed "the Harp of the Spirit," St Ephrem the Syrian (†373) chants in his fourth-century liturgical hymns:

> Glory to you who came down and plunged into the depths to seek Adam whom you freed from Hades in order to lead him into paradise (*Carmina Nisibena* 65).

Another Church Father, St Cyril of Jerusalem (313-387), develops the theme of the Descent into Hell in his *Catachesis:*

> Death was afraid when it saw this New Man descending unfettered into hell.

> Why does the sight of him make you afraid, O guardian of hell? What unwonted fear has come upon you? Death has fled and this flight only betrays its fear. The holy Prophets come to meet him, Moses, the Law-giver, Abraham, Isaac, Jacob, David, Solomon, Isaiah, and John the Baptist, the witness who had asked: "Are you the one who is to come or should we await another?" He redeemed all the righteous ones that death had swallowed up...Then all the righteous said: "O Death, where is your victory? Hell, where is your sting?" The Conqueror has set us free! (14:19).

In another text—which approximates or imitates in certain respects the Gospel of Nicodemus, which he must have known—Cyril goes a bit further, leaving a great deal of leeway for images:

> (Observe) great silence, for the king is asleep. The earth shook, then it was quiet, for God fell asleep in the flesh, and He has gone to awaken those who have slept for centuries...He is going to deliver from their pain the fettered Adam, and Eve held captive with him, He who is both their God and their son. Let us descend with him, that we might see the alliance between God and man. There is Adam, the first father who, being the first one ceated, is buried deeper than all those condemned. There is Abel who is the first to have died and who, as the first righteous pastor, prefigures the unjust murder of Christ. There is Noah, a figure of Christ, who built the great arch of God, the Church...There is Abraham, the Father of Christ, the one who offered to God, by a dagger yet without a dagger, a sacrifice of blood yet one without death. There dwell Moses...Daniel...Jeremiah...There is Jonah in the monster which is able to contain the world, meaning hell...And among the prophets there is one who cries out: "From the

belly of Sheol hear my supplication, heed my cry!" And another: "Out of the depths I cry to thee, O Lord, hear my voice!" And another: "Let thy face shine and we shall be saved!"...

Speaking to all those who had been in chains since the beginning of the world, Adam spoke thus: "I hear the steps of one coming toward us!" And as he spoke, the Lord entered, bearing the victorious weapon of the cross...And having taken hold of his hand he said to him: "Awake, O sleeper, and arise from the dead, and Christ shall give you light (Eph 5:14). I am your God, and for your sake I became your son. Arise, you who were sleeping, for I did not create you to remain bound in hell. Having arisen from the dead, I am the Life of the dead...Arise and let us depart from here, from death to life, from corruption to immortality, from darkness to eternal life..." (*Homily on Holy Saturday, PG* 43, 444-464).

Without returning to the texts of the New and Old Testaments that heralded the Resurrection (see ch. 2), it seems necessary, nonetheless, to recall the silence of the Gospels concerning Christ's descent into hell. Yet the apostles Peter and Paul mention it. Right after the Twelve received the Holy Spirit on the day of Pentecost, Peter spoke to the crowd that was "bewildered, because each one heard them speaking in his own language":

He [David] foresaw and spoke of the resurrection of the Christ, that he was not abandoned to Hades, nor did his flesh see corruption. This Jesus God raised up, and of that we all are witnesses (Acts 2:6 and 31-32).

Later, in his First Epistle, he declares:

Christ also died for sins once and for all, the righteous for the unrighteous, that he might bring us to God, being put to death in the flesh but made alive in the Spirit; in which he went and preached to the spirits in prison (1 Pet 3:18-19).

And St Paul adds:

In saying 'He ascended,' what does it mean but that he had also descended into the lower parts of the earth? He who descended is He who also ascended far above all the heavens, that He might fill all things (Eph 4:9-10).

The Old Testament, as a mirror image of more recent times, has made abundant contributions to the development of this iconography. The allusions are striking, both in Isaiah and in the Psalms:

Arise, shine; for your light has come, and the glory of the Lord has risen upon you (Is 60:1).

Lift up your heads, O gates! and be lifted up, O ancient doors! that the King of glory may come in. Who is the King of glory? The Lord, strong and mighty, the Lord, mighty in battle! (Ps 24:7-8).

20. The Descent into Hell; mid-11th c. fresco, Church of St Nicholas, Kakopetria, Cyprus.

> Some sat in darkness and in gloom, prisoners in affliction and in irons, for they had rebelled against the words of God, and spurned the counsel of the Most High. Their hearts were bowed down with hard labor; they fell down, with none to help. Then they cried to the Lord in their trouble, and he delivered them from their distress; He brought them out of darkness and gloom, and broke their bonds asunder. Let them thank the Lord for His steadfast love, for His wonderful works to the sons of men! For He shatters the doors of bronze and cuts in two the bars of iron (Ps 107:10-16).

The entire Old Testament follows Hosea when he prophesies:

> After two days he will revive us; on the third day he will raise us up, that we may live before him (6:2).

As for the famous text of Nicodemus, *The Acts of Pilate,* the second part deserves more than a brief summary. When considered as a continuation of the texts we have just mentioned, and read with the eyes of faith, it takes on a new dimension, unveiling and making tangible the reality of salvation offered to us through Christ's victory over death.

And at the hour of midnight a light as radiant as the sun pierced the darkness. We were illumined so that we could see each other. And immediately our father Abraham, along with the patriarchs and the prophets, was filled with joy, and they said to one another: This shining comes from a great light. The Prophet Isaiah, who was present, said: This is the light of the Father and the Son and the Holy Spirit...

While Satan and Hades were speaking thus to one another, there sounded a loud voice like thunder: Lift up your gates, O rulers, and be lifted up, O everlasting doors, and the King of glory shall come in (Ps 23:7 LXX). When Hades heard this, he said to Satan: Go out, if you can, and withstand him. So Satan went out. Then Hades said to his demons: Close the bronze gates tightly, set the iron bars, double the locks, and maintain a constant watch. For if He enters here, He will become our Master.

When the forefathers heard that, they all began to mock him, saying: O all-devouring and insatiable one, open, that the King of glory may come in...

The bronze gates were broken in pieces and the bars of iron were snapped; and all the dead who were bound were loosed from their chains, and we with them. And the King of Glory entered like a man, and all the dark places of Hades were illumined...

Then the King of Glory seized the chief ruler, Satan, by his head and handed him over to the angels, saying: Bind his hands and his feet and his neck and his mouth with iron fetters...

The King of Glory stretched out his right hand and took hold of our forefather Adam and raised him up. Then He turned to the rest and said: Come with me, all you who have suffered death because of the tree which this man touched. For behold, I raise you all up again through the tree of the cross...

As they were entering the gate of paradise, two old men met them. The holy fathers asked them: Who are you, who have not seen death nor gone down into Hades, but dwell in paradise with your bodies and souls? One of them answered: I am Enoch, who pleased God and was removed here by him. And this is Elijah the Tishbite...While they were saying this, there came another man, humble and carrying a cross upon his shoulder. The holy fathers asked him: Who are you, who have the appearance of a robber, and what is the cross you are carrying on your shoulder? He answered: I was, as you say, a robber and a thief in the world...But when the flaming sword (that of St Michael) saw the sign of the cross, it opened to me, and I came in. [Excerpt (slightly modified) from *New Testament Apocrypha,* E. Hennecke, Lutterworth Press, 1963]

The suggestive power of this text and the realities it conveys profoundly mark every heart and spirit that is enlightened by the teaching of the Fathers and Holy Scripture. It is important that nothing be isolated, that one lay hold of every facet, like scattered streams giving birth to the great river of divine love revealed to men by the Risen One.

The matins and vespers of Holy Saturday, reflecting what has preceded them, are truly a verbal icon of the "Descent into Hell":

> Today hell groans and cries aloud: 'My power has been destroyed. I accepted a mortal man as one of the dead; yet I cannot keep Him prisoner, and with Him I shall lose all those over whom I ruled. I held in my power the dead from all the ages; but see, He is raising them all' (Vespers, tone 8).

Likewise, the fifteen readings of Holy Saturday illustrate the close connection that exists between the Old and the New Testament concerning the Death and Resurrection of Christ. These readings are related, in order, to the following themes:

1. The account of Creation up to the third day (Gen 1:1-13), when the light first pierces the darkness.

2. Isaiah proclaims the light of the Lord (Is 60:1-6).

3. Exodus, the Passover of the Jews freed from the Pharaonic yoke (Ex 12:1-11). Satan, who is identified with Pharaoh in the liturgical texts, keeps these souls in Egypt, which symbolizes captivity.

4. The sign of Jonah (Jon 1:4) who, having been swallowed by the great fish, remains there three days and three nights before beseeching God "from the midst of hell."

5. Joshua's encounter with the Archangel Michael "the day after the Passover" (Jos 5:10-16).

6. With the "pillar of cloud" guiding them and lighting the way, the Jews cross the sea "on dry land" before a defeated Pharaoh (Ex 13:20-15:19).

7. Forgiveness and deliverance prophesied by Zephaniah (Zeph 3:8-15).

8. Given shelter by the widow of Sarepta, the prophet Elijah brings her son back to life (1 Kg 17:18-24).

9. The prophecy of Isaiah: "The Lord will show justice and mercy before the face of all peoples" (Is 61:10-62:5).

10. The test of Abraham (Gen 22:1-18) in which his son, Isaac, becomes the prefiguring image of Christ. Unlike Isaac, the Son of God will not be spared and will truly give His life.

11. Isaiah proclaims "the Good News to the poor, the afflicted...and liberty to the captives" (Is 61:1-10).

12. The promise of a son, made by Elisha to the Sunamite woman, a son he later brings back to life (2 Kg 4:8-27).

13. A call to the Lord for deliverance (Is 63:11-64:5).

14. A new covenant and forgiveness prophesied by Jeremiah (Jer 38:31-34).

15. The account of the three Chaldean youths who, having been cast "into the fiery furnace" because they refused to make a sacrifice to the idol, "walked in the midst of the flames, praising God" (Dan 3:1-88).

The liturgical texts are echoed in iconography; the latter is nourished by them and becomes their icon as they themselves are the icon of the celebrated mystery. There is no doubt that the "Paschal Canon" and the hymns of St John of Damascus, written in the eighth century, along with those of St Andrew of Crete and St Cosmos of Maioum, contributed to the development of the iconographic theme of the "Descent into Hell":

> Thou didst descend, O Christ to the depths of the earth. Thou didst break the everlasting bars which had held death's captives, and like Jonah from the whale on the third day, Thou didst arise from the grave...O my Savior, as God Thou didst bring Thyself freely to the Father, a victim living and unsacrificed, resurrecting Adam, the father of us all, when Thou didst arise from the grave (Paschal Matins, Ode 6, Canon of St John of Damascus).

St John of Damascus simply reworked the canticle of Jonah (2:3-10) out of appreciation for its power to evoke the event:

> I went down to the land whose bars closed upon me for ever; yet thou didst bring up my life from the Pit (Jon 2:6).

Let us conclude with an excerpt from the "funeral Eulogies" of Holy Saturday which sum up the event:

> Of old, Joshua stopped the sun in its path in order to triumph over his enemy. On this day, you cover its radiance, becoming the vanquisher of the Prince of darkness (Matins, 2nd verse, tone 5, no. 116).

> To earth hast Thou come down, O Master, to save Adam: and not finding him on earth, Thou hast descended into hell, seeking him there. (Matins, first stasis, tone 5, no. 25).

The existence of several "descents into hell," born out of different cultures, could lead one to regard that of Christ rather subjectively. In reality, history as a whole proclaims the coming of the Savior. Every initiation amounts to a "passage" and a death, to the same degree that baptism, the rite of incorporation into Christ, signifies the death of sin.

A Description of the Icon

In his guide to iconographic customs, Denys de Fourne aptly describes the icon of the Descent into Hell:

Hell, like a dark cave, under a mountain. Radiant angels bind Beelzebub, the chief of darkness; they strike some demons and pursue others armed with spears. Naked and fettered, several men raise their eyes. Many broken locks. The doors of Hell are knocked down; Christ is trampling them. The Savior takes Adam with His right hand and Eve with His left. On the Savior's left, the Forerunner, pointing to Him. David stands near Him as well as other righteous kings with crowns and halos. On the left, the prophets Jonah, Isaiah and Jeremiah; the righteous Abel and many others have halos. All around, a brilliant light and a multitude of angels (*Guide to Painting,* Paris, 1845).

How can we hope to restore the spiritual content of the Resurrection, the Mystery of mysteries, if not through symbols? In Orthodoxy, these are not mere representations of a reality; they are themselves a manifestation of this reality. A full reading of this icon can be made, therefore, only through the powerful symbolism that opens the soul and the heart to its inexhaustible hidden meaning.

At the moment of Jesus' death, "the earth shook, and the rocks were split" (Mt 27:51). Is this not the sign of a theophany, a sort of reverse transfiguration that is no longer played out on Mount Tabor, but at the center of the earth and of the cosmos, free from every geographic particularity? The master of life, radiant with light, now manifests toward the dead, the solidarity He had with the living during His earthly life. And He does so by penetrating to the very depths of the under-world, where darkness abounds. As in the icons of the Transfiguration, the Ascension and the Dormition, a bright mandorla indicates the transformation of His body into one of glory. The mandorla is frequently replaced by a set of concentric circles, often three in number. Their blue or green color becomes more intense from the first outside circle to the very dark center, as an illustration of the apophatic description of God: "radiant darkness!" In these instances, rays of light emanate from Christ, who is adorned with a vestment of gold or brilliant white. The gold vestment is a sign of divinity to the same extent as the white one, and is streaming with light. As a flash of lightning illumines the dark of night, Christ springs forth in a movement that expresses His universal presence and power. When He raises Adam by firmly grasping his wrist, it is all of humanity that He resurrects. The keen observer will note that Adam's sleeve is often of a much lighter color than the rest of his clothing, as proof of the transfiguration or deification that is taking place, effected by Christ Himself, filled with the Holy Spirit.

This movement of the raising of the first man, with his soul animating his body, captures the whole content of redemption. Like the Incarnation, the Descent into Hell has no other purpose and expresses no other meaning. And the event is not "physical" but fully spiritual.

Christ's large vestment, with a fold often floating upward, clearly indicates the descending movement so well rendered by the paschal liturgy. Indeed, the latter does not

21. The Descent into Hell; late 15th c. icon, from the iconostasis of the Church of the
Dormition of Volotovo, near Novgorod. History and Architecture Museum, Novgorod.

state that the gates of Hades were merely opened, but that they were shattered along with the locks. As a result, they can never again be shut! This liberation marks a final, brilliant victory, expressed unambiguously by the fact that Christ's feet are trampling the gates of Hell. The scroll in His left hand symbolizes the preaching to the "spirits in prison" (1 Pet 3:19); when it is replaced by the cross, under Western influence, it becomes a sign of victory, as the means by which Christ conquered and broke down the gates of bronze.

A little behind Adam are the two ancestors of the Savior, each wearing a crown: Solomon, the beardless one, and his bearded father, David, the founder of Jerusalem who sings in the psalms: "Out of the depths I cry to thee, O Lord, Lord hear my voice!" (Ps 130). Near them, St John the Forerunner indicates the liberator, whom he proclaims to the world both above and below. We can hardly fail to recognize the importance of the one who was beheaded in order "that he might proclaim the coming of the Savior even unto Hades" (Beheading of John the Baptist, Matins, Ode 7). The order of the characters varies. Those from the Old Testament are often situated to the right of Christ, and His contemporaries or those that came after Him, to the left. They stand behind Eve, who raises her hands, shrouded in a fold of her mantle, in a humble gesture that welcomes this One who brings eternal life. This gesture hearkens back to a custom of the Byzantine court, which called for hiding the hands as a sign of submission in the presence of one's superiors. Created in purity, the first woman Eve is freed by the One who is without sin: He who is born of the new virgin Eve, the Mother of God.

The presence of the prophets seems self-evident. Having awaited the Resurrection, were they not the first to announce it? And what about Abel, the first victim of injustice? Moses, wearing a phrygian cap, in the manner of the prophets, is generally included as representing the first covenant and as a witness to the first Pascha. Standing in the background, kings, prophets, and righteous men immediately recognize the Risen One whom they have borne in their hearts and whom they have summoned with their whole being. The asymmetry of this scene serves to express the outpouring of life, while the fact that Paul is often depicted standing behind Eve shows that the event concerns every time and every place, indeed, the whole cosmos.

Death is sometimes represented as a black silhouette, occasionally accompanied by helpers. He lies defeated, held in chains underneath the gates, his hands and feet tied and his neck bound. Death has been put to death. As the father of lies and the enticer of men, Satan is sometimes depicted with two faces, a powerful sign of his lack of unity and disintegration, integrity being the mark of the saints.

The final element, symbolized by the rocks, is the entire cosmos that reflects the light rising from the depths of the earth. Both the visible and the invisible world participate in the Resurrection of Christ, the One whom we need only welcome and follow in order to be saved. "Let us enter into the joy of our Lord..."

Light, Freedom, Joy: Fullness of Life

Light, life, joy, freedom: these words resound throughout the Gospels and the liturgy during the paschal season. "Now all is filled with light, heaven, earth, and the lower regions" (Paschal Matins, Ode 3). "From death to life...has Christ our God led us." (Paschal Matins, Ode 1). All of creation is borne up in this freeing motion. The icon confirms that Pascha (from the Hebrew *peschah*, passage), is connected to the Old Testament liberation of the chosen people then enslaved in Egypt, and now signifies deliverance from sin and death. "How great the joy, how full the gladness, that Thou hast brought to those in Hell, shining as lightning in its gloomy depths" (Matins of Holy Saturday, first stasis, tone 5, no. 48).

Whether it be on a physical, spiritual, social or even economic level, light plays a fundamental role in the process of life. Diverse cultures were not mistaken in raising it to the level of a powerful symbol. In the face of darkness, the symbol of death and damnation, the "truth," meaning the "reality" of beings and of things, is revealed in and through light. Man finds his way (the truth) only in reference to the light. If the latter allows beings and things to be known, it also conditions their existence and provides a foundation for their life. Yet Christ refers to Himself as "Light, Life, Way, Door, Truth!" He is the fullest expression of "reality"; all that is has its source in Him.

At his entrance into hell, Dante has the ancient poet, Virgil, declare that he is penetrating into a place that is "mute as to light," (*ogni luce muto*) but full of groaning. The lack of light actually implies a lack of awareness of the other, total isolation, the absence of communication and of love. Hell is none other than the state of separation from God, a condition into which humanity was plunged for having preferred the creature to the Creator. It is the human creature, therefore, and not God, who engenders hell. Created free for the sake of love, man possesses the incredible power to reject this love, to say "no" to God. By refusing communion with God, he becomes a predator, condemning himself to a spiritual death (hell) more dreadful than the physical death that derives from it.

But let us return to the text whose assimilation is accomplished as much by sight as by sound, enabling us to receive the Word of God through the icon in which Christ appears adorned in light:

> You are a chosen race, a royal priesthood, a holy nation, God's own people, that you may declare the wonderful deeds of him who called you out of darkness into his marvelous light (1 Pet 2:9).

"I am the light of the world; he who follows me will not walk in darkness, but will have the light of life" (Jn 8:12).

"I have come as light into the world, that whoever believes in me may not remain in darkness" (Jn 12:46).

The Lord is my light and my salvation, whom shall I fear? (Ps 27:1).

Evening worship do we offer Thee, the Unwaning Light, Who in the end of the ages, through the flesh as in a mirror, hast shined upon the world; and hast descended even unto Hades, and dispelled the darkness there, and hast shown the light of the Resurrection unto the nations. O Giver of light, Lord, glory be to Thee (Bright Wednesday, Lord I Call, tone 5).

The people who walked in darkness have seen a great light; those who dwelt in a land of deep darkness, on them has light shined (Is 9:2).

The shadows and darkness have no hold on Christ. As light, He is salvation:

Even though I walk through the valley of the shadow of death, I fear no evil; for thou art with me (Ps 23:4). For with thee is the fountain of life and in thy light shall we see light (Ps 36:9).

The evangelist Matthew relates that when Jesus gave up the spirit, "the curtain of the temple was torn in two, from top to bottom; and the earth shook, and the rocks were split; the tombs also were opened, and many bodies of the saints who had fallen asleep were raised..." (Mt 27:51-52). By His death, Christ did away with the chasm that separated man from God, while the torn curtain of the Temple proclaimed the end of any separation. Having been defeated, death freed those it held captive, allowing many saints to return to life.

Situated at the very heart of Christianity, the Resurrection is cause for joy, because death no longer has dominion over those who adhere to Christ. For His light has already defeated the darkness of this world. Only faith enables us to perceive this light that penetrates all things, that frees us from the fear of death. Being Christian means believing in the light in the midst of darkness, hoping when all seems lost, gazing on the fallen world with compassion and tenderness, and with the assurance of a future transfiguration. And this is possible because, as we are reminded by the inscription in the fresco of the superb Descent into Hell of Kahrié Djami, in Constantinople: "The land of the dead has become the land of the living."

"Through the cross, joy has come into all the world!" (Paschal hours, tone 8). Suffering-joy, death-life, kenosis-exaltation: this notion of "joyful sorrow," so dear to the great spiritual minds, finds its place quite naturally in the icon. Yet joy always prevails—"This is the day of Resurrection!"—and we observe faces lighting up as they exchange the paschal greeting:

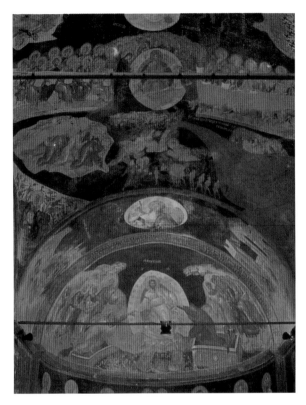

22. The Descent into Hell and the Last Judgment; fresco, 1315-21,
Church of the Holy-Savior-in-Chora, Kahrié Djami, Constantinople.

"Christos anesti!—Alithos anesti!"
"Christos voskresse!—Vo istinu Voskresse!"
"Christ is risen!—Indeed He is risen!"

Christ in Hades

Christ's billowing garment shows that the Resurrection is expressed, in this icon, not by an upward movement, but by a downward one. This descent bears within itself the beginning of an ascent that connects heaven and hell by a single flow of light.

Life erupts within the kingdom of death. Death is a contemporary taboo that has remained, humanly speaking, unacceptable. No one escapes it. Death is an object of scandal that constitutes the primordial and fundamental question for every human being. Is death not an obvious proof that God does not exist? Or all the more, doesn't the reality of death make a mockery of the "loving" God professed by Christians?

Far from being the opposite of life, death is situated on another plane of existence that is made evident by the captives in hell. How can one admit that Lucifer, the fallen "light-bearing angel," was able to reduce God's creation to oblivion? This is utter nonsense! As it is with death, so it is with life: it is not limited to biology, but embraces the soul and the spirit. The fall of humanity takes place on a spiritual plane: it constitutes a disruption of the primordial harmony and henceforth affects all of creation. It is the source of every imbalance that troubles the spirit, the will and the body. Physical death may result either in spiritual life or death, in light or darkness. Perceived here below through the body, the soul after death reflects the body. In hell it is the soul of Adam, bearing the mark of his body, that is freed. Although Christ accepted to die and to descend into the tomb to conquer spiritual death, He did not abolish physical death. That remains an integral part of this world which He did not destroy. Instead, He turned it into a "passage," the means of attaining new life. His victory over death is our freedom, because we are no longer victims of nature or of chance.

In hell, Christ meets the godless ones that are deprived of light. He, the Most High, descends as far as man can possibly fall in his solitude and abandonment. Already, during His earthly life, He experienced hunger, thirst, temptation and pain. He shed tears at the tomb of Lazarus, showed anger toward the money-changers in the Temple, sweat water and blood on Golgotha (Lk 22:44), was tortured, humiliated with spitting and a crown of thorns (Mt 26:67), the sign of derision and insolence (Mt 27:39-41); He was nailed to the cross before being pierced by a spear.

Can one imagine any more than this? Because He assumed humanity—not merely pretending to be a man but fully becoming one, while remaining fully God—Christ went to the very end of the experience of spiritual death, the most horrible kind, before yielding to physical death. In Gethsemane, full of sadness and anguish, He confided in three of His disciples: "My soul is very sorrowful, even to death" (Mt 26:38). Then, at the height of despair, at the very moment of His physical death, He cried out from the cross: "My God, my God, why hast thou forsaken me?" (Mt 27:46). This cry is one of dismay, of ultimate anguish; it is the cry of a godless one, of an a-theist, of a being who, reminded of the one needful thing, feels cut off from God who alone gives meaning to life. Can we dare to imagine deprived of life, of the way and of light, the One who is all these things?

There is only one answer: "God is love" (1 Jn 4:16). And without love, the human creature perishes. Christ gives His life "willingly" (Jn 10:15); He dies "for all" (2 Cor 5:15). Fully man, yet without sin like Adam before the fall, He bears on His body and within Himself the mark of this separation (Is 53:4), since "what is not assumed cannot be saved" (Gregory the Theologian), and "there is no other name under the heavens given among men by which we must be saved" (St Peter, Acts 4:12).

The words of St John Chrysostom's Paschal Homily are extremely powerful:

> Let no one weep for his iniquities, for pardon has shone forth from the grave.
>
> Let no one fear death, for the Savior's death has set us free. He that was held prisoner of it has annihilated it. By descending into Hell, He made Hell captive.
>
> ...It [hell] took a body, and met God face to face... It took that which was seen and fell upon the unseen (Paschal Matins).

The Risen One, who is the "first born from among the dead" (Col 1:18), appears indeed as the master of life who fills all things: "Fear not, I am the first and the last, the living one! I was dead, but now I live unto ages of ages, and I hold the keys of death and to the sojourn of the dead" (Rev 1:17-18). Christ holds all power in heaven, on earth and in Hell. His Resurrection is the only valid answer in seeking direction for one's life; it enlivens time and space. The countless spiritual deaths we experience and witness every day are vanquished. They are mystically transformed, for they are borne by the person of the incarnate God.

Cosmic Man and Exalted Humanity

Through His presence in Hell, Christ moved the locus of the divine Theophany from a higher to a lower level, from earth to hades. This Transfiguration does not take place on a mountain, the meeting point between heaven and earth, nor at the top of the icon, but exceptionally at the bottom. The discontinuity between the levels of heaven, earth and hell, is abolished, and everything is now "open."

"In the tomb with the body, in hell with the soul as God, in paradise with the thief, on the throne with the Father and the Spirit, wast Thou, O boundless Christ, filling all things!" (Paschal Hours, tone 8). While the first Adam assumes the cosmic tragedy and indeed sums up fallen humanity within himself (which is why he is usually the only one being "raised"), the new Adam, Christ, takes on a new humanity. He completes by His Resurrection what was so marvelously inaugurated by His Incarnation, before reaching its fulfillment at the time of the Ascension. That which was mortal, corruptible and final is transformed into immortality, incorruptibility and eternity by the resurrection of His divine-human body. The Risen One descends to meet Adam as He comes to meet each one of us, yesterday, today and forever. Man will never again be alone.

As the last stage of Christ's abasement, the descent into Hell marks the ultimate phase of His humiliation, which simultaneously initiates the ascent of humanity in His wake. "God raised him up, having loosed the pangs of death, because it was not possible for him to be held by it" (Acts 2:24). The Father raises the Son by the Holy Spirit: such is the

23. The Descent into Hell; icon, ca. 1680, from the iconostasis of the
Cotroceni Monastery, near Bucharest, Romania.

mystery of the triune divinity. Woven with light, the garments of the cosmic Man form a sharp contrast with those the iconographer gives Him during His earthly sojourn.

Having assumed a body "subject to death," Christ changed it, through His death, into a "glorified body," henceforth free, like the soul itself, from the laws of this world. His new, resurrected body is free from time and space, and is therefore capable of overcoming any obstacle, even of passing through closed doors. It is with this incorruptible, glorified body—inseparable from the soul—that Christ descended into Hades. Here we find ourselves face to face with a great mystery. As the Russian theologian Sergius Bulgakov wrote:

> The corporeality of Christ on earth, even after His Resurrection, is characterized by "flesh," and therefore by a spatial quality: "Touch me, and see; for a spirit has not flesh and bones as you see that I have" (Lk 24:39). We may speak of a different spatial quality with respect to the resurrected body, a corporeality other than our earthly one...The body can only be spatial, and no spatial quality is compatible with spiritual being (see *Du Verbe Incarné,* L'Age d'Homme, Lausanne, 1982, p. 330).

"Yesterday I was buried with Thee, O Christ. Today I arise with Thee in Thy Resurrection. Yesterday I was crucified with Thee. Glorify me with Thee, O Savior, in Thy kingdom" (Paschal Matins, Ode 3). With time abolished, it is in the eternal divine present that every person makes these words his or her own. Once restored, Christ's image is exalted by His Ascension to the Father. That which was obtained for humanity as a whole, however, requires a "personal" (not an "individual") completion, for salvation is realized through communion.

The Resurrection of the Flesh

There will come a day when "we shall all be changed" (1 Cor 15:51). As St Gregory Palamas (†1359) notes, every human being will be resurrected at the close of the age, at the time of Judgment. But only those who have put on Christ, who have received Him in others, will know the resurrection in glory and the ascension. How will this take place? For St Gregory of Nyssa, "it is not in a part of the nature (of man) that the image is to be found, but it is the nature in its entirety that is the image of God" (*On the Creation of Man*, PG 44, 185). The result, adds St Justin (†165), is that "it is the entire person, and not simply a part of the person, that God calls to the life of Resurrection. It is the fullness of man that is called, meaning the soul as well as the body" (Fragment 8).

A person is neither mere body nor soul taken separately, but both, indissolubly united one to the other. The body reflects the soul through the face, which enables one to identify a person. The "shapeless" soul is a "model" of the body and vice versa. If Christ assumed a human face, if the icon, therefore, favors every face, is it not precisely so that we might be reminded that what is resurrected is the entire person, the soul as well as the body?

Faith in the resurrection of the flesh, which we confess at every eucharistic liturgy, is especially important today, given the many dilemmas (ecological, social, etc.) that mankind has been unable to resolve. The temptation is there to say, "after us comes the flood," that is, to surrender the cosmos to the forces of evil. As "microcosm" and "microtheos" (since he is "in the image of God") the human person sums up creation within himself. Each of his actions can either improve or impoverish his surroundings. The transfiguration of the flesh of this world includes everyone, who, when presented with a choice between the materialization of the spirit or the spiritualization of the body, boldly enters into the dynamism of the resurrection by the power of the Holy Spirit.

A New Creation: the Eighth Day

Ignoring the symbolic power of numbers amounts to depriving oneself of a major element in the effort to assimilate the reality of salvation. A first indication is given to us by the number six that expresses the totality of creation and the perfection of the work. Thus, the Word of God who was to become incarnate, created Adam on the sixth day, at the end of His creative activity. A victim of the fall, Adam is recreated on the sixth day of the week, the day of Christ's crucifixion.

As we go on to the number seven, we recall that the Creator rested on the seventh day, which became the Sabbath day for the Jews, and Holy Saturday for the Orthodox liturgy which is centered on the "Descent into Hell." The number seven is the image of the fullness of the present time, while it also initiates a departure from that time. It opens up into the eighth day, the day of Resurrection that introduces a new era, inaugurating a new time, and thereby becoming the first day of the week. The Pentecostarion includes seven weeks, from the day of Pascha to the eighth Sunday which is that of Pentecost itself. These closely connected feasts of the Resurrection, Ascension and Pentecost lead us to the Eighth Day, which coincides with the outpouring of the Spirit on all flesh. There are three consecutive actions in which: *a*) the Father, through the power of the Spirit, raises the Son, *b*) who ascends to the Father in order *c*) to send the Holy Spirit. The Greek word for "Sunday" (which in Russian also means "Resurrection") is *Kyriake hemera*, meaning "the day of the Lord." This refers to the first day, or the "Unique Day," which is Holy Pascha. According to Gregory Nazianzen, known as the Theologian (†390), if the first Christians were accustomed to referring to the Resurrection as the eighth day, it is because "it is the first of those that follow and the eighth of those that precede it, a glorious day among all others" (*PG* 36, col 612C, *Oration 44*). And St Justin adds: "We all gather on the day of the sun because it is the first day, on which God, by giving substance to the darkness and to matter, created the world, and on that same day, Jesus Christ our Savior rose from the dead" (*First Apology,* 67:7).

"Yesterday I was buried with Thee, O Christ. Today I arise with Thee in Thy Resurrection" (Paschal Matins, Ode 3). The Eighth Day, the "Unique Day" without end, is not merely a promise; it has already begun: "Therefore if anyone is in Christ, he is a new creation; the old has passed away, behold, the new has come" (2 Cor 5:17).

Having appeared at the end of the first creation, man stands at the beginning of the second, since the world is transfigured through him. And while the first creation marks the beginning of time, the second enables one to depart from it and attain to the light of the never setting Sun.

The Myrrhbearing Women

The image of the Myrrhbearing Women is the most ancient depiction of Pascha, appearing already in a fresco of Dura Europa, in Syria, which dates back approximately to the year 230. While the iconography of the "Descent into Hell" has as its aim a strictly spiritual content and deals with an event that escapes the senses as well as historical criteria, the icon of the Myrrhbearing Women refers to a precise moment in history. Without any kind of extrapolation, it is based on the accounts of the Gospels that it follows in every detail. Its development parallels that of the liturgical texts, describing what the women and the disciples saw as they neared the tomb.

For the first century Christians, and for their immediate heirs, the believers of the Orthodox Church, the empty tomb symbolizes the Resurrection to a greater degree than it does the cross, the instrument of salvation. Thus, when Orthodox faithful visit the church of the Holy Sepulcher in Jerusalem, whose foundation was laid on the place of the Crucifixion and Resurrection, they first venerate the tomb, called in the liturgical texts the "source of life." "Forgiveness has shown forth from the grave!" (St John Chrysostom, Paschal Homily).

"And when evening had come, since it was the day of preparation, that is, the day before the sabbath, Joseph of Arimathea, a respected member of the council, who was also himself looking for the kingdom of God, took courage and went to Pilate, and asked for the body of Jesus" (Mk 15:42-43). In this atmosphere of fear, intensified by the defeat inherent in the Master's death, it is not an apostle but Joseph who confronts Pilate, asking for the body of Jesus. And as "the sabbath was beginning" (Lk 23:54), with the help of the women that had followed Jesus, Joseph quickly prepared and cleaned the body that was covered with blood and spittle. Nicodemus "came bringing a mixture of myrrh and aloes, about a hundred pounds' weight. They took the body of Jesus, and bound it in linen cloths with spices, as is the burial custom of the Jews" (Jn 19:39-40). Wrapped in a new linen cloth, the body was laid "in a tomb which had been hewn out of the rock; and he [Nicodemus] rolled a stone against the door of the tomb" (Mk 15:46).

Under such conditions, one can imagine with what great difficulty the cloths that clung to Christ's body might have been removed. Is it really conceivable that thieves would have patiently taken the time to free the body, to remove the bandages and, moreover, to roll up the shroud with such care? Would the bandages not have been torn as well? These are some of the many questions that come to mind.

The icon of the Myrrhbearing Women, striking in its sobriety, enables one fully to understand its message. All essential details are there: the rocks that reflect the diffused light of the tomb, a section of the walls of Jerusalem, the women bearing jars full of spices, the empty tomb with the shroud and the rolled up napkin, one or two angels with outstretched wings. Were there two, three, four, or more women at the tomb? The Gospels differ. Matthew speaks of two women, Mark of three, while Luke says nothing. It is important to note that Jewish law, for which the testimony of a woman was not even valid, accepted the veracity of an event based on the deposition of at least two witnesses. The majority of the icons respect these figures, but finding six or more women depicted is not uncommon.

Who are these Myrrhbearing Women? They are the women who accompanied the Mother of God during the Passion: Mary Magdalen, and Mary, the mother of James and Salome. Though she is never mentioned in the Gospel accounts, the Mother of Jesus is sometimes present in the composition, always recognizable by the letters ΜΡ-ΘΥ (from the Greek *Meter Theou*, "Mother of God"). In a thirteenth-century homily, St Gregory Palamas strongly upheld the notion that the Theotokos was naturally the first to be informed of the Resurrection and to witness it. So these women arrived with their spices after the Sabbath rest. The myrrh and herbs were to allow them to approach the body they came to venerate, but whose decomposition would soon have caused an unbearable odor.

Other differences in the Gospels include the number of angels. Only one, according to Matthew and Mark, two according to Luke and John. Far from invalidating their testimony—the early Church was not duped—this difference rather reinforces their agreement on the very reality of the Resurrection. Messengers from the most high "in dazzling apparel," these angels of such extraordinary beauty evoke the transcendent world.

> "Before the dawn Mary and the women came and found the stone rolled away from the tomb. They heard the angelic voice: 'Why do you seek among the dead as a man the one who is everlasting light? Behold the clothes in the grave! Go and proclaim to the world: The Lord is risen! He has slain death, as He is the Son of God, saving the race of men!" (Paschal hours, tone 8).

24. The Myrrhbearing Women at the Tomb;
contemporary icon, private collection, Switzerland.

The linen cloths are the conclusive evidence in the angel's attempt to convince the Myrrhbearing Women, who were in no way prepared for such a turn of events. The liturgy, as a verbal icon of this mystery, quotes the Gospels directly: "Why do you seek the living among the dead?" (Lk 24:5). He is the living One, the Emmanuel, "God with us" (Mt 1:23). We must not limit our perception to what is visible, as did Thomas; we must look instead to what lies beyond, to the invisible.

Initially, the apostles did not believe the Myrrhbearing Women: "but these words seemed to them an idle tale, and they did not believe them" (Lk 24:11). The disciples, unable to understand that Christ had to be put to death, remained incredulous as they heard the message of the Resurrection. They had not yet grasped the full meaning of the Scriptures. Furthermore, it was not a rationalistic individual but one who perceived with his heart, John "the Theologian," who, upon seeing the linen cloths, suddenly understood. Similarly, when Jesus raised the putrid body of Lazarus, He commanded those that had witnessed the miracle: "Unbind him and let him go" (Jn 11:44). In Lazarus' case, the linen cloths and the shroud were indeed obstacles that could only be overcome by some outside force. Yet this was not so for Jesus: the linen cloths lay on the ground and the napkin was rolled up in a place by itself (Jn 20:5-7). In the account of his arrival at the tomb, John states simply that "he saw and believed" (Jn 20:8).

The numerous attempts to prove that Christ was not resurrected, but rather remained in the tomb, have failed. The apostles died with this very truth on their lips. During his fierce persecution of Christians, Paul of Tarsus was questioned on his way to Damascus: "Why do you persecute me?" (Acts 9:4). His striking conversion made him an ardent defender of the Resurrection of Christ, for which he suffered and willingly gave his life.

To be sure, the empty tomb is not sufficient in itself to justify faith in the Resurrection. Had the body of Jesus of Nazareth been found, everything would have fallen apart. The empty tomb is an invitation to seek the living Christ elsewhere, it is a reminder of the angel's words: "He is risen as he said" (Mt 28:6). The Scriptures have been confirmed and enlightened by the light of the tomb that reveals their meaning. Hence the insistence, at the very heart of the liturgy, on eliminating every trace of doubt:

> O ye blind unbelievers, deceivers and transgressors, who disbelieved Christ's arising as though it were a lie: What do you see that is unbelievable? That Christ, Who raised up the dead is risen?

> O ye enemies of Christ, though ye disbelieve, ask your soldiers what they suffered. Whose hand rolled away the stone of the sepulchre?

> Who is it that withered the fig tree? Who is it that healed the withered hand? Who is it that once filled the multitude in the wilderness? Is it not Christ God, Who raised up the dead?

> Who is it that enlightened the blind, and cleansed the lepers, and straightened the maimed, and walked on the sea dry-shod as though on land? Is it not Christ God, Who raised up the dead?

> Who is it that raised the four-day dead from the grave, and the son of the widow? Who is it that, as God, strengthened the paralytic on his bed? Is it not Christ God, Who raised up the dead?

> The stone itself crieth, the seals call out; when ye placed them, ye appointed

a watch to guard the tomb. Truly Christ is risen, and He liveth unto the ages.

Truly Christ is risen, Hades is despoiled, the serpent is slain, Adam is delivered, those below are saved. Wherefore, why do ye disbelieve, O ye enemies and transgressors? (Sunday of the Myrrhbearing Women, Matins, Ode 8, tone 2).

Depictions of Christ coming directly out of the tomb are defective in at least three ways. First of all, when the angel comes to roll away the stone it is not so that Christ might come out, but rather to show that the tomb is empty. Furthermore, Christ would not be coming out of the tomb since, having descended into hell, He ascends to the Father, followed by the captives He has freed. Finally, the soldiers are struck with fear at the sight of the angel and not of the Risen One. Could they have otherwise accepted to spread the lie that the body had been removed by thieves? All those who recognized the divinity of Christ confessed Him to their death. Thus, when the centurion, Longinus, and his soldiers that were present at Golgotha, "saw the earthquake and what took place, they were filled with awe, and said, 'Truly this was the Son of God!'"(Mt 27:54).

When two angels are present, the interpreter must decipher the symbolism in the icon of the Myrrhbearing Women as the realization of one covenant by the other. God said in the Old Testament:

Then you shall make a mercy seat of pure gold; two cubits and a half shall be its length, and a cubit and a half its breadth. And you shall make two cherubim of gold; of hammered work shall you make them, on the two ends of the mercy seat. Make one cherub on the one end, and one cherub on the other end; of one piece with the mercy seat shall you make the cherubim on its two ends. The cherubim shall spread out their wings above, overshadowing the mercy seat with their wings, their faces one to another; toward the mercy seat shall the faces of the cherubim be. And you shall put the mercy seat on top of the ark; and in the ark you shall put the testimony that I shall give you. There I will meet with you (Ex 25:17:22).

God speaks to His people from the place named "Tent of Meeting." However, the Pascha of the Lord bears witness to the alliance between God and His people, an alliance that was renewed at the time of the Incarnation, then completed at the time when the first Adam and the new Adam come face to face. The precise reproduction of this Old Testament prefiguration is accomplished before our eyes, in the icon, thus recalling the covenant.

The Icon of the Paschal Mystery

Already in the second century, well before the first appearance of the two primary representations of the Resurrection we have just mentioned, the frescoes of the Roman cata-

25. The Myrrhbearing Women at the Tomb; fresco, 1637 (?), from the side wall
of the nave of the Church of the Nativity, Arbanassi, Bulgaria.

combs of Priscilla and Callixtus treat the theme of the Resurrection allegorically. The
scene of Jonah freed from the belly of the whale is not, strictly speaking, a representation of
the Resurrection; yet it prefigures it as only the Old Testament could. The monster found
in the icon is the one referred to as "the Glutton" or "Hades," in the apocryphal Gospel of
Nicodemus. Up until the first council of Nicea (325), the feasts of the Resurrection and the
Ascension, two fundamental stages in the mystery of salvation, were celebrated on the same
day. This explains their juxtaposition in a number of composite icons such as the one shown
here. In his account, the evangelist Luke gives the impression that, in spite of the span of
time in which it is lived out, this entire series of events takes place on the same day. Also, just
as in Genesis, where God breathes "the breath of life" (Gen 2:7) into the man's nostrils,
Christ "breathes" the Spirit upon His disciples (Jn 20:22) on the night of His Resurrection.
As in baptism, the new creation is accomplished in and by the Spirit.

This composite icon of the paschal mystery belongs to a series of double icons that was
produced in the sixteenth century, in Russia, under Western influence. The theme of
Christ coming out of the tomb complements, among others, the theme of the descent

26. The Descent into Hell; composite icon, early 19th c., Russia.
Private collection.

into hell. Any icon that depicts Christ coming out of the tomb, including those of a single theme, is deplorable insofar as it betrays the truth of the Gospel and rejects its mystery. Yet we see here that the iconographer has made good use of the entire motif by an overall reading in which the parts shed light on the whole. The primary event depicted by the icon is the liberation of captives. Far from obscuring this point, however, the central scene in which an ethereal Christ seems to elude the view of the onlookers, rather accentuates that liberation, making unmistakable the ultimate purpose of the Resurrection.

The eye naturally follows the ascending dynamic of the composition. As He stands upon the gates of hell, Christ appears to be the director of a great ballet. He is the central figure, streaming with a light intensified by the white mandorla. At the heart of the image, in a state of weightlessness, Christ is outlined against a traditionally Byzantine cave into which has been inscribed a traditionally Latin tomb. The stone rolled away, the white linen cloths surrounded with red ties, the fallen soldiers collapsed on the ground as if they were dead: every detail is there. The ceremonial dress of the guards corresponds to the liturgical hymnography dedicated to the reposing King. Under Christ's right hand, raised as for a blessing and apparently orchestrating the movement, a number of angels make their way toward the gates of Hades, which one of them has already broken down. A few demons attempt, in vain, to shore up the breaches with large posts. One of the devils, painted brown, tries to protect the doors with his body but succumbs to the assault of the first angel, who grabs him by the hair and strikes him with a cross. The demons are defeated in the belly of the infernal monster that spits out its captives. According to a common custom, a comment appears on the edge of the icon: "The heavenly powers descended into Hades, took hold of the devil and of all his powers and cast him into the pit of eternal punishment." This text recalls the vision of the Book of Revelation: "Then I saw an angel coming down from heaven...And he seized the dragon...bound him...and threw him into the pit" (Rev 20:1-3).

The doors of Hell are represented a second time underneath Christ as He comes down to free the righteous of the Old Covenant, granting them the Resurrection. As He raises Adam up with His right hand, Christ guides the long procession of righteous souls toward Paradise with His left. At His feet, to the left, two angels restrain a pair of demons destined for the gaping fiery pit. On the other side, Eve touches her head to one of the Savior's feet in a gesture of tender veneration. She is followed by Sarah, companion to the father of all believers, and by Rebecca, Isaac's companion. The superimposed halos in the groups of angels and of the elect suggest a vast crowd. Behind Adam, who is first in the procession, comes the young Abel who can be recognized by his shepherd's clothing. Then come Solomon, the beardless one, and his father David, with a silver beard and bearing in his hand a scroll of the psalm text: "Arise, O Lord..." (Ps 132:8); both are adorned with crowns. Higher still, another prophet is also carrying a scroll with an excerpt from Scripture: "Let God arise and his enemies be scattered" (Ps 67:2). Behind the lead angel, John the Forerunner is holding out a parchment with the words: "I bore witness to him..." At the gate of Paradise, upon which is mounted a fiery cherub to guard its access (according to Gen 3:24), stands the first man to have entered there (Lk 23:43), the Wise Thief who can be identified by the cross he bears in his right hand. He is represented a second time, beyond the walls of the heavenly Jerusalem, conversing with the two righteous men of the Old Testament who were taken up to heaven while they were still alive: the prophet Elijah, the Tishbite (2 Kg 2:11), and the ancestor Enoch (Gen 5:22).

Let us now examine the final scenes that are closely linked to the Resurrection. Above the entrance to hell, located opposite that of Paradise, three Myrrhbearing Women are seen facing the empty tomb to which an angel is pointing. Among them are Martha and "the other Mary." A little higher, Peter, in disbelief, examines the linen cloths left in the tomb. Just slightly higher, the Lord invites Thomas to place his hand in His side, so that he might no longer be "faithless but believing" (Jn 20:27). On the lower right side, the Risen One, still robed in glory, appears to His disciples on the shore of the Sea of Tiberias (Jn 21:1-14). At His word, they cast their nets to the right side of the boat only to find a catch so large that they are unable to draw it in. Recognizing the Lord, Peter impulsively throws himself into the water in order to join the master.

The Ascension, as the crowning event and the fulfillment of the Resurrection, is naturally situated in the upper middle of the icon. What we have here is the usual theme of the apostles surrounding the Mother of God, with an angel in white apparel on either side, watching Christ being "taken up into heaven" (Mk 16:19).

The more we return to the liturgical texts, too numerous to be cited in their entirety, the better we can understand the icon: "Today a tomb holds Him who holds the creation in the hollow of His hand; a stone covers Him who covered the heavens with glory. Life sleeps and Hell trembles, and Adam is set free from his bonds. Glory to Thy dispensation, whereby Thou hast accomplished all things, granting us an eternal Sabbath, Thy most holy Resurrection from the dead!" (Matins of Holy Saturday, Praises, tone 2). "All-devouring hell received within himself the rock of life, and cast forth all the dead that he had swallowed since the beginning of the world" (Matins of Holy Saturday, first stasis, tone 5, no. 23). This insatiable, greedy "glutton" is identified as the Leviathan, the prince of evil referred to in the book of Job (Job 40:25-41:26).

This icon complements the paschal liturgy that incessantly proclaims the incredible news. Yet human creatures are so slow to believe. Christ is not immediately recognized by His followers because "their eyes do not see," they have not yet received the Spirit.

In the tender account of Emmaus, the two disciples are sad and disappointed: "We had hoped he was the one to redeem Israel" (Lk 24:21). Blinded by their lack of faith, they do not recognize Christ until the breaking of the bread, which He gives them just before He vanishes from their sight. They are filled with joy as they understand why their hearts burned within them while they walked with Him on the road. Who would dare claim that the disciples were the victims of an hallucination?

27. The Descent into Hell; composite icon, center
portion of a portable tryptich, 17th c., Abou Nidal
collection, Lebanon. (Photo: U. Held. Reproduced with
permission of the Archeology and History Institute of
the University of Lausanne.)

In his commentary on the appearance of Christ on the shore of lake Tiberias, St John
Chrysostom (†407) removes any ambiguity:

> Jesus calls to the disciples: "Do you have any fish?" He still speaks a human
> language, as if he had wanted to buy some fish from them. They motion that they
> have nothing. He says to them: "Cast your net to the right side." They obey and
> take in a great catch. It is then that they recognize Him; and once again Peter and
> John reveal their personalities. Peter has a fiery temperament, while John shows a
> loftier character; the first is more abrupt, the second more discerning. Also, John
> is the first to recognize Jesus while Peter is the first to reach Him.

28. The Descent into Hell; composite icon, early 19th c.,
Russia. Private collection. (Photo: Victor Bakchine)

They were witnessing extraordinary signs. What were they? First of all, the catch was large; then, the net was not torn; finally, having reached the shore, they found a charcoal fire with fish laid out on it, and bread. Indeed, Jesus produced these things out of nothing, rather than from existing material things as he had before his death, when he wanted to adapt himself to our condition.

Thus, Peter recognizes him. He drops everything, the fish, the net, and he girds himself. Do you see the respect and the love he had? The shore was a hundred yards away. But he did not have the patience to reach it by boat; he threw himself into the water. Listen now to Jesus: "Come and eat," he said. None dares question him. They no longer sense the familiarity they once had with him; they are unsure and no longer approach him with questions. They were seated in silence, full of fear and respect, attentive to his person. "They knew it was the Lord," the Gospel tells us. So also they did not dare ask him:

"Who are you?" His face was different, and this impressed them with fear and amazement. They would have liked to question Him in this regard. But they kept their silence out of fear, and because they knew that it truly was He. In silence they ate the meal He had prepared for them by virtue of His omnipotence (Homily 87 on John 2-3; *PG* 59, 457-476).

The composition of this icon manifests the fulfillment of a promise and gives proof that the limits of time and space have been overcome, that Christ is all and in all. Along with the elect, He is our contemporary.

"For as in Adam all die, so also in Christ shall all be made alive. But each in his own order: Christ the first fruits, then at His coming those who belong to Christ" (1 Cor 15:22-23). Liturgy and iconography focus our attention continuously on the double motif of Death and Resurrection.

Other Icons of the Resurrection

The Appearance to Mary Magdalen and the Doubt of Thomas

The misunderstanding of the disciples on their way to Emmaus follows that of Mary Magdalen, who mistook Jesus for the gardener. Each time, the recognition is made at the level of the heart. If the Risen One appears and disappears without warning, is it not to demonstrate that He is no longer subject to the laws of the fallen world, that He is no longer merely physically apprehensible, but can also be touched in and through the Spirit?

The icon of the appearance to Mary Magdalen was developed together with sixteenth century Western images of Christ emerging from the tomb, though its roots are much older. Thus, in Ravenna, a city of the Eastern empire, the church of St Appollinarius contains a mosaic of this theme that was composed around the year 400: it depicts Mary Magdalen speaking with the angel, who is giving her the news of the Resurrection.

Although it is drawn from the gospel accounts (Mk 16:9; Jn 20:14-17), this icon attempts to satisfy the Western desire to see and touch. Not that the subject lacks warmth or beauty; far from it. Rather, in its desire to render the mystery visible, it deprives us of a large part of what the main paschal icons proclaim with such power.

The iconographer depicts Christ streaming with light, as in the icon of the "Descent into Hell." Yet the Risen One, whom Mary Magdalen mistakes for the gardener, cannot be recognized by His clothing. A revealing dialogue takes place between this woman in tears and the angels "sitting where the body of Jesus had lain":

"Woman, why are you weeping?"
"Because they have taken away my Lord, and I do not know where they have laid him" (Jn 20:13).

29. The Appearance to the Mother of God and to Mary Magdalen; icon painted in 1546 by
Theophan the Cretan, Stavronikita Monastery, Mount Athos.

30. The Appearance to Mary Magdalen (*Raboni*); fresco, 1335-1350, Church of the
Pantocrator, Decani Monastery, Serbia.

31. The Doubt of Thomas; late 15th c., early 16th c. icon, two-sided tablet, from the Church of St Sophia, Novgorod. Architecture and History Museum, Novgorod.

We see here the result of the misinformation spread by the leaders of the synagogue, who did not hesitate to bribe the soldiers into saying that Jesus' body had been stolen by His disciples (Mt 28:11-15). Or we may conclude simply that, without imagining the possibility of the Resurrection, Mary came seeking a dead man whom she mourned bitterly.

> Saying this, she turned around and saw Jesus standing, but she did not know that it was Jesus. Jesus said to her, "Woman why you weeping? Whom do you seek?" Supposing him to be the gardener, she said to him, "Sir (*Kyrie*, in Greek), if you have carried him away, tell me where you have laid him, and I will take him away." Jesus said to her, "Mary." She turned and said to him in Hebrew, "Rab-bo'ni!" (which means teacher) (Jn 20:14-16).

In its own way, this icon possesses a latent emotional power, while its realism contrasts with the symbolism seen in previous icons. Half kneeling, Mary moves toward Christ, whose extended hand bears the mark of the nail. The scene of the empty tomb, with or without angels, is set somewhat to the side.

Each time the disciples believe they are seeing a spirit and are afraid, Jesus invites them to touch Him in order to convince them, then He eats. Even if they did recognize the Lord, they would not expect to see the tortured body that was put to death and laid in a tomb. When this disbelief is considered along with the many doubts that marked their realization of the facts, the agreement in the testimonies to their faith in the Resurrection is astounding.

Thomas—being the image of the modern man who is conditioned to believe only what he can see, touch and smell—has inspired a paschal icon that faithfully relates the gospel scene taking place in the upper room, symbolized by the buildings.

In spite of the joyful account given by his fellow disciples, Thomas is unable to overcome his disbelief. However, his doubt is changed into an abiding faith upon his encounter with Jesus.

> He touched the man and called him God. He touched the one and believed the other. Had he written a thousand volumes, he could not have better served the Church (Thomas of Villeneuve, 1555, Sermon).

Christ allows Thomas to touch Him so that he might believe. But how could he have touched the mark of the wounds if this had not been the body that was previously crucified? Furthermore, how might one explain this sudden presence when all the doors were locked? Once reason is vanquished, it can only acknowledge Him: "My Lord and my God!" (Jn 20:28). By these very words Thomas recognizes the two natures of Christ. The mark of the nails, the wound left by the spear, the signs of the abuse endured during the passion: all these serve to show the divine-human existence of Christ. By breathing the Spirit upon His apostles, He opens their minds to the Scriptures.

Nativity of the Virgin	Presentation of the Virgin in the Temple	Annunciation	Nativity of Christ
Presentation of Christ in the Temple	Descent into Hell		Baptism of Jesus
Entrance into Jerusalem			Transfiguration
Ascension	Pentecost	Dormition	Elevation of the Cross

Canonical order of the Twelve Great Feasts.

> The considerable time it took for the disciples to believe in the Lord's Resurrection may have been a weakness on their part; nevertheless, it served to our strength. In response to their doubts, they received numerous proofs of the Resurrection: when we become aware of them, we can say that the apostles' doubts are the opportunity for us to affirm our faith. Mary Magdalen, who believed immediately, is less useful to us than Thomas, who doubted for some time. For his doubt led him to touch Christ's wounds, thereby healing in our hearts the wound of doubt (St Gregory the Great, *Homily* 29; *PL* 76, 1213-1216).

Judas was the only one, among the disciples that Jesus loved, to turn from Him and from His message. Is he not the image of the unfaithful man who prefers earth to heaven, the creature to the Creator? Every man also resembles Peter who gave in to fear, lacking courage in the face of temptation. Blessed is he to have shed tears over his betrayal and his lack of love for the One who so loved us as to give His life for us, for "the measure of love is to love without measure" (St Augustine).

32. The Doubt of Thomas; early 16th c. Russian icon (Novgorod). Icon
Museum, Recklinghausen, Germany (Museum photo).

33. Icon of the Twelve Great Feasts with the Descent into Hell in the center; 18th c., Russia. Private collection, Switzerland.
(Photo: Elsa Bloch-Diener Gallery, Berne)

"But there are also many other things which Jesus did; were every one of them to be written, I suppose that the world itself could not contain the books that would be written" (Jn 21:25).

May those who are able, understand: "Blessed are those who have not seen and yet believe" (Jn 20:29).

An Icon of the Great Feasts

The Resurrection of Christ is truly the center around which all other feasts revolve: they reveal its meaning insofar as they draw from it their own significance. Within this correlation, the twelve Great Feasts of the Orthodox Church create a natural crown around the "Descent into Hell," which most powerfully expresses the meaning of the Resurrection as fulfillment, recapitulation and "eschatology" (that which pertains to the end times).

In the following pages, we shall observe how these feasts are intimately related to the Resurrection.

5

Icons Related to the Resurrection

Whereas the twelve Great Feasts constitute an unparalleled synthesis of the history of the mystery of salvation, recapitulated in Christ's Resurrection, several other feasts shed a particularly interesting light on the subject: the Raising of Lazarus, the Last Supper, the Crucifixion, and Christ's Burial. The feast of Pentecost is represented by two liturgical images: the icon of the descent of the Holy Spirit on the apostles gathered in the upper room and, by association, that of the Holy Trinity.

The Nativity of the Mother of God

The first feast of the Orthodox liturgical year, which begins on September 1, is the feast of the Nativity of the Mother of God. This celebration falls on September 8, one week before the feast of the Elevation of the Cross (September 14). Salvation begins at this point, with a premonition of the Cross. The reason for which the liturgical cycle begins and ends with feasts of the Mother of Jesus Christ, the Son of God, is that she is the purest of creatures and, therefore, the closest to God. She is the woman through whom the Savior entered into the world, as well as the one whose soul Christ bears up at the time of her Dormition. She is the first to be redeemed, opening and revealing the "Way."

Her example is particularly striking. In His divine providence, God chose not only a people and prophets, but a woman. Even more astonishing, and further indication of God's gift of life, is that she was born of a barren mother. Barrenness is synonymous with the absence of life and a close kin to death. Therefore, Christ leads us from death (sin) to life, freeing us from spiritual barrenness.

Joachim and his wife Anna (whose name appropriately means "grace") learn from an angel that they will have a child. The icon of Mary's Nativity thus expresses the joy of regained fertility and the forthcoming deliverance of mankind, because the restored capacity for life heralds the Resurrection. St John of Damascus regarded the healing of this barrenness as proof that "the barrenness of this world, which was unable to produce good, was also going to end...This is why the Mother of God is born through a promise" (*Homily on the Dormition,* I, 5-6).

The one through whom God chose to give us the Emmanuel is born: "From thee has shone forth the Sun of Righteousness, Christ our God. He has loosed us from the curse

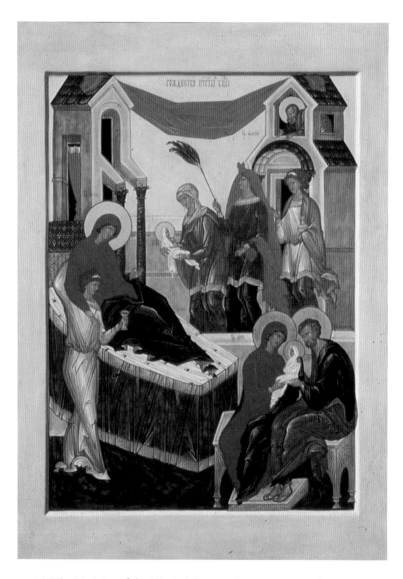

34. The Nativity of the Virgin Mary; 20th c. icon, painted in Russia.

and given the blessing; He has made death of no effect and bestowed on us eternal life" (Troparion of the feast, tone 4). Indeed, Christ is the light that has shown forth from the shadows of death, the light of the never ending day inaugurated by the Resurrection.

The Orthodox Church teaches that man is not heir to the sin of Adam, but to the consequences of his fall: the inclination toward evil, which is inseparable from human freedom. It differs in this respect from the Roman Catholic Church, for whom every person inherits original sin. From this Western perspective, Anna cannot conceive a child who is free from this guilt and ontologically removed from other human beings from the time of her birth (which gives rise to the doctrine of the Immaculate Conception). The Orthodox Church, on the other hand, professes that Mary, from the time of her birth, was like all other mortals; yet she remained unfailingly devoted to God, and therefore absolutely pure. This theological difference, far from being a mere quarrel over terminology, is crucial insofar as the whole understanding of salvation is at stake. According to a famous patristic adage, "what is not assumed is not saved." The full Incarnation of the second Person of the Holy Trinity implies that His Mother was like all other human beings, a true daughter of Eve, apart from voluntary subjection to the passions. Any restriction on this condition encroaches on the fullness of the Incarnation. It invalidates the affirmation that Christ was like us in every respect.

> She had to be a first-born in order to give birth to "the First-Born of all creation," in whom "all things subsist" (Jn 12:24); (John of Damascus, *Homily on the Nativity of the Virgin Mary*, 2).

> Worthy daughter of God, beauty of human nature, the rehabilitation of Eve our first mother! For by your birth, she who fell is raised up. All holy child, splendor of women! If the first Eve was indeed guilty of a transgression, and if "death entered" through her because she served the serpent against our first father, Mary, in turn, became a servant of the divine will; she deceived the deceptive serpent and brought immortality into the world (*Ibid.*, 7).

> You are truly more precious than all of creation, for from you alone the Creator received a share of human nature. His flesh was made from your flesh, His blood from your blood; God was nourished by your milk, and your lips touched the lips of God. Incomprehensible and ineffable wonders! (*Ibid.*, 7)

This feast is the apex of the union between man and God, who chose a woman to assume our humanity, and is naturally commemorated with joy. Let us leave the last word to the liturgy itself which serves as a verbal icon:

> The barrenness of our nature has been loosed: for the barren woman is revealed as mother of her who, after bearing the Maker, still remained Virgin (Great Vespers, Lord I Call, tone 6).

35. The Presentation of Mary in the Temple; mid-18th c. icon, from an iconstasis
and workshop in Valachia, Romania. National Museum, Bucharest.

> Let Adam our forefather be glad and let Eve rejoice with great joy. "For," says she, "unto me is born deliverance, through which I shall be set free from the bonds of hell" (Great Vespers, Litia, tone 1).

> Today is born of the seed of David the Mother of Life, who destroys the darkness. She is the restoration of Adam and the recalling of Eve, the fountain of incorruption and the release from corruption: through her we are made godlike and delivered from death (Great Vespers, Litia, tone 8).

> She is the holy Temple, the receiver of the Godhead, the instrument of virginity, the Bridal Chamber of the King, wherein was accomplished the marvellous mystery of the ineffable union of the natures which come together in Christ (Great Vespers, Aposticha, tone 8).

> O Undefiled, by thy holy Nativity Joachim and Anna were set free from the reproach of childlessness, and Adam and Eve from the corruption of death (Matins, Kontakion, tone 4).

> Thou art truly the mediatrix of grace and joy (Pre-feast, Vespers, Lord I Call, tone 1).

The Presentation of Mary in the Temple

This icon, which is not historical in content but only in form, is comprised of spiritual elements that convey the reality of salvation. Mary, at the age of three, was brought to the temple by her parents, Joachim and Anna, who wanted to dedicate her to God. There she was greeted by the High Priest, Zachariah (the one who would become the father of John the Forerunner), who led her into the Holy of Holies, where she would grow up learning to serve the most High God. Although the entrance into the Holy of Holies, made only once a year, was reserved for the High Priest, the Tradition maintains that to everyone's bewilderment, Mary entered there alone as a sure sign of her divine election. She appears a second time on the highest level of the Holy of Holies, with an angel giving her bread to eat. One must recognize in this the image of the "Bread of Life" that God gives to His people. For, as a faithful companion of His human creatures, God guides and prepares those who do not seek their own will, but who discover, through the tribulations and signs of daily life, the path they must follow.

Mary lived under the rule of the Law and the Temple. The former would be superseded in favor of love, the latter would actually become Christ. The passage from the Old to the New Testament is already accomplished in the person of Mary. She is in the Temple, yet she is soon to become the Temple of the Lord. As the cloud once filled the Temple so that the priests could no longer enter it, so God would fill this chosen creature with His presence. Yet on this occasion the work would remain hidden from human eyes, since apart from John the Baptist, who recognized his Master from within his mother's womb, the shepherds, the wise men, the righteous Symeon and Anna the prophetess were the only ones to worship Christ after His birth.

As Theotokos, the temple holier than the one in Jerusalem, Mary is the ultimate Temple; and since the time of the Resurrection and the outpouring of the Spirit on all flesh, all persons have as their vocation to become like her.

> After thy birth, O Lady and Bride of God, thou hast gone to dwell in the temple of the Lord, there to be brought up in the Holy of Holies, for thou art thyself holy (Great Vespers, Lord I Call, tone 8).

> The Virgin is revealed in the temple of God, and beforehand she announces Christ to all (Great Vespers, Troparion, tone 4).

> To her Zacharias in amazement cried: 'O Gate of the Lord! Unto thee I open the gates of the temple: rejoice and go round it in gladness. For I know and believe that the deliverance of Israel shall now come to dwell openly in our midst, and that from thee shall be born God the Word, who grants the world great mercy' (Great Vespers, Aposticha, tone 5).

> The living Bridal Chamber of God the Word receives bread from the hands of a divine angel, as she dwells in the Holy of Holies (Vespers, Aposticha, tone 2).

> The Theotokos, glorious fruit of a sacred promise, is truly revealed unto the world as higher than all creation (Matins, Praises, tone 1).

The Annunciation

The Creator Word who was in the beginning, who guided the Hebrew people in the desert and revealed Himself in the cloud, assumes our humanity, that it might be deified.

> Gabriel today announces the good tidings to her who is full of grace: "Hail, O unwedded maiden who hast not known marriage. Be not struck with dismay by my strange form, nor be afraid: I am an archangel. Once the serpent beguiled Eve, but now I announce to thee the good tidings of joy: O Most Pure, thou shalt remain inviolate and yet shall bear the Lord' (Great Vespers, Litia, tone 2).

> Today is the crown of our salvation and the manifestation of the mystery that is from all eternity. The Son of God becomes the Son of the Virgin, and Gabriel Announces the good tidings of grace (Troparion of the feast).

Before explaining the content of this feast that constitutes a turning point in the history of humanity, one must distinguish between two types of icons of the Annunciation. The first is found already in the sixth century. It is characterized by the presence of

36. The Annunciation, known as Oustiog; late 12th c. icon, Novgorod.
Tretiakov Gallery, Moscow.

the angel Gabriel, announcing the divine motherhood, and by a ray of light directed toward the head of the Virgin Mary, from which the Holy Spirit comes forth, symbolized by a dove. The second type, of which the "Oustiog Annunciation" (end of the twelfth century) is part, also reproduced here, seems to have been known in Byzantine circles already in the ninth century. The Child, with an adult head and his hand raised for a blessing, is inscribed within the womb of his mother, the one who will give birth to the Lord in a divine conception effected by the Holy Spirit, according to the angelic message.

Let us return, however, to the first icon. The scene takes place among the houses of Jerusalem, the place of pilgrimage of the Jews. Mary is seated in front of the Temple of the Old Testament, while within her is the dawning of a new age, a new covenant that will be sealed by the blood of the Child to be born of her. In contrast to the temple of stone, she is the new Temple of flesh, in whom the incarnate God dwells:

> The tabernacle of the human nature which the Lord took upon Himself, making divine the substance He assumed, is consecrated as a Temple of God...full of grace: the Lord is with thee. From thee has Christ our God and our Salvation taken human nature, raising it up unto Himself (Vigil, Litia, tone 4).

Relative to nearly all other icons that express peace and repose, this image, like that of the Descent into Hell, reveals an unusual movement and dynamic. The message of the angel, who seems to catch Mary off guard by his appearance, is as surprising as Christ breaking into Hades. Yet, the overwhelming power of the message is free of any emotionalism; it leads rather to an attitude of welcome, an unreserved openness to the divine plan. The visible portion of sky, the rays of light and the dove are all symbols that make of this feast the first theophany in the cycle of Great Feasts.

If the Annunciation is traditionally depicted on the Royal Doors of the iconostasis, above the four evangelists who represent the Word of God, it is because these doors mark the passage from this world to the Kingdom of Heaven. This feast establishes the connection between the flesh and the Holy Spirit, between earth and heaven. The Theotokos, assuming the attitude required of those who desire to enter the Kingdom, empties herself of her own will in order to receive within herself the One whom the world cannot contain.

Gabriel follows after Isaiah, the prophet of the Incarnation who announced the Emmanuel, together with His Passion and His definitive victory. By the power of God, this leader of the bodiless hosts announces the Incarnation. He is the "mediator" of the New Creation, of Christ's restoration of all of humanity. The liturgical texts constantly evoke the union of matter and Spirit: "The immaterial light...is joined to a material body" (Matins, Ode 7), "earthly things become heavenly things" (Vespers, Aposticha). There is no doubt that...

> ...today is revealed the mystery that is from all eternity. The Son of God becomes the Son of man, that, sharing in what is worse, He may make me share in what is better. In times of old Adam was once deceived: he sought to become God, but he received not his desire. Now God becomes man, that He may make Adam God (Praises, tone 2).

Foreseeing its deliverance, through Mary, humanity shall attain unto deification: "Rejoice, O blessed Virgin, through whom Adam is recalled to Paradise, and Eve set free!" (Great Vespers, Litia, tone 1).

In the Incarnation the creature contained the Creator, the finite encompassed the Infinite, and the Eternal entered time. This unfathomable mystery enables us nevertheless to understand the connection between liturgical time and cosmic time. The spring equinox, which now takes place on March 21, took place, in the second century, on March 24. The feast of the Annunciation coincided with the celebration of spring, giving the latter a unique significance. Isn't this the gentle season during which the trees blossom, when the seeds sown in the earth begin to yield their fruit? The Annunciation bears within it the promise of a fullness affecting the whole of the cosmos. The embryo taking shape in the Virgin's womb is the God of all ages, beyond time and space. In the confrontation between light and darkness that marks the history of salvation, three key stages are apparent: at the time of the Annunciation that presages victory and constitutes the first element of Pascha, the light surges invisibly; it pierces the darkness once at the time of the Nativity, finally filling all things on the day of the Resurrection. To say that Christ is born into Hades and that "the light shines in the darkness" becomes highly meaningful as one contemplates the icon of the Nativity. The same is true of the icon of Pascha which marks the outpouring of light on everyone and everything.

While the new Eve, by answering "yes" to the archangel Gabriel and choosing what is good, enabled humanity to regain its divine kinship, the first Eve compromised human nature by giving in to the malevolent demands of the fallen angel, Lucifer. Unlike Eve who ignored the divine appeal out of her desire for autonomy, Mary responds: "I am the handmaid of the Lord" (Lk 1:38). She submissively and unconditionally welcomes the Word, and through a self-emptying, allows God to become incarnate; she freely chooses God rather than the creature.

> "I shall bear Him that is without flesh, who shall borrow flesh from me, that through this mingling He may lead man up unto his ancient glory, for He alone has power so to do" (Great Vespers, Lord I Call, tone 6).

The akathist hymn sung on the Saturday of the fifth week of Great Lent commemorates the Annunciation. In the form of a dialogue, the archangel is contrasted with Satan, and the Virgin Mary with Eve. Mary takes care in responding to the angel, thereby avoiding Eve's lack of discernment: "How can this be since I have never known a man?"

37. The Annunciation; icon, ca. 1560, from the iconostasis of the Cathedral of the
Nativity of the Mother of God, Antoniev Monastery, Novgorod.
Architecture and History Museum, Novgorod.

38. The Archangel Gabriel; detail from a fresco, 1388-1391, Church of the Cozia Monastery, Transylvania, Romania.

39. The Double Annunciation, at the well and in the house; late 14th c. fresco, Church of the Holy Cross, Pelénderi, Cyprus.

(Lk 1:34). Has one ever witnessed a child being born under such conditions, disregarding the laws of nature fixed by the creator? Is this invitation truly from God and not from the tempter?

> "The Holy Spirit will come upon you, and the power of the Most High will overshadow you; therefore the child to be born of you will be called holy, the Son of God" (Lk 1:35). And Mary said, "Behold, I am the handmaid of the Lord; let it be done to me according to your word" (Lk 1:38).

Without doubting God, Mary seeks the assurance that she is serving Him with righteousness.

In His virginal birth, without a human father, Jesus is born of Mary in the absence of the human process of transmitting life. Born of a virgin and not from the union between a man and a woman, He enters the world that He Himself created, overthrowing the wisdom of this world by being born of a woman that is His creature, the New Eve, the mother of mankind. He is preexistent—"Before Abraham was, I Am" (Jn 8:5)—and His appearance in the flesh restores what had become withered. "True God and true man," the Second Person of the Holy Trinity, He is both the Son of God and the son of Mary.

> He who made the heavens and contains them, the maker of all creation, both visible and invisible, who is not contained, for He contains every being within Himself—since, by definition, the place contains what is within it—made Himself one of its little children, without human seed: He makes of it the spacious abode of His divinity which is unique and limitless, filling all things; fully contained within it without being reduced, and remaining fully beyond it, being Himself its infinite locus (St John Damascene, *Homily on the Dormition,* II, 2).

> If He were born of a seed, He would not have been a new man; modeled after the first man and heir of his error, He could not have received intact, within Himself, the fullness of divinity nor become an inexhaustible source of sanctification (St Gregory Palamas, *Homily on the Nativity*).

The Virgin Mary puts her trust in God with the assurance of His Word. She complies without realizing fully the implications of her fiat. "She is the passage to heaven and the ladder perceived by Jacob...who frees the mother of the living [and] the first father of the ancient curse" (Annunciation Vespers, Exapostilarion). Through her, God seals a new covenant that puts an end to the exile from Eden. In her, Adam, meaning all of humanity, becomes the abode of God, effecting a "metanoia," since, in the words of the angel Gabriel, "the Lord is with you" (Lk 1:28).

This "yes" precedes our own spiritual progress. "Yes" to Christ means "no" to the latent impulses of our human nature that lead toward death. It allows the Spirit to act within us.

As the Incarnation is realized by Mary's fiat, a free act, open to God's intervention, divinity is grafted to our humanity in accordance with our own will, which implies a preparation, an emptying of ourself, a rejection of idolatry. It is a gift of our entire being, body, heart and soul.

A passage from the Gospels read at feasts of the Virgin Mary tells of the woman who one day, in Jesus' presence, cried out: "Blessed is the womb that bore you, and the breasts that you sucked!"; to which Christ responds: "Blessed rather are those who hear the word of God and keep it!" (Lk 11:27-28). Such a reply applies perfectly to Mary, who pondered these things in her heart (Lk 2:19). Following her example, each of us may receive the Word and become a theophany, a place of the Incarnation, manifested to the whole world.

The Nativity of Christ

This icon has sparked numerous debates about the Incarnation. It reached its nearly definitive form at the close of the iconoclastic upheaval, marked by the Triumph of Orthodoxy, in 843. Initially celebrated on January 6, together with the feast of Theophany (or Epiphany), the celebration of the Nativity of Christ was moved, in 354, to December 25, in the Roman Catholic Church, in order to supplant the cult of the sun (*Natalis Invicti*) and other pagan feasts that took place on that day. The winter solstice does indeed allow us to establish a close connection between the natural world and the mystery of salvation, the increase of light foretelling the coming victory over night. A separate celebration of the Nativity was also introduced in the sixth century in Antioch, then in Constantinople, having already been firmly established in Cappadocia. The Armenians and the Copts, however, have maintained a single feast to this day. Furthermore, many Orthodox, such as those of Russia and Serbia, together with the monks of Mount Athos, celebrate the Nativity on January 7. They follow the Old or "Julian" calendar, which runs thirteen days behind the "Gregorian" calendar.

The iconography of the feast draws on the Gospel of Luke for the birth itself, and on that of Matthew in regard to the Wise Men. The scene of the infant being bathed and that of Joseph sitting apart, however, are drawn from the apocrypha, whose didactic emphasis should not be minimized. The cave, a sort of dark abyss, pierced by the whiteness of the child's clothing, is absent from the Gospels. It suggests darkness, "the valley of the shadow of death" (Ps 23:4), from which Christ comes to free us. Referred to as "the Star of Life" by several Fathers who see Lucifer as "the star of death," Christ enters into battle against evil and darkness, until the final victory by which all things will be filled with light. This icon is inherently analogous to the icon of the Descent into Hell. In both cases, a descent takes place, into the heart of darkness from which the light shines forth. God is incarnate in a world held captive by sin: humanity is

40. The Nativity of Christ; 20th c. icon, inspired by that of the
Rublev School (early 15th c., Russia).

forlorn, devoid of the Kingdom. "For behold, darkness shall cover the earth, and thick darkness the peoples; but the Lord will arise upon you, and his glory will be seen upon you" (Is 60:2). For "the Virgin gives birth to the transcendent One, and the earth offers a cave to the unapproachable One" (Matins, Kontakion).

It is a strange crib in which the Child is laid. It is rather like an altar, bearing the supreme sacrifice. This altar in the shape of a tomb reveals "the living bread which came down from Heaven," the flesh that is "for the life of the world" (Jn 6:51). Furthermore, note that the swaddling clothes have been changed into a burial garment. The altar of sacrifice, the linen cloths, the tomb and the light all point forward to death and to the Resurrection.

The icon of the Rublev School, shown here, depicts the Child at the center of the composition, with His head at the center of an invisible cross that underlies the whole. In connection with the star mentioned by the evangelist Matthew (2:2), an element that was already a symbol of divine presence in pagan art, the three rays of light shining down from heaven onto the Child indicate the Trinitarian participation in the event. The Virgin Mary is resting on a purple bedding, the color of royalty, since in giving birth she has become the Mother of God, as affirmed by the Ecumenical Council of Ephesus (431). She is indeed the one who gave birth to this Child. Therefore she is depicted without Joseph, whose separation from the central scene is meant to be pedagogical, a point that has been underestimated in Western style Nativity scenes. Mary seems to be pondering within her heart the forthcoming events: the Cross, the Tomb... Her gaze is focused beyond the present without resting on her Son, as a mother's often does, giving the scene a prophetic quality.

By their presence, the angels attest to the presence of God. Their hands are covered by a fold of their robes in a sign of respect and submission—a tradition taken from the Byzantine court. The three angels in the middle, bowing in adoration, are reminiscent of the ones standing near the empty Tomb. The first human witnesses to the birth of Christ are not philosophers, but shepherds: simple, guileless people, who are receptive, devoid of preconceptions and who, not unlike the women at the Tomb, live somewhat apart from society.

While the shepherds represent the Jewish people, the Magi personify the pagan world. Of different origins and races, they emphasize the universality of the salvation brought by this Child. These Magi, Persian priests, perhaps astrologers, were convinced of the influence of the stars in human destiny. The star of Bethlehem led them to Christ, "the bright morning star" (Rev 22:16). He is the creator of the stars, the light of light that guides mankind. It is clearly revealed to the Magi that it is He who rules the world and gives meaning to life, whereas the stars merely obey Him. "Those who worshipped the stars were taught by a star to adore thee..." (Troparion of the feast). Faith sometimes flows out of a test tube, because the more scientists expand the limits of knowledge, the more they are given to contemplate the mystery of life and creation. Observing the stars and the "great open book" of nature leads every perceptive soul to encounter God.

These Magi, who in those times guided peoples and kings, came from afar to recognize their king: a poor infant laid in a manger. How can it be true? How could they have acted in this way without being guided by the Spirit? An initial response is given in the liturgical texts: "The whole creation leaps with joy, for the Savior and Lord is born in Bethlehem. Every error of idolatry has ceased, and Christ reigns unto all ages" (Vespers, Litia, tone 6). The second response is provided for us by St Ambrose of Milan (†ca. 397): Christ, the "Way," guides the Magi toward Himself:

> By one road the Magi came, by another they returned, for having seen Christ, having beheld his mystery, they return better men than when they had come. There are in fact two ways. One leads to death, the other to the Kingdom; the first is that of sinners, which leads to Herod; the second is Christ Himself, through whom we return to our homeland (Exposition of the Gospel of Luke).

As a testimony to their faith, their gifts prove to be full of meaning. Gold is a royal gift, of great importance in the icon's background, that becomes pure through fire. Incense is an offering to God, made in prayer; while myrrh, which is also a healing ointment, is for the One dead and resurrected.

"When they saw the star, they rejoiced exceedingly with great joy" (Mt 2:10). They came in haste, without stopping, seeking "the one thing needful." They then decided to return by another way, deaf to the command of Herod who, by the subsequent massacre of innocent children, foreshadowed the Cross. The Magi are as different in their origins and their race as they are in their age. One young man, another in his prime, and an old man: the three together represent a mosaic of three stages of life. Every place and every time converges in Christ, the eternal One who enters into our time.

The animals that are present with the infant fulfill the prophecy of Isaiah: "The ox knows its owner, and the ass its master's crib; but Israel does not know, my people does not understand" (Isa 1:3). St Gregory of Nyssa sees in the ox the image of the Jews bound by the Law, and in the ass, the pagans enslaved to idolatry, "the nations" whom Christ comes to free from their yoke.

Succumbing to agonizing doubt, Joseph confronts the mystery of this virginal birth. Mary's gaze, which is usually turned toward him rather than toward the child, seems to comfort him, sharing his pain and saying: "Do not be afraid, believe in the miracle taking place before your eyes." The evangelist Matthew recounts Joseph's reaction upon discovering that Mary was pregnant: "Before they came together," he "resolved to put her away quietly" (Mt 1:18-19). But he was reassured by an angel. This doubt mixed with confusion recurs in several instances in the Gospels: Mary's hesitation at the time of the Annunciation (Lk 1:29-30); the reluctance of John the Baptist at the Jordan (Mt 3:14-15); the fear of Peter, James and John during the Transfiguration (Lk 9:34); the terror of the apostles as Jesus came walking toward them on the water (Mt 14:25-27); Peter's turning away at Gethsemane (Mt 26:69-75).

> Joseph spoke thus to the Virgin: "What is this doing, O Mary, that I see in thee? I fail to understand and am amazed, and my mind is struck with dismay. Go from my sight, therefore, with all speed. What is this doing, O Mary, that I see in thee? Instead of honour, thou hast brought me shame; instead of gladness, sorrow; instead of praise, reproof. No further shall I bear the reproach of men. I received thee from the priests of the temple, as one blameless before the Lord. And what is this that I now see?" (Christmas Vigil, Royal Hours, Stichera, tone 8).

Joseph's experience takes on universal significance as the confrontation at the level of the human heart of two divergent realities and understandings. On the one hand, Josephs's gaze is fixed on what is visible and earthly; on the other, Mary exhibits that faith through which all things are possible.

The scene in which Jesus is bathed by the midwives is taken from the apocrypha, making the point that He is outwardly identical to any other infant and subjects Himself to human customs. As for the earth that is represented in the form of mountains, it seems to be rising up in the joy created by the presence of this child. The rocks are split open by the intrusion of the light that, as in the icon of the Descent into Hell, penetrates all of creation to its very depths. For although the world does not accept the light, the earth reflects it already.

Somewhat artificially we may distinguish three panels in the icon: the upper portion is characteristic of a theophany, the center pertains to mystery, while the lower portion is devoted to the human realm.

All of history bears witness to the singularity of Christ, as is evidenced by the division of time before and after His coming. Before looking to the liturgical texts, we must be made aware of the true relationship between liturgical and cosmic time. The liturgical calendar symbolically commemorates the Nativity as a Wednesday, or the fourth day of creation, at the time of the winter solstice. The light that is at first only partially revealed, progressively increases up to the time of Pascha, when all things are filled with light and evil is defeated. The same passage from Genesis (1:14) that is read at the Vespers of the Nativity, Epiphany and the Resurrection, describes creation until the appearance of the stars.

The liturgical texts deserve more than a mere overview. The reader will note, upon closer inspection, that the Nativity is referred to extensively on the five days preceding the

41. The Nativity of Christ; 16th c. icon, painted by Longinus,
Decani Monastery, Serbia.

feast. The epistle to the Hebrews (1:1-12), read on Christmas day, requires a careful reading. Furthermore, the feasts of the Nativity, Epiphany and Pascha are the only ones with the intricate compilation of the Royal Hours.

But let us seek to penetrate to the heart of the mystery:

> The earth has bowed down to receive the Creator, who receives glory from the Angels on high; from the sky a star, from the shepherds praise, gifts from the magi, and from the world the recognition of his divinity (Christmas Vigil, Matins, Ode 3, tone 2).

> Today the Virgin gives birth to the transcendent One, and the earth offers a cave to the unapproachable One. The Angels and shepherds glorify Him. The wise men journey with the star, since for our sake the eternal God was born as a little child (Matins, Kontakion, tone 3).

> The middle wall of partition has been destroyed; the flaming sword turns back, the cherubim withdraw from the tree of life, and I partake of the delight of Paradise from which I was cast out through disobedience. For the express image of the Father, the Imprint if His eternity, takes the form of a servant, and without undergoing change He comes forth from a Mother who knew not wedlock. For what He was, He remained, true God: and what He was not, He has taken upon Himself, becoming man through love for mankind (Vespers, Lord I Call, tone 2).

> Adam, once imprisoned, is now deified and all the faithful redeemed, O our Savior who came, wrapped in swaddling clothes, to dwell in a cave (Christmas Vigil, Matins, Ode 8, tone 6).

> Beholding him that was in God's image and likeness fallen through the transgression, Jesus bowed the heavens and came down, and without changing He took up His dwelling in a Virgin womb, that thereby He might fashion corrupt Adam anew (Vespers, Litia, tone 1).

> Thou didst assume the nature of Adam, Thou who art perfect God in nature, and Thou didst will to be held, Thou who dost hold the universe in Thy power...How can I nurse Thee who didst feed the whole universe? How can one fail to admire Thine incomprehensible poverty, how canst Thou be called my Son, if I am now Thy handmaiden? (December 28, Lord I Call, tone 5).

God puts on our humanity in order to introduce us to the mystery of man, the deified man that we are now intended to become. In other words, the God-man reveals our first and final destiny of becoming man-god. "Heaven and earth are united today, for Christ is born. Today has God come upon earth and man gone up to heaven" (Vespers, Litia, tone 1). Christ's entrance into the world allows for our birth in Him. Far from being born in any palace, He chooses a cave that served as a stable for animals, in whose trough He is humbly laid. Because the creator of all things became man, it is man himself who brings fallen creation back to the Creator. "Who has ever seen a potter put on clay? Who has ever seen fire remain covered by linen cloths? This is the way, however, in which God emptied Himself in His love for man" (St Ephrem, First Hymn for the Birth of Christ). These are not the honors and riches due to a king, but abasement and detachment: such is the teaching here summarized. Born in order to die as every man, the Child once grown would die under the blows of His enemies. He would allow the forces of evil to rise up against Him so that He might defeat them and free mankind. The icon of the Nativity, whose black chasm already prefigures the Descent into Hell, implies a complete kenosis. The Second Person of the Holy Trinity, the "New Orient," clothed in our humanity, is born in the heart of darkness. The "Sun of suns rends the darkness of Hades and gives life to everything around Him. From the very beginning, everything takes place in this dark abyss, the symbol of sin, of death and of nothingness, into which the light breaks forth.

It is impossible to speak of the Resurrection without evoking the Incarnation, because it is our very nature that is saved, it is sin itself that is conquered, it is the "ultimate enemy," death, that is trampled down.

> O Christ our Defender, Thou hast put to shame the adversary of man, using as a shield Thine ineffable Incarnation. Taking man's form, Thou hast now bestowed upon him the joy of becoming godlike: for it was in hope of this that of old we fell from on high into the dark depths of the earth (Matins, Ode 7).

> Thou hast come, O Resurrection of the nations, to bring back the nature of man from its wanderings (Matins, Ode 8).

> Being life by nature, He took a body subject to corruption in order to destroy the power of death within it and to transform it into life. Like iron that becomes the color of fire when it touches it, so the flesh, after receiving within it the life-giving Word, is freed from corruption. Therefore He assumed our flesh in order to free it from death (St Cyril of Alexandria, *Homily on Luke* 5:19; *PG* 72,172).

> A miracle, not of creation, but of recreation (St Gregory Nazianzen, Oration 38, *On the Nativity, PG* 36, 664-665), for I have come to raise up and glorify the fallen nature of mortal man (Vigil of the feast, Matins, Ode 9, tone 6).

Unlike the first Adam, who was created from the earth and not from a mother, the new Adam comes from the "All Pure" Virgin Mary who is elevated to the honor of first creature. Born from the earth, Adam lost his integrity; born from heaven and a sanctified earth, that is from the Father and the purest woman of the human race, Christ is the incarnation of humanity in its most perfect expression.

> In Christ, we were all contained: in Him, the collective human person returns to life. That is why we call Him the New Adam: sharing the common nature of all men, He enriches it, leading it to blessings and glory, as the first Adam had led it to shame and corruption (St Cyril of Alexandria, "On John").

Exiled from his true homeland, which is life in God, man wallowed in slavery and deception, imprisoned in time and condemned to die. Today, the Word become flesh brings him back to truth, freedom and to eternity. Christ, the image of the Father (Jn 14:9), is henceforth also the image of man, within whom He restores the purity of nature "in the image of God."

> The Lord gave us a sign as deep as Sheol and as high as heaven (Is 7:14,11), though man did not dare hope for such a gift. How could he have expected a virgin to give birth to a son, to see in this Son "God with us," who would go down into the depths to seek out the lost sheep, the creature he had fashioned, and then arise to offer to His father the "man" who had thus been recovered (St Irenaeus of Lyons, *Adv. Haer.* III, 19).

The icons of Christmas and Pascha speak to and complement one another. Are there not, in both of them, a struggle between light and darkness, a tomb, myrrh and linen cloths? The ascending and descending movements present in the icon of the Descent into Hell appear here as well, as God becomes man who, in turn, rises up toward Him. The glory of man is realized through the "kenosis" of God, who loves him to a degree that surpasses our understanding. The newborn child, laid on the tomb or sacrificial altar, opens for us the "passage" to the Winter Pascha. Every attack on humanity now also personally affects Christ, who became incarnate in our history and bore our flesh. The New Adam, therefore, can only be counted among those who are oppressed and persecuted. "To put on Christ" means to share the purpose of the poor, of those who suffer in their humanity, even if they do not share our faith. Having come to save not only the just but all mankind, Christ leaves the ninety-nine sheep to seek the one that is lost:

> The people who walked in darkness have seen a great light...For to us a child is born, to us a son is given; and the government will be upon his shoulder, and his name will be called "Wonderful Counselor, the Mighty God "(Is 9:2, 5).

> The day shall dawn upon us from on high to give light to those who sit in darkness and in the shadow of death, to guide our feet into the way of peace (Lk 1:78-79).

On this point, Western representations raise some questions: is this plump child, moving about under a young woman's tender gaze, truly the Son of the Most High? The technical mastery of the artwork makes no difference. This omnipresent sentimentality that pervades Western iconography, together with the mildness of so many Italian Nativity scenes, reveals a disquieting theological void. Traditional icons, being of a more

42. The Nativity of Christ; early 16th c. icon, Moscow School. National Gallery, Oslo.
(Photo: Jacques Lathion, National Gallery, Oslo)

sacred character, seem more austere, as they must, yet they reveal a tremendous richness to those who know how to find it. They truly preserve the mystery.

Saint John Chrysostom stated that "human reason has greater difficulty understanding how a God might have become man than to explain how a man might become a child of God" (Homily 2, 2 *On Matthew, PG* 57, 25). "We cannot fathom this mystery" (Praises, tone 4), for "the Incarnation of the Word is a greater and more profound mystery than that of the creation of the world" (V. Lossky, *Mystical Theology*, p. 156). Over against Arianism, which reduced Christ to the level of a superior man, the First Ecumenical Council of Nicea (325)—which was confirmed by each of the six subsequent Councils—affirmed Christ's consubstantiality (*homoousios*) with the Father. To deny this is to follow Arius, who cut himself off from the Church; it means rejecting the very essence of our faith. Because God's Incarnation made possible the deification of man, the main objective of the forces of evil is to "dis-incarnate" the Incarnation. The world has yet to recognize, or rather does not want to recognize, the light that shines in the darkness. And yet, it is still shining. Separated from God, the human creature becomes "diabolical" (from the Greek *diabolos*, "that which divides"), an instrument of death and deception, deprived of the self-giving life.

> In this the love of God was made manifest among us, that God sent his only Son into the world, so that we might live through him...not that we loved God but that he loved us (1 Jn 4:9-10). He who abides in love abides in God and God abides in him (1 Jn 4:16).

Through the birth of Emmanuel—God with us—our isolation comes to an end; we can have peace in our hearts. Yet this is possible on one condition: that we remove from this battle-field between light and darkness all that is not of God so that we may love Him "with our whole heart." In order to be born and to grow within us, the Word-made-flesh must penetrate our flesh and enliven it. Our eyes must become His eyes; our heart, His heart; our mouth, His mouth; our hands, His hands. Whence the necessity of *askesis*, of a personal effort, of repentance and tears that will earn for us the gift of the Spirit. The Resurrection, together with the Incarnation, can then have a profound effect on history (time) and on the world (space).

> (Let us contemplate) in the cave, the sublime and divine mystery: Paradise truly opens up as the Virgin gives birth to the true God, perfect God and perfect man (Vigil, Aposticha, tone 8).

> How can one describe this glorious mystery? The Incorporeal becomes incarnate, the Word takes on flesh; the invisible becomes visible, the inaccessible allows himself to be touched, He who is beyond time has a beginning in time; the Son of Man becomes Son of God (December 26, Vespers, Aposticha, tone 8).

> The true light that enlightens every man...the Word became flesh and dwelt
> among us (Jn 1:9, 14).

In silence and secrecy, God enters the heart of darkness in order to join His human creature, who was cast out of Paradise. His Nativity, the Winter Pascha, recreates the humanity that must now be reborn and resurrected with Him.

The Presentation of Jesus in the Temple

> O Lord,
> now lettest Thou Thy servant depart in peace,
> according to Thy word,
> for mine eyes have seen Thy salvation,
> which Thou hast prepared before the face of all people,
> a light to enlighten the gentiles
> and to be the glory of Thy people Israel (Lk 2:29-32).

With thanksgiving and a joyful heart, Symeon receives in his arms "the Light of the world," the One to redeem Israel and all of mankind. The Mosaic law prescribed that every first-born male child be offered to God (Ex 13:1, 11-16). Yet in accordance with the Jewish laws of purification (Lk 12:2-8), forty days after His birth, the Virgin Mary presents to the Temple made with human hands the First-born of the dead, who was to take His place at the right hand of the Father forty days after His Resurrection. The Evangelist Luke relates that Symeon, a "righteous and devout" man, was "looking for the consolation of Israel, and the Holy Spirit was upon him. And it had been revealed to him by the Holy Spirit that he should not see death before he had seen the Lord's Christ" (Lk 2:25-26), that is, the Messiah. As a priest of the Temple, Symeon did not enter there by chance, but rather he was "inspired by the Spirit" (Lk 2:27), the source of every encounter with Christ. Although Mary is no different from any of the other women, the old man finds her without hesitation.

Also known as the "Meeting," because the Christ Child encompasses within Himself both the Old and New Testaments, the feast celebrates the fulfillment of the messianic promise. The sacrificial altar on which the first-born appears is situated in the center of the icon. Is He not, according to the testimony of John the Forerunner, "the Lamb of God that takes away the sin of the world" (Jn 1:29), the prototype of the new man who will conquer death and the grave? In this poignant meeting between Symeon and the Virgin Mary, accompanied respectively by the prophetess Anna and by Joseph—who is often seen bearing the prescribed offering of two turtledoves, symbols of the Jewish and pagan world—everything expresses a joyful sorrow. There is joy in the meeting of the old and the new, sadness in the coming Passion. The joy of the light that will "enlighten the gentiles"

43. The Meeting or Presentation in the Temple; mid-16th c. icon,
Moldavia, Romania (Photo: National Art Museum, Bucharest).

before bursting forth in Hades, yet the sorrow of the old man's prophecy addressed to Mary: "A sword will pierce through your own soul" (Lk 2:35).

With her hands covered, the Virgin Mary remains subject to the One who is born of her, her Son and her God. It is folly to the wise of this world. As Symeon bends over the Child he is cradling in his arms, he becomes totally open; he is himself an offering and a prayer: "Now lettest Thou Thy servant depart in peace...."

> Today the elder Symeon enters into the Temple rejoicing to receive in his arms the One who of old gave Moses the law and now fulfills it. Moses had been deemed worthy of seeing God through the cloud and to hear his voice; then, with his face veiled, Moses rebuked the Hebrew people for their infidelity. Symeon, however, carried the God of all eternity, the Word of the Father, incarnate, and he manifested Him as the light of the nations, the Cross and the Resurrection. And the prophetess Anna proclaims the Savior who redeems Israel (Great Vespers, Litia, tone 2).

> Our God shall descend into the depths of Hell to save mankind (Matins, Ode 7).

Let us heed the Spirit, keeping our houses clean and our lamps lit for the day when the Lord returns, no longer as a little child, but in the glory of His resurrected body. As we await Him, let us bear Him up as Symeon did, through our neighbor.

Theophany or the Baptism of Christ (Epiphany in the West)

Toward the beginning of the second century, an influential group of Egyptian Christians, known as Gnostics, professed a false doctrine: that Christ, having been born a mere mortal, like all other men, received a share of divinity on the day of His baptism through the action of the Spirit that descended upon Him in the form of a dove. The event was worthy of commemoration. The date that was chosen was the sixth of January, in opposition to the pagan feast of the god of the Nile, celebrated on that same day. The Church reacted against the Gnostics by emphasizing that Christ, the Son of God and the Second Person of the Trinity, had simply awaited that day to reveal Himself as such. It instituted the celebration under the name of Theophany—manifestation of God—or Epiphany. Although there is chronologically a thirty year period between Christ's birth and His baptism, the two feasts make up a whole, a solemn pair whose popularity in the third century is conveyed to us by the Fathers. A correction in the date of the winter solstice, from January 6 to December 25, was presumably responsible for the separation of the two feasts as early as the fifth century. The icon of the Theophany, which was composed already in the fourth century, was further enriched from the twelfth century onward.

44. The Baptism of Christ; fresco, 1637 (?), side wall of the nave
of the Church of the Nativity, Arbanassi, Bulgaria.

"Water is at the origin of the world, the Jordan is at the origin of of the Gospels," wrote St Cyril of Jerusalem (†387). Through His descent into the Jordan, the God-man renews creation, anticipating His Death and Resurrection.

Purification by means of water, far from being a Christian invention (it is known in many ancient traditions), is a cultural as well as a cultic element, and it is no surprise to find Jesus submitting Himself to it and transforming it into baptism. The theme of water occupies a particularly important place in the Gospels: as Jesus said to Nicodemus who came by night to question Him: "Unless one is born of water and the Spirit, one cannot enter the kingdom of God" (Jn 3:5). And "on the last day of the feast, the great day, Jesus stood up and proclaimed, 'If any one thirsts, let him come to me and drink. He who believes in me, as the scripture has said, 'Out of his heart shall flow rivers of living water.' Now this He said about the Spirit, which those who believed in Him were to receive" (Jn 7:37-39). Though it is the source of life, water can also become an instrument of devastation and death. Through His baptism, which inaugurates our own, Christ leads us into the Red Sea as if on dry land; the arrows from Pharaoh's (the Evil One's) chariots cannot reach us as long as we follow after Him.

The Book of Genesis recounts that at the origin of creation, "the Spirit of God was moving over the face of the waters" (Gen 1:2). This fallen creation, having been condemned, by the fall of man, to suffer the pangs of child bearing, could only be renewed by an outpouring of the Spirit through Christ who restored the waters. Having been sanctified, they purify man in His Name.

Like the liturgy of the feast, dedicated to the sanctification of water, the icon does not attempt to relate a specific historical moment. It requires a spiritual reading, with an emphasis on three aspects of Christian spirituality: the dual nature of Christ, the Holy Trinity, and the New Creation. The symmetry of the scene is not haphazard. Christ represents the vertical axis of the composition, around which everything else revolves: the Jordan, its banks, the mountains and the characters. It focuses one's attention on the central theme: "This is my beloved Son, with whom I am well pleased" (Mt 3:17).

Under the watchful eye of the heavenly powers, represented by the angels, Jesus enters the Jordan and comes back out after the appearance of the Holy Spirit, anticipating His descent into Hell and His rising in glory. This descent, His *kenosis* or self-abasement, is expressed in Christ's willingness to be baptized by the Forerunner, His own creature. It also serves to remind us that He did not come to be served but to serve.

On the edge of the river, to the right of the naked Christ, John the Baptist raises his eyes to heaven in a tension affecting his whole being, his right hand resting on Jesus' head. As Mary had asked the angel Gabriel, "How shall this come to pass?", so the bewilderment of the Forerunner is echoed in the liturgy: "Descending today into the waters of the Jordan, the Lord said to John: do not be afraid to baptize me; I have indeed come to save Adam, the first father" (January 2, Matins, Kontakion, tone 4). In both cases, the inconceivable comes to pass through obedience to the divine will. Both Forerunner and a disciple at once, John recognizes Christ immediately: "Behold the Lamb of God, who takes away the sin of the world" (Jn 1:29). To John's testimony concerning the divinity of Christ and the salvation that He brings to all men is added a testimony to the light and to the Spirit: "I saw the Spirit descend as a dove from heaven, and it remained on him" (Jn 1:32).

In the presence of the Messiah, who is stripped naked to bear the sins of mankind, "the Jordan stopped, its waters turned back" (January 6, the Blessing of the Waters, tone 8), while John proclaims his unworthiness: "Can the lampstand illumine the Light?" (*Ibid.*). Just as in the scenes of the Annunciation, the Nativity and the Resurrection, the Angels stand to one side in silence, their hands covered as a sign of submission, bowing to the master of heaven and earth. Jesus is "conceived of the Holy Spirit" (Mt 1:20). He is not

45. The Baptism of Christ; 15th c. icon, St Thekla Chapel, Greek Patriarchate, Jerusalem.

merely filled with the Holy Spirit, He receives praise and glory along with the Father and the Spirit. The whole of His life is touched, molded and guided by the Spirit, who is united with Him in the divine tri-unity, the one Trinity. The manifestation of the Spirit in the form of a dove (Mt 3:16) and the words of the Father–"This is my beloved Son" (Mt 3:17)–reveal Jesus' divinity to the whole world.

At the bottom of the Jordan are often depicted two men, naked, with overturned jars in their hands. This is an iconographic rendition of the image of the mythological god. Christ descends into the waters of the Jordan to conquer the sea monster. By entering the water, He exorcises the elements in the same way the waters of baptism free us from the grasp of the Evil One and make us "children" of God. The icon, as a mystical vision of the New Creation inaugurated by Christ, sheds light on His triumph over the forces of darkness, represented by the dragon that is trampled and put to flight.

> Thou hast bowed Thine head before the Forerunner and hast crushed the heads of the dragons. Thou hast descended into the waters and hast given light to all things, that they may glorify Thee, O Savior, the Enlightenment of our souls (Vespers, Lord I Call, tone 2).

Christ's descent into the Jordan reveals His intention to restore the universe, to assume human nature in its fullness in order to purify it. The New Noah, the fulfillment of the Law and the Prophets, saves all beings from the flood, establishing a new humanity in the waters of the Jordan.

> Of old Thou didst create me out of the void to fashion me in the image of God, but I violated Thy law and Thou didst return me to the clay whence Thou hadst made me. Return me now to Thy likeness and restore my initial beauty.
>
> I am the icon of Thine ineffable glory, although I bear the mark of sin; have pity on Thy creature, O Lord, purify me in Thy loving-kindness, grant me a heavenly dwelling and a return to Paradise (Saturday morning, third week of Great Lent, Evloghitaria, tone 5).

"Now when all the people were baptized... Jesus also was baptized" (Lk 3:21). This submission to the baptism of John goes beyond mere conformity. It represents a true *kenosis*, illustrating the importance of humility.

> Wishing to save man gone astray, Thou hast not disdained to clothe Thyself in the form of a servant, for it befitted Thee, as Master and God, to take upon Thyself our nature for our sakes. For Thou, O Deliverer, hast been baptized in the flesh, making us worthy of forgivness (Vespers, Lord I Call, tone 2).

"Theophany" means "divine manifestation." At the beginning of His public ministry, Christ is revealed to men by the Father, while the Spirit, symbolized by the dove, dwells within Him. The work of Christ, who came to free mankind, does not begin with an extraordinary act, but rather by His participation in human living, His submission to the laws, His humble self-abasement. By inaugurating His ministry with the regeneration of water, which is the foundation of life, Christ blesses all of creation and invites man to a *metanoia*, a conversion through his own descent into the purifying waters. While at Christmas, God enters time, mankind on this day penetrates divine Eternity, anticipating the Eighth Day.

The prophecy of Isaiah read during the feast of the Nativity is accomplished before our eyes: "O that Thou wouldst rend the heavens and come down, that the mountains might quake at Thy presence" (Is 64:1). The evangelist Matthew, supported by Luke (3:21-22), claims that "the heavens were opened" and "a voice from heaven" (3:16-17) was heard. The voice declared: "This is my beloved Son" (Mt 3:17), thereby proclaiming Jesus to be "the Son of God," "the Christ," which means "the anointed One of God." In this encounter between heaven and earth, humanity is renewed by Christ's baptism; therefore in every subsequent baptism, human persons receive God as Father.

The troparion of the feast gives powerful expression to this first and unique manifestation of the triune God:

> When Thou, O Lord wast baptized in the Jordan, the worship of the Trinity was made manifest; the voice of the Father bore witness to Thee, and called Thee His beloved Son; and the Spirit in the form of a dove confirmed the truthfulness of His word.

We find here the first record of the revelation of the Trinity, after it was symbolically proclaimed at the Oak of Mamre, at the time the three angels visited Abraham. The words "my beloved Son" strongly convey the love that unites Father and Son, the same bond they have with the Spirit that rests on the Son in the form of a dove, "for God is Love" (1 Jn 4:8). In the icon, the ray, or rays of light directed toward Christ emanate from a semi-circle often made up of three sections of varying shades, a symbol of the Trinity. The dove is often depicted near the end of this ray of light. How can one not sense this profoundly Trinitarian aspect, in which the Father anoints, the Son is anointed and the Spirit serves in anointing the Son? Both light (*phos*) and glorification (*doxa*) play a fundamental role in this feast. When Christ descends into the dark, watery grave of the Jordan, the Father glorifies Him while the Spirit illumines Him. The same light and the same glory illumine the Transfiguration and the Resurrection, in which Christ's glorification is accompanied by an abundance of light.

> A voice came from heaven, as did He to whom that voice bears witness. The Spirit is manifested in the form of a dove, thereby honoring all things corporeal, for the body itself becomes God through the work of deification. It is not the first time the dove has been present; of old, it brought the good news of the end of the flood (Gen 8:11)(see St Gregory Nazianzen, *Oration 39, PG* 36).

The feasts of the Nativity and Theophany of Christ are closely connected and prefigure His Death and Resurrection: His descent into the flesh of the world which He raises up with Himself. The liturgical texts of the two feasts draw significantly on the week of the Passion and of Pascha. Thus, the account of the beginning of creation (Gen 1:1-13), read on Holy Saturday, stops at the third day, because the great lights—the sun, the moon and the stars—were created on the fourth day. To varying degrees, every feast celebrates light. If Christ, through His birth, made light shine upon a world that was still unaware of His presence, His baptism brought the light out from under the bushel, while His descent into Hell on Holy Saturday put an end to all darkness.

Theophany in the Jordan, theophany on mount Tabor, theophany in Hades: the same superabundant light leads to regarding Jesus' baptism as the "Feast of lights." He initiates our own baptism, which must be regarded as our "illumination" (*photismos* in Greek). This purification puts the shadows to flight and brings the neophyte into the light of Christ and of the Holy Trinity. "God is light," the apostle declares (1 Jn 1:5).

Neophytes at the time of St Augustine of Hippo (354-430) were baptized during the Paschal vigil. Communion in Christ's Death and Resurrection, baptism in fact saves through the Resurrection (1 Pet 3:21), which marks the passage from darkness into light (Eph 5:8-9). Christian initiation ended with receiving the body of Christ during the eucharistic liturgy. This close connection to Pascha is continually affirmed by the apostle Paul and the Fathers:

> We were buried therefore with Him by baptism into death, so that as Christ was raised from the dead by the glory of the Father, we too might walk in newness of life. For if we have been united with Him in a death like His, we shall certainly be united with Him in a resurrection like His (Rom 6:4-5).

> You were buried with Him in baptism, in which you were also raised with Him through faith in the working of God, who raised Him from the dead (Col 2:12).

> The act of descending into the water, then coming out again, symbolizes the Descent into Hell and leaving it again...Baptism represents death and burial, life and resurrection...When we put our head in the water as in a tomb, the old man is submerged, entirely buried; when we come out of the water, at once there appears the new man (St John Chrysostom, *Homily on John*).

> The water receives our body as a tomb, and so becomes the image of death, while the Spirit pours out life-giving power, renewing in souls that were dead in sin the life they first possessed. This is what it means to be born again of water and the Spirit: the water accomplishes our death, while the Spirit raises us to life (St Basil the Great, *On the Holy Spirit,* 15:35; D. Anderson, trans., SVS Press, New York, 1980; p. 58).

In the rite of baptism, the catechumen is undressed, immersed in water, then clothed in a new garment. Once stripped, the old man who had been clothed in corruption abandons his robe of flesh, which is the result of the fall, and regains his initial innocence. Yet baptism is like a seed: without good soil, light and water, it cannot grow. In other words, every Christian must "actualize" his baptism through a complete break with the past and through tears of repentance, what St Isaac the Syrian (seventh century) referred to as a "second baptism." Only under these conditions can one be born again of water and the Spirit. Only then does the sacrament of "illumination" take effect, enabling us to escape the Evil One and become a new creature that has put on Christ. Once baptized, we become the Temple of the Spirit, ever suspended between Death and Resurrection. We are summoned to constant vigilance, not to let this Temple be turned into a den of thieves, a place for the money-changers whom the Master rebuked.

> Exult, Adam and Eve, do not hide any longer as you once did in Paradise; for seeing you naked, the Lord has come to clothe you in the first garment. Christ is manifested to renew all of creation (January 2, Vespers, Troparion, tone 4).

One final look at the icon reveals a tree behind the Forerunner, with an axe at its base, as a powerful summary of the teaching addressed to every baptized individual:

> Even now the axe is laid to the root of the tree; every tree therefore that does not bear good fruit is cut down and thrown into the fire...I baptize you with water...He will baptize you with the Holy Spirit and with fire (Mt 3:10-11).

Transfiguration

The feast of the Transfiguration was widely celebrated in the East by the eighth century. Yet despite its official recognition by the Roman Church in 1475, it only became slowly incorporated in the West over the course of the following centuries, and was never accorded any major significance. This divergence between East and West, which resulted from their different sensibilities, also had a theological foundation. The history of sacred art in the West, with the militant iconoclasm of the Reformation, is well documented. Unlike the Christian East, Rome never fully assimilated the theology of the icon that was developed and justified by the great Ecumenical Councils. Nevertheless, the icon is a "theology in color" which conveys the content of our faith.

"His face shone as the sun and his vestments became as white as light" (Mt 17:2). Who has not tried to look at the sun in the middle of the day? Can we imagine for a moment a vestment of pure light? The icon of the Transfiguration confronts us with this unearthly light, whose radiance made the apostles fall to the ground. In anticipation of the "reverse

Transfiguration" which is the descent into Hell, this event takes place on a mountain, the bridge between the human and the divine, where we see Christ clothed in the same robe of light as at His resurrection. Though His vestments and His face are still those known to His followers, they are now radiant with divine glory. The glory itself is emphasized by the usual mandorla with a blue background that varies in intensity depending on the gradation in color that is used. The light does not emanate from Elijah or Moses (who is holding the "Tables of the Law"), but from Christ, whose glory and radiance illumine everything around Him.

> He who once spoke through symbols to Moses on Mount Sinai, saying, 'I am He who is,' was transfigured today upon Mount Tabor before the disciples; and in His own person He showed them the nature of man, arrayed in the original beauty of the Image. Calling Moses and Elijah to be witnesses of this exceeding grace, He made them sharers in His joy, foretelling His decease through the Cross and His saving Resurrection (Great Vespers, Aposticha, tone 1).

How are we to explain the presence of Moses and Elijah? The one (Moses) represents the Law that Christ Himself superseded. Both of them are prophets and prefigured what Christ accomplished. The Old Testament relates the moving account of Moses impatiently desiring to behold the face of God: "I pray Thee, show me Thy glory" (Ex 33:18). "But, He said, you cannot see my face; for man shall not see me and live...Behold, there is a place by me where you shall stand upon the rock; and while my glory passes by I will put you in a cleft of the rock, and I will cover you with my hand until I have passed by; then I will take away my hand, and you shall see my back; but my face shall not be seen" (Ex 33:20-23). "When Moses came down from Mount Sinai...(he) did not know that the skin of his face shone because he had been talking with God" (Ex 34:29), but the Israelites saw him and were afraid to approach him.

He who saw the Glory of God now finds himself in the presence of the Word incarnate. The same is true for Elijah, who perceived the presence of the God of Israel in "a still small voice" (1 Kg 19:12-13). While Elijah represents the world of the living, having been taken up alive into heaven after intense suffering imposed by other men, Moses represents the domain of the dead.

"Peter and those who were with him were heavy with sleep, and when they wakened they saw His glory" (Lk 9:32). The three apostles are Jesus' closest disciples, the same ones who, according to the evangelist Mark, were present at the raising of Jairus' daughter (Mk 5:37), as well as in the garden of Gethsemane (Mk 14:33). Upon witnessing the Transfiguration of their Master, they were frightened by the cloud that surrounded them. Their fear was multiplied at the sound of the voice from above, at the moment when Peter suggested making "three booths" (Lk 9:33).

46. Transfiguration; icon, ca. 1680, from the iconostasis of the Cotroceni Monastery (Bucharest). National Art Museum, Bucharest (Museum photo).

Peter is kneeling in the icon, raising his hand to protect his eyes from the blinding light. In the center, John has fallen down, away from the light, while James, usually seen on the left, begins to flee, until he also falls to the ground. The absence of halos shows that they have not yet attained saintliness, hence their reaction of panic. The apostles' reaction reminds us of the saying from Exodus according to which man cannot see God and live, and demonstrates the weakness of the creature before God.

Unlike the icon of the Nativity, in which the light remains circumscribed, in this instance it appears to penetrate the rocks. The whole cosmos participates in the Transfiguration of Christ, who assumes the "flesh" of the world. Its three levels are depicted: heaven, where Elijah was taken when he still lived—not to be confused with the wise thief who was the first among the dead to enter the Kingdom; the earth, with the disciples; and finally Hades, where Moses is also depicted in the icon of the Descent into Hell, along with the righteous members of the Old Covenant who awaited the coming of the Savior.

The importance attributed to the symbolism of light, in the Old Testament as much as in the New, emphasizes the close connection between the Scriptures and the icon. In this regard, the great proponent of the "uncreated Light," Gregory Palamas, comments on the words of the Gospels: "He was still speaking, when lo, a bright cloud overshadowed them" (Mt 17:5): "Inaccessible Light wherein God dwells…This light that came into the world is also darkness, it overshadows out of the very brilliance of its light" (*Homily 35, PG* 151:439).

According to St John the Theologian, "God is Love," (1 Jn 4:8) and "Light" (Jn 1:9, 1 Jn 1:5). In the face of Evil, which is ontologically a darkness that separates us from one another, Love, which is communion, implies light. St Symeon the New Theologian (†1022) claimed that "God is Light and those that he finds worthy of beholding Him see Him as light…Those who have not seen this light have not seen God, for God is Light" (Catechesis 28:109ss). During the Transfiguration, it is the apostles who, through the Spirit, suddenly perceive the divinity of Christ in His glory, as He will be in His return at the end of the age.

The Transfiguration is the vehicle of a Trinitarian theophany: the Father bears witness to the Son, the image of the Father, who is radiant with the light He shares with the Spirit. As with the baptism in the Jordan, the Father speaks, and the Spirit is manifested in His "energies" through Christ, who is recognized as the Word that becomes light. While Epiphany implies a sanctifying activity, and Pentecost leads one to the knowledge of God, the Transfiguration manifests the light, for "the Father is Light, the Son is Light and the Spirit is Light."

It is impossible to speak of the Resurrection without reference to the Transfiguration, present in the depths of Hades into which the Risen One descends. On Mount Tabor, robed in light, Christ anticipates His descent into the heart of darkness, where He bestows

47. Transfiguration; 16th c. icon. Pereyaslavl-Zalesski Museum, Russia.

truth and life upon His creatures. The same light that surrounded Christ on Mount Tabor flows forth from the Risen One, who has conquered death through the cross. Is this not the proclamation of His death? "Was it not necessary that the Christ should suffer these things and enter into his glory?" (Lk 24:26). With a careful reading of the Scriptures, we may be struck by the fact that the event of His glorification is situated in the context of His progression towards the Passion, the Cross and the Resurrection. The first prediction of the Passion comes just before the Transfiguration scene (Mt 16:21-23), while Jesus speaks plainly to the disciples about His Resurrection during the descent from Mount Tabor. A golden thread connects the Transfiguration, the Passion and the Resurrection. To Death and Resurrection there correspond the Cross and the Transfiguration in glory. The cross inscribed in Christ's halo is meant to indicate the giving of His life on the cross, through which He conquered death and attained to the glory of the Resurrection.

"Today Christ on Mount Tabor has changed the darkened nature of Adam, and filling it with brightness He has made it godlike" (Vespers, Aposticha, tone 2). The Transfigured Christ, prefiguring the future of humanity, is the image of man immersed in divine light, purified from the darkness of evil and sin, and restored within the primordial beauty of creation. This vision of the integrity of a redeemed humanity, the future condition of the children of God, is given to us by Jesus Himself: "The righteous will shine like the sun" (Mt 13:43), He declares. The presence all at once of Moses, Elijah, Peter, James and John expresses their continual union in the One who connects the old and the new, the living and the dead.

The proclamation of the coming illumination, made during the night of Pascha to those in exile and captivity in Hell, confirms the prophetic nature of the feast. The eschatological dimension of the Transfiguration is important insofar as Christ will appear in the same way when He returns in glory. According to St Anastasios of Sinai, "it is here that the symbols of the Kingdom were prefigured, that the mystery of the crucifixion was foretold, the beauty of the Kingdom revealed and Christ's second coming in glory was manifested" (*Homily on the Transfiguration,* 3). If the curtain of the Temple was torn in two at the moment of the death of Jesus, who by His death conquers death, it is because a deified human flesh enables us to abide in God. The disciples do not see the transfigured Christ with their eyes of flesh but with "spiritual sight," a gift of the Spirit. And for anyone who may doubt the deep connection between prayer and the knowledge of God, let us recall the words of St Luke: "as he was praying, the appearance of his countenance was altered" (Lk 9:29).

St Seraphim of Sarov considered the acquisition of the Holy Spirit to be the ultimate goal of the Christian life. Yet, the Transfiguration realizes the fullness of the Spirit, anticipating what we are called to become, directing us toward the purpose of existence: "then from my flesh I shall see God, whom I shall see on my side" (Job 19:26ff). Yet God already reveals Himself to those who follow Him: "Whoever has seen me has seen the Father." And Jesus answers Philip: "Have I been with you so long, and yet you do not know me, Philip?" (Jn 14:9). The apostles had not yet received the Spirit. Yet to those who received Him in their baptism and open themselves to His activity through their obedience to the command-ments of the Master, the triune God becomes manifest, speaking to the heart. We know only the One we love! Hence the futility of a theology that is not grounded in prayer, for we must enter into the light in order to receive our share of the light.

We live in a world of suffering, a world broken and disintegrated, in which Christ's Transfiguration uncovers reality and reveals to our skeptical minds a new humanity that has either entered into the light of the Risen One or is still called to do so. Ever since Pentecost, the Transfiguration no longer takes place on Mount Tabor, but within every person who welcomes Christ, the image of the Father who sends the Spirit upon his beloved. Our darkness is removed to the extent that we become Christ-like. The light enables us to assume our human condition, a condition that remains limited until our death, but is nonetheless restored in its essence as it awaits a "body of glory." The Transfiguration reminds us that for true disciples, tears, suffering, wounds of body and soul will all be transformed in the joy of the Resurrection. In the Transfiguration and through Christ's Resurrection—this "reverse Transfiguration"—we draw not only the strength to face every new day, but to make every moment a "Eucharist," to be priests of the world, offering to God His own creation. The Transfiguration, whose presence at the heart of Christianity reveals its ultimate goal, is also at the heart of iconography, providing its fundamental themes of light and glory.

The Raising of Lazarus
(The Saturday before Palm Sunday)

The raising of Lazarus, which is celebrated on the sixth Saturday of Great Lent, is the only occasion for which a Paschal liturgy is celebrated on a day other than Sunday. This leaves little doubt as to the anticipatory character of the event.

The icon, while remaining faithful to the Gospel account (Jn 11), nevertheless acquires a broader meaning in the light of the liturgical texts. "Four days dead, already stinking, bound in grave clothes, lacking the breath of life, at Thy call, O Lord, he lept up filled with life" (Compline, Ode 8). Though the tone is thus set, the circumstances and the participants have yet to be considered. The Jews are seen crowding behind the tomb, which is located outside the walls of Jerusalem. Two groups are discernable: on one side are Christ and the apostles, and on the other, Lazarus and the Jews. As for Mary and Martha, the sisters of the one who was raised, both express their gratitude by falling at the feet of the giver of life. The author of this miracle is an imposing presence, a point emphasized by the fact that every eye is resting on Him rather than on Lazarus, who looks on with gratitude and loving veneration. This "resuscitation" of Jesus' friend marks the historic moment that provoked the reaction of the synagogue, eventually leading Christ to the cross and to Hades, from which He would arise in victory.

The resuscitations performed by Elijah and Elisha foretold those of Lazarus and of Christ, who Himself is life and Resurrection: "This is He who raised the dead of old: for when Elijah and Elisha brought the dead to life, He it was that spoke and acted through them" (Compline, Ode 9). This is the power of the "Word" that is now incarnate. Christ creates and revives through his Life-bearing "Word."

> O Lord, Thy voice destroyed the dominion of hell, and the word of Thy power raised from the tomb him that had been four days dead; and Lazarus became the saving first-fruits of the regeneration of the world (Vespers, Lord I Call, tone 6).

> Since, Lord, Thou art Life and true Light, Thou hast called dead Lazarus and raised him up. For in Thy power Thou hast shown to all that Thou art God of the living and the dead (Compline, Ode 5).

On the eve of His Passion, Jesus clearly demonstrated His power over death, announcing at the same time the universal resurrection by which everyone who is "in Christ" will be raised bodily at the time of the Last Judgment. Christ is the friend of Lazarus, as He is of all mankind. Many of the prayers of the Orthodox Church end with the formula: "For Thou art good and lovest mankind!" He weeps over each one of us as He "wept" over Lazarus (Jn 11:35). His will was to bring him and every one of us back, not only to an earthly life, but to life in all its fullness, to a spiritual life. *Ho philanthropos*!

The One who said to a weeping Martha: "I am the Resurrection," (Jn 11:25) is also the One who, a moment later, commanded Lazarus to "Come forth!" (Jn 11:43). The victory over death follows the stench of decay. The call to "come out" is addressed to each one of us. It is His outstretched hand that keeps us from the darkness of death and doubt. However sinful we may be, we can be raised up, resurrected in soul and body; for what seems impossible to us, is possible with God!

> O Lord, wishing to give to Thy disciples an assurance of Thy Resurrection from the dead, Thou didst come to the tomb of Lazarus and called to him by name. Then was hell despoiled, and it released the one that had been four days dead (Vespers, Lord I Call, tone 6).

> Who has ever known or heard of a man raised from the dead, when his corpse already stank? Elijah and Elisha raised the dead, yet not from the tomb or four days after death (Compline, Ode 4).

Wishing in Thy love to reveal the meaning of Thy Passion and Thy Cross, Thou hast broken open the belly of hell that never can be satisfied, and as God Thou hast raised up a man four days dead (*Ibid.*).

Calling Lazarus by name, Thou hast broken in pieces the bars of hell and shaken the power of the enemy; and before Thy Crucifixion Thou hast made him tremble because of Thee, O only Saviour (*Ibid., Ode 1, tone 1*).

The gates were shaken and the bars were shattered, and the bonds which held the dead were loosed. When Christ spoke in power, hell groaned bitterly and cried aloud: 'Woe is me! What and whence is this voice that brings the dead to life?" (*Ibid.*, Ode 9).

The similarity of this event to that in the icon of the Descent into Hell is evident. Whereas the risen Christ did not return to a previous state of being, Lazarus would eventually die again. Consequently, it has been deemed necessary in his case to use the term "resuscitation" rather than "resurrection." Though Christ remained the same in many ways, His glorious body was completely different.

"Unbind him and let him go" (Jn 11:44). Through His death and Resurrection, Christ broke the bonds that held us captive. Nonetheless, He conferred on the apostles the power to bind and to "loose," thereby giving His Church the responsibility of transmitting salvation.

The Entrance Into Jerusalem

Six days before the Passover, Jesus came to Bethany, where Lazarus was, whom He had raised from the dead (Jn 12:1). The next day, five days before the Passover, a great crowd who had come to the feast heard that Jesus was coming to Jerusalem. So they took branches of palm trees and went out to meet Him, crying: "Hosanna! Blessed is he who comes in the name of the Lord, even the king of Israel!" (Jn 12:12-13).

That same day or the next, Jesus declared:

The hour has come for the Son of Man to be glorified. Truly, truly, I say to you, unless a grain of wheat falls into the earth and dies, it remains alone; but if it dies, it bears much fruit (Jn 12:23f).

As He spoke, a voice was heard: "I have glorified [my Name] and I will glorify it again" (Jn 12:28). And Jesus added, for the sake of the crowd: "This voice has come for your sake, not for mine. Now is the judgment of this world, now shall the ruler of this world be cast out; and I, when I am lifted up from the earth, will draw all men to myself" (Jn 12:30-32).

This point is clearly made in the icon. Before His ultimate *kenosis*, Christ was welcomed into Jerusalem as the Messiah-king, having just raised a man dead four days.

48. The Raising of Lazarus; 17th c. icon, from Prissovo,
Veliko Trnovo region, Bulgaria. National Gallery, Sofia.

But what the adults are seeking, as they look to earthly possessions, is one who would restore the kingdom of Israel rather than the One who conquers death, the Lord of a kingdom that is not of this world. On the other hand, the children begin singing: "Blessed is He that comes in the name of the Lord…" They are the ones who laid their vestments in his path, a tribute that was reserved to the anointed king (2 Kg 9:13). "Enthroned" on an ass, a common animal in Palestine that was replaced by a horse in Russia, Christ is holding a scroll of Scripture in His left hand while giving a blessing with His right. The prophecies concur in drawing a connection between the docile nature of the ass and the kingdom of peace ushered in by the One seated on its back. The palms, the symbol of His victory over death, have naturally made their way into the icons of saints who bear them up as a sign of their own victory.

50. The Entrance into Jerusalem; 15th-16th c. icon, central Greece.
Byzantine Museum, Athens (Museum photo).

49. The Nativity of the Virgin Mary, the Presentation of the Virgin Mary in the Temple, the Raising of Lazarus and the Entrance into Jerusalem; late 15th c. fresco, Church of St Pareskevi, Yeroskipos, Cyprus.

51. The Entrance into Jerusalem; mid-11th c. fresco, Church of St Nicholas, Kakopetriá, Cyprus.

"And when He drew near and saw the city, He wept over it" (Lk 19:41). This is a deeply moving scene in which the lover of mankind is seen lamenting the earthly Jerusalem that has rejected the light that came into the world. He would soon be rejected by the people crying "Crucify him," then He would be put to death outside the city walls. Nevertheless, in light of His Death and Resurrection, the Jerusalem that is represented in the icon symbolizes the heavenly Jerusalem, the Kingdom of the New Covenant, the fulfillment of the prophecy of Zachariah: "Rejoice greatly, O daughter of Zion!...Lo, your king comes to you; triumphant and victorious is he, humble and riding on an ass" (Zach 9:9).

> Today, Christ enters the city of Bethany riding on a foal, and destroys the wicked and barren folly of the Gentiles (Matins, Troparion, tone 2).
>
> O Immortal Lord, Thou didst triumph over Hell; Thou didst trample down death and resurrect the whole world, O Christ, and the children with palms celebrate Thy victory, crying out: Hosanna, Son of David...(Matins, Ikos).
>
> O immortal Lord, Thou hast bound Hell, slain death, and raised the world: therefore the children, carrying palms, sing praise to Thee as Victor, O Christ, and they cry aloud to Thee this day: 'Hosanna to the Son of David!' (Matins, Kontakion, tone 8).
>
> Light thy lamps, O Jerusalem, and receive the Lord who comes at midnight as a bride-groom, to renew His covenant with thee (Vespers, Aposticha, tone 7).

The Last Supper (Holy Thursday)

The Last Supper does not figure among the twelve Great Feasts, but it incorporates them. During the celebration of the Divine Liturgy, the priest says quietly: "Remembering these saving commandments and all that has come to pass for us: the Cross, the Tomb, the Resurrection on the third day, the Ascension into heaven, the sitting at the Right Hand of the Father, Thy second and glorious coming; Thine own of Thine own, we offer unto Thee, on behalf of all and for all!" (Liturgy of St John Chrysostom). This represents a remarkable synthesis of the Eucharist and of the entire mystery of salvation. Shortly before this, just prior to the Great Entrance, the choir sings: "We who mystically represent the cherubim" (meaning we who are their icon) "now lay aside all earthly cares, that we may receive the king of all." While the eucharistic liturgy is an icon of salvation, the icon, which is itself a liturgical image, draws its meaning only from the Eucharist, the bloodless sacrifice which commemorates the Lord's Supper and manifests the presence of Christ among us and within us through our partaking of the gifts.

The icon is not only the image of Christ that bears witness to His Incarnation and to the penetration of the Spirit into matter, into a transfigured human existence. It is also the image of the Eucharist, where cosmic, material reality becomes the Body and Blood of Christ through the working of the Holy Spirit.

In accordance with the Gospels, the icon of the Last Supper describes the exact moment when Christ foretold Judas' betrayal: "It is he to whom I shall give this morsel when I have dipped it" (Jn 13:26). "Behold the hand of him who betrays me is with me on the table" (Lk 22:21). We can imagine the apostles' reaction: "One of you will betray me"—"Lord, who is it?" (Jn 13:21, 25).

The prayer offered before communion also reflects this situation: "At Thy mystical supper, O Son of God, accept me today as a communicant; for I will not speak of Thy mysteries to Thine enemies, neither like Judas will I give Thee a kiss, but like the thief will I confess Thee: remember me, O Lord, when Thou comest in Thy kingdom." This prayer affirms the indissoluble connection that exists between the Last Supper and the Eucharist: the Christ who was in the upper room, who is seated at the right hand of the Father, is the same One who now gives His flesh for food. This correspondence is particularly striking in the icons which, together with the liturgical texts, were developed from the sixth century until the height of the iconoclastic crisis, between the ninth and eleventh centuries. The apse of the Churches of the Holy Wisdom (eleventh century) and Saint-Clement of Ohrid (thirteenth century) offer a remarkable lesson in theology through a fresco of rare beauty. The prevalent position of the Theotokos affirms her fundamental role in the incarnation of the Son of God, who is present in the Holy Gifts on the altar. In the scene of the apostles' communion, Judas is replaced by Paul, while Christ is clearly portrayed as the celebrant, the One who "gives and is given." The scene shows Christ on one side giving of His body in the form bread, and on the other, His blood in the form of wine.

The Transfiguration on Mount Tabor, as well as in the depths of Hell, reveals the same Spirit that transforms and transfigures the bread and wine into the Body and Blood of the Risen One, as He transforms and transfigures all of creation, beginning with humanity that is "raised up." The bread is a material reality that becomes a spiritual reality by the power of the Spirit, to the same degree that the divine becomes incarnate in man and man becomes god. The dual nature of Christ is inseparable from a spiritualization of matter whose height is reached in the Last Supper. Every Eucharist constitutes a new Pentecost insofar as the Spirit comes down not only on the gifts that it sanctifies but also on the faithful. "The Holy Gifts are for the holy."

The Paschal mystery encompasses three elements: the Last Supper (Holy Thursday), the Crucifixion (Holy Friday) and the Tomb (Holy Saturday). Likewise, the Jewish Passover included three exceptional events: the eating of the lamb, whose blood was used on the lintel of the houses to protect the Jews from the devastation, the liberation or exodus from Egypt (representing Satan), and the entrance into the Promised Land. However, the Supper, the sacrament of the New Covenant, incorporates us into Christ, the token of our salvation; the Crucifixion frees us from the grip of spiritual death and from Satan; while from the tomb flows forth light, the dawn of a new day.

While the Last Supper precedes the Passion and the Resurrection chronologically, it also mystically includes them. The Eucharist is the "remembrance of the Cross and the Tomb." At the beginning of the third century, St Hippolytus of Rome wrote in a liturgical text: "In order to destroy death, to free us from the bonds of Satan, to trample down the powers of Hades, to lead the righteous to the light and to proclaim the Resurrection, He took bread..." The Orthodox Church understands the "Divine Liturgy" to be a "sacrifice of praise" (these are the words of the liturgy). It is not the renewal or the repetition of a bloody sacrifice, but the commemoration of a death and Resurrection, the "promise of resurrection," because it is the One who died and rose who is given up and gives Himself up. "Christ, our paschal lamb, has been sacrificed" (1 Cor 5:7). The Passover is the foundation of the Eucharist.

Christ does not merely give up His life on the cross; He is Life itself and gives Himself to whomever is willing to receive Him. He offers Himself unconditionally because He loves without measure. He is the "Lord of Glory" (Jas 2:1) and the "Light," according to the hymn sung after communion, "We have seen the true Light." Similarly with the vesperal hymn: "O Gladsome Light of the holy glory of the immortal, heavenly holy Father: Blessed Jesus Christ. Now that we have come to the setting of the sun and behold the light of evening, we praise God, Father, Son and Holy Spirit. For meet it is at all times to worship Thee with voices of praise, O Son of God and giver of life. Therefore all the world doth glorify Thee!"

The *Trisagion*—"Holy God, Holy Mighty, Holy Immortal"—usually sung at the Divine Liturgy, is replaced during the feasts of the Nativity, Theophany and Pascha, by the Pauline verse: "As many as have been baptized into Christ have put on Christ, Alleluia!" (Gal 3:27). In accordance with a tradition that was already firmly established in the fourth century, according to St Augustine, the Orthodox Church gives communion to the newly baptized, since baptism represents an incorporation into Christ.

> It was not from the same matter as that which He first created that He created afresh. Then He made man out of dust taken from the earth (Gen 2:7), but when He created him the second time He gave His own Body. As He restores his life He does not improve the soul, since it remains in its natural state, but as He pours His Blood into the hearts of those who have been initiated He makes His own life to dawn upon them. At the beginning it says that "He breathed into him the breath of life" (Gen 2:7), but now He communicates His Spirit to us (Nicholas Cabasilas, *The Life in Christ,* IV; *op. cit.,* p. 141).

52. The Communion of the Apostles; 11th c. fresco (detail),
apse of the Church of St Sophia, Ochrid, Macedonia.

54. The Last Supper; fresco, 1106, Church of the Mother of God, Assínou, Cyprus.

53. The Communion of the Apostles and the Virgin Orans; fresco, 1295, from the apse of the Church of St Clement, Ochrid, Macedonia.

"The Son of God, in his incomparable love for mankind, did not merely unite His divine Person to our nature, assuming a body and an intelligent soul, appearing on earth and living among men. He unites himself...to human persons, himself becoming one with each of the faithful through the communion of His Body. He becomes one body with us, making us a temple of the whole Divinity—for in Him, in His own body, dwells the fullness of Divinity. Under such conditions, how could the divine radiance of this body not illumine the souls of those who belong to Him, encircling them with His light as it illumined the bodies of His disciples on Mount Tabor? During His mortal life, although His body possessed within it the source of radiant grace, it had not yet become united to the bodies of men, and it is from without that He illumined those who were worthy of approaching Him: He communicated illumination to their souls through their eyes of flesh. But now Christ has, in a sense, merged with us, He is within us as our own possession; it is therefore from within that He cradles our souls in light" (Gregory Palamas, *In Defense of the Hesychasts,* I, 35).

The Supper presupposes the Incarnation, insofar as its entire meaning is revealed in the light of the Passion and the Resurrection. This is a reality Orthodoxy has maintained by the high honor in which it holds the Theotokos in most of its churches.

Finally, St John Chrysostom challenges us when he writes:

"How many exclaim: What a joy it would be to behold his face; even his clothing, or merely his sandals! Yet, in the Eucharist, He is the one you see, He is the one your hands touch, He is the one who becomes one flesh with you" (St John Chrysostom, *Homily on Matthew*, LXXX, *PG* 58,743).

Chrysostom places particular emphasis on two elements that he considers to be inseparable: the sacrament of the altar and the sacrament of one's neighbor. The presence of Christ is mystical in the icon, it is real in the Eucharist and it is personal in the poor and the oppressed. The emphasis the Orthodox Church places on the person is derived from a Trinitarian theology that expresses the singularity and the identity of the persons in a union of love. The Eucharist is the means of access to this communal, Trinitarian mystery. The litanies and prayers of the Divine Liturgy themselves end in Trinitarian doxologies. This liturgy leads us into the Kingdom, which is beyond time but also present with us, present within history, because the Eucharist does away with every limit of time and space. The Risen One is present, He is secretly manifest, uniting the body of the Church, while enabling us, by partaking of His glorious Body, to realize that all things are accessible to us.

According to an Arab proverb, two people must share a cup of salt before they can be friends. This is a subtle way of stressing the importance of a shared meal in the context of human relations. After His Resurrection, Christ often appeared during a meal where His followers recognized Him and, with their hearts burning within them, they drew from

Him a new energy. After the Ascension, the meal became the moment of greatest importance for Christians: communing of the Risen One and, through Him and in Him, communing with one another.

> This is the day of Resurrection...let us embrace each other; let us call brothers even those that hate us, and forgive all by the Resurrection (Paschal Stichera, tone 5).

The warmth of the Spirit is given to us during the "breaking of the eucharistic bread," as it was to the disciples of Emmaus who questioned one another once they were alone: "Did our hearts not burn within us?" (Lk 24:32). Such is our contact with fire! If a woman was healed by touching "the hem of his garment" (Mt 9:20), how much more will we be renewed by receiving His body in faith and love?

> If the mere touch of Christ's holy flesh gave life to decaying bodies, shall we not profit even more by tasting of his life-giving eucharist? As we partake of it, it shall fully change us unto itself: unto immortality.
>
> Do not be astonished at this, nor inquire as to how this may be, as do the Jews. Instead, consider this: water is cold by nature, but pour it into a kettle and place it over a fire: it will forget its nature, so to speak, and being overcome by the fire, it will take on its properties. Although our flesh is corruptible by nature, we likewise are freed from our infirmity through union with Christ, our true life, and we are renewed in this life. It was not enough for our soul to be regenerated by the Spirit unto new life; our carnal and earthly body also had to be sanctified through its participation in a flesh of like origin, and thereby be called to incorruptibility (St Cyril of Alexandria, *Commentary on John* 4:2-3).

Christ is the "medicine of immortality," according to the Fathers, who does not give Himself to the righteous but to sinners, for He alone is righteous. This is affirmed by the prayer before communion said by each of the faithful: "I believe, O Lord, and I confess that Thou art truly the Christ, the Son of the Living God, who camest into the world to save sinners of whom I am first. I believe also that this is truly Thine own most pure body and that this is truly Thine own precious blood..." (Liturgy of St John Chrysostom).

To commune of Christ's body means to drink from the cup of His suffering and of the suffering of the world, to commune in His sacrifice for mankind and for oneself. It is also through His Passion, His *kenosis*, that we commune in His Resurrection; thereby we are already mystically seated at the right hand of the Father and receive the Pentecostal outpouring of the Spirit.

When He gave His flesh "for the life of the world" and washed the disciples' feet, the Master simply requested that they imitate Him. "He who has ears to hear, let him hear!" (Mt 13:43).

55. The Last Supper, The Washing of the Feet and Praying in Gethsemane; late 15th c., early
16th c. icon, two-sided tablet, from the St Sophia Cathedral in Novgorod.
History and Architecture Museum, Novgorod.

56. The Washing of the Feet; 20th c. icon.
Private collection, Switzerland.

The Crucifixion

Given the inseparability of Christ's Death and Resurrection, the icon of the Crucifixion is of considerable importance in spite of the fact that it is neither part of the cycle of the Great Feasts nor recognized in the same way as the Exaltation of the Cross. In contrast with Latin Christians who often linger at the foot of the Cross, the Orthodox Church gives greater attention to the Resurrection; although it is a later event, it is the only way to approach the Crucifixion.

The diversity of the icons of the Crucifixion reveals a wide range of sensibilities and theological content. Though they were scarce in the fifth century, icons representing Christ, still alive, His eyes open and His naked, outstretched body hanging on the Cross, began to spread as early as the sixth century. Without ignoring the fact that His side was pierced by a spear (Jn 19:34) soon after He gave up the Spirit, the first objective of the icon of the Crucifixion is to show His victory over death. At least until the ninth century, one could find representations of Christ with His eyes wide open; the best example is a fresco from the eighth century, painted by a monk of the East at Santa Maria-Antiqua in Rome. The traditional Coptic icon, however, continued to show Christ crucified, still alive, looking upon all men with compassion and love. In other depictions beginning in the eleventh century, Christ appears with His eyes firmly shut, perhaps as a reminder of His mortal human nature. The increasingly curved position of His body served as a further indication of His death.

The crown of thorns, which was hardly present until the fourteenth century, suddenly took on a great significance in western frescos. The arms of Christ which, until then, had been fully outstretched, were depicted in a more convulsive, curved position. Christ's frail and gently curved figure often gave way to a ragged, suffocating body. This suppression of beauty contradicts any notion of Resurrection, which alone has the power to make of the body a new and transfigured flesh.

The fifteenth century, in the West, witnessed a particular emphasis on the Passion rather than on the Lord's glorification. In producing retables and statues in which the crucifix occupies a central position, the artists were inspired by the reenactment of the mysteries, taking place at the time in the public squares during Holy Week. These were deeply moving events. These artists, as well as their successors during the following centuries, became progressively more interested in the bloody character of the Passion, undoubtedly influenced by their reading of Isaiah.

> As many were astonished by him—his appearance was so marred, beyond human semblance, and his form beyond that of the sons of men—so shall he startle many nations; kings shall shut their mouths because of him; for

that which has not been told them they shall see, and that which they have not heard they shall understand (Isa 52:14-15).

He was despised and rejected by men; a man of sorrows, and acquainted with grief; and as one from whom men hide their faces he was despised, and we esteemed him not. Surely he has borne our grief and carried our sorrows; yet we esteemed him stricken, smitten by God, and afflicted. But he was wounded for our transgressions, he was bruised for our iniquities; upon him was the chastisement that made us whole, and with his stripes we are healed (Isa 53:3-5).

It would be interesting indeed to undertake a detailed comparison of the iconography of the Crucifixion, from the Enlightenment to the present, both in the West and in countries of Orthodox tradition. The record would not be entirely spotless on either side, although one must humbly admit that the Byzantine iconographic heritage was, if not spoiled, at least marred under the influence of the Latins and the art of the Renaissance in particular. In the West, the glorious cross became a cross of pain. The tragic destiny of man finds its fulfillment in the image of the crucified God-man, brutally subjected to the reality of a death which has become a passage to life. Even if this salvific perspective was present in the minds of the painters, images such as those of Grünewald depict a crucified human being, so human that Christ's divinity is ultimately overshadowed. One must not lose sight of the theological implications of such iconography. In the eyes of several fourth-century Syrian and Palestinian Church Fathers, it could not possibly represent such a crippled human form without also denying the mystery of salvation. The images of our temples of flesh and of our temples of stone must express both divinity and humanity.

"Of all the depictions of the human body, painted or sculpted, the most elaborate is that of the crucified Jesus. And this because, of all that is known to us in the history of painting and sculpture, this image includes the most facets; it took shape under the influence of the greatest diversity of tendencies and trends of thought, whether philosophical, religious or aesthetic. The most extreme tensions are found there: from the most common image of the triumphant Christ, clothed in rich apparel, to the crucifixion of Grünewald that appears to be frighteningly Nestorian. Yet the most synthetic image, the one that combines these contradictions, is the one that has been produced in its various forms from the Byzantine iconographic tradition at the height of its development. In this single image, representative of the artist's homogeneous vision, are brought together both serenity and dogma, triumph and horror, the fall and victory, the humiliation of the helpless and the majesty of the all-powerful, the shame of nakedness and the glory of the deified human body, death and resurrection. This is why the Orthodox mind attributes such great honor to this image. It honors it on Holy Friday as it remembers Jesus' death, and at Pascha, rejoicing in the Resurrection. There was a time when Christians celebrated a single Pascha, on the day of the

57. The Crucifixion; 9th and 13th c. icon. Byzantine Museum, Athens (Museum photo).

Crucifixion. For them it was the Pascha of the Cross and a joyous Pascha all at once." (from "Mystagogie de l'image peinte de la Crucifixion" Jerzy Nowosielski; in *Contacts*, no. 133, 1988, p. 33)

The services of Holy Week, filled already with the breath of the Resurrection, echo the Gospels in which the suffering of Christ is always linked to His Resurrection (Mt 16:21, 17:23; Mk 8:31, 9:31, 10:34; Lk 9:22, 18:33, 24:7). The icon of the Crucifixion provides a synthesis of the four Gospels, retaining only what is essential. Its aim is to raise us up from a tangible to a spiritual perception; it leaves no room for the corruptible world. Its form and colors are intended above all to express immortality and victory over death. The crucified body is already changed, restored to its initial beauty in spite of the stigmata of the Passion. A naturalistic painting which depicts only a disfigured body, marred by suffering, represents only the man, and not the God-man who conquered death. In the icon, Christ's suffering is already transfigured. His naked body, though we might think it should appear wounded and twisted in pain, is not seen hanging like that of a thief. Rather, it is renewed, transcending the cross which He appears to bear up more than it bears Him up. There is no place given to theatrical anguish or sensuousness, but only a sadness that is full of hope, only tears of thanksgiving that remind us that Christ died for us. In complete serenity the King sleeps, His arms outstretched as the sign of both an offering and a welcome: "Let us behold our Life lying in the tomb" (Holy Saturday, Praises, tone 2).

The archetypal image of the "center of the world" is realized in the Cross. It is also symbolized by the tree or the pillar, each of which represents the axis that connects the three cosmic levels: heaven, earth and hell. By burying its roots all the way into the center of the earth and reaching up toward heaven, the Cross, which the liturgical texts refer to as "the Tree," "the ladder" and the "pillar of Paradise," reestablishes the continuity between these three levels that had been separated by the fall. The Cross, which was foreseen and proclaimed in the archetypal image of the Tree of the World, drawn from the most ancient times, has itself become the center of the world, pronouncing its judgment and bestowing its salvation. It sums up and fulfills the "complete renewal" that was proclaimed by that tree. The "Tree of Life" referred to in Genesis, a symbol of Christ who is the source of life, was often depicted in the form of a cross in pagan circles.

As a parallel to St Cyril of Jerusalem (†387), for whom Christ "stretched out his arms on the Cross in order to embrace the ends of the earth" (*Catechesis,* Lect. 13:28), St Athanasius of Alexandria (†373) considered the purpose of the Crucifixion to be this: "it was that He might draw His ancient people with His one hand and the Gentiles with the other, and join both together in Himself" (*On the Incarnation*, 25; SVS Press, New York, 1982; p. 55). Christ reconciled four worlds by destroying two barriers: one horizontal, separating the Jews from the pagans, the other vertical, which had removed mankind from God.

> Christ defeated the devil using the very same means by which the Evil One had triumphed; he fought him with his own weapons. How is this possible? A virgin [Eve], the wood and death were all signs of the victory of the devil; the wood was the tree in paradise, while death was the sentence imposed on Adam. But the virgin, the wood and death, which were the signs of our defeat, were also those of our victory. Mary took the place of Eve; the tree of the Cross took the place of the tree of the knowledge of good and evil; the death of Jesus Christ took the place of that of Adam. Thus was the devil defeated by the very instruments of his victory.

> At the foot of the tree in paradise, the devil had overthrown Adam; on the Cross, Christ has trampled down the devil. The wood of old forced humanity into the abyss; that of the Cross led mankind out from it. Through the first wood, man was thrown, bound and naked, into darkness; by the second, the one that had defeated mankind was conquered, stripped of his weapons and offered as a spectacle for the whole universe. The death of Adam came also to his descendants; the death of Christ gave life even to those that were born before him (St John Chrysostom, *Homily on the Word Cemetery*, 2, *PG* 49, 395-396).

St Gregory of Nyssa (†394) suggested that the Cross symbolizes the unity of the cosmos through the unification of its four points. Its vertical axis, north-south, connects heaven and hell, while the crossbars, east-west, span the whole world. The "Tree of Life," the Cross planted on Golgotha, does indeed represent the *axis mundi*; Christ is at its center, reigning over the whole universe and assuming it to the end.

John, the beloved disciple, received as his spiritual master the mother of his Lord: "Behold your son" (Jn 19:26). He became "the theologian" par excellence. "Behold your Mother" (Jn 19:27). It is no doubt from this relationship that he drew the unparalleled depth and originality of his Gospel, relative to the Synoptics. The presence of the centurion, Longinus, in the icon, is too important to be ignored:

> Seeing the heavens grow dark, the earth tremble, the rocks being split and the veil of the Temple being torn in two, as Christ suffered His divine Passion, the centurion recognized Him as the true Son of God who endured all this in His compassion, He who was impassible by nature, the One that sustains the universe in glory, together with the Father and the Holy Spirit, as true God and King; then Longinus cried out in his joy: O Christ, Thou art my strength, my power and my help (Feast of Longinus the martyr, October 16, Matins, Ikos).

The presence of a skull in the cave below the Cross reminds us that, according to Tradition, Christ was crucified in the very same place where the first Adam was buried. "As in Adam all die, so also in Christ shall all be made alive" (1 Cor 15:22). While the catalyst for the death of mankind was taken from Adam's side as he slept, the side of the reposing Christ becomes the source of life. This water and this blood, this new creation, become the regenerating waters of baptism and the life-giving blood of the New Covenant that we drink "in memory" of Him. The water that flows down from Jesus' side onto Adam's skull is an obvious reflection of the icon of the Descent into Hell, in which the New Adam raises the first father from his tomb. The crucifixion outside the walls of Jerusalem expresses not only the people's rejection of the Messiah, but also the universal character of His sacrifice. As both High Priest and victim, He offers Himself up and is offered up for all.

> And Jesus cried again with a loud voice and gave up the spirit. And behold, the curtain of the temple was torn in two, from top to bottom; and the earth shook, and the rocks were split; the tombs also were opened and many bodies of the saints who had fallen asleep were raised (Mt 27:50-52).

The death on the Cross is written into the biblical tradition which sees in the darkening of the sun and the moon, as well as in the earthquakes, signs of the Day of the Lord. "It is finished!" (Jn 19:30). Through the common depiction of a darkened sun and moon, the icon espouses both the Gospels and the liturgy: "When Thou wast crucified, all of creation trembled at the sight!" (Matins of Holy Saturday).

The "triple barrier" that separates us from God, and about which St Nicholas Cabasilas wrote in *The Life in Christ* (III), in this instance takes on a particular character. Following the Incarnation, which overthrew the first barrier by restoring our fallen nature, Christ's death overthrew the barrier of sin and, through His Pascha, leads us into a new life in the Resurrection. Note that in the Orthodox tradition, the death of the God-man does not serve to settle an account nor to satisfy divine justice. It frees man from the yoke of darkness, from the Evil One who is already defeated. "He has trampled down death by death..." The most difficult thing to believe is not Christ's Resurrection, but His death, the incredible abyss that stands between the inaccessible God and the suffering Servant on the Cross. The only answer is provided for us by St John the Theologian: "God is Love" (1 Jn 4:8). But then why are there so many crushed, maimed and malformed innocent children? The mystery of suffering remains intact, even if its origin is known. Faced with so many questions, one can only contemplate the One dead and resurrected. He was stripped, emptied of His power and majesty; He experienced the absence of God (Mt 27:46), lowering Himself to the point of becoming a slave, so that we all might again be joined with Him.

> Thou didst ascend the Cross, O Jesus, Who didst descend from Heaven. Thou camest unto death, O Immortal Life. Thou camest unto those in darkness, O Thou Who art the True Light. Thou camest unto the fallen, O Resurrection of all. Our Light and our Saviour glory be to Thee! (Bright Week, Friday evening, Aposticha, tone 8).

58. The Crucifixion; 12th c. fresco, caves of the St Neophyte Monastery, Cyprus.

59. The Crucifixion; fresco, 1209 (detail),
Church of the Mother of God,
Studenica Monastery, Serbia.

Christ Himself spoke of His abasement and death as an exaltation: "And I, when I am lifted up from the earth, will draw all men to myself" (Jn 12:32). In a continuous motion, His descent into Hell is followed by His ascension into heaven, which in turn determines the descent of the Holy Spirit. His shameful death raises up mankind, anticipating its glorification. This is the meaning of the inscription at the top of the Cross that generally does not bear the words of Pilate—"the King of the Jews" (Mk 15:26)—but rather "the King of Glory."

The Cross, the power of Resurrection, is in turn inscribed in a trinitarian dynamic that was well expressed by St Philaret of Moscow: "The crucifying love of the Father, the crucified love of the Son, the love of the Holy Spirit, triumphant over the wood of the Cross."

From the distant third century, Origen urges us:

> May you receive the power to understand, along with all the saints, what is "the breadth, the length, the height and the depth" (Eph 3:18). The cross of Christ bears each of these dimensions. Through it He ascended the high mount, leading captives in His train (cf. Ps 68:18), and through it He descended to the depths of Hell; for the Cross has "height" and "depth." And it stretches out over the entire expanse of the universe, thus spreading its "breadth" and its "length." And the one "crucified with Christ," who knows the tension of this crucifixion, is the one that understands "the breadth, the length, the height, the depth" (Fragment of a *Commentary on the Epistle to the Ephesians*).

The icon of the Crucifixion, rather than being a mere memorial, is the proclamation of universal salvation, leading into the future which is born in the present of each and every life.

Christ's Burial

Only a few words need to be said about this less common icon that is not unlike that of the Myrrhbearing Women. Among its variations, the beloved disciple (John) and Joseph of Arimathea are often seen bent over the figure of Christ wrapped in linen cloths, while His Mother, Mary, embraces Him one last time. In this respect, the icon supercedes the four Gospel accounts that mention neither Mary nor John (Mt 27:59-61; Mk 15:46-47; Lk 23:53-56; Jn 19:39-42). The scene in which Mary is embracing Jesus is derived from the apocryphal gospel of Nicodemus, but it is certainly possible, in all good faith, to imagine that these events actually took place. Other figures such as Mary Magdalen and Nicodemus can be seen motionless in the background, against the mountains.

The body of Jesus is not claimed by an immediate disciple, but by Joseph of Arimathea who overcomes his fear. Christ's burial confirms His death in the same way the empty tomb confirms His Resurrection. It is a powerful event with universal significance:

> When Thou, the Redeemer of all, wast laid for the sake of all in a new tomb, hell was brought to scorn and, seeing Thee, drew back in fear. The bars were broken and the gates were shattered, the tombs were opened and the dead arose (Holy Friday, Vespers, Aposticha, tone 2).

The liturgical texts and the icon both reject any notion that Christ's body might have begun to decompose before His Resurrection. This would amount to denying his dual nature and ignoring His incorruptibility. His presence in the tomb is the presence of God among the dead, a light in the darkness, the dawn of a triumphant victory that transforms our suffering into joy.

The Elevation of the Cross

It was noted earlier that the Orthodox Church has dedicated its first Great Feast to the *Theotokos*; the second is dedicated to the Cross. This is a way of emphasizing the prominent role of the Cross in the economy of salvation and in the liturgical year throughout which the Cross remains ever present.

From within the tangle of available information concerning the origin of this feast it is quite difficult to distinguish history from legend. The fact remains that when the empress Helena went to the Holy Land, in 326, with the express purpose of discovering the true Cross, she was guided by an old rabbi named Jude, from whom she learned that the Jews had buried the Cross under a mountain of refuse. Jude or someone else recommended searching in a place that was covered with basil (this is highly symbolical!). The search led to the discovery of not one but three crosses, along with a sign bearing the inscription: "Jesus of Nazareth, the King of the Jews." The bishop of Jerusalem, Macarius, was summoned and began with the premise that the true Cross must be identified by its power of life. No sooner said than done. Each of the three crosses was touched to a dead body that was soon to be buried. When the third cross touched the body, the deceased came to life, much to everyone's surprise. Shortly thereafter, an ailing woman was instantly healed in the same way. The true Cross, thus authenticated, was then venerated by all the people before being elevated by bishop Macarius in a blessing of the four corners of the earth. It remained in the church of the Holy Sepulcher (completed in 335), where it was venerated until its dedication in Constantinople in 614 (Sept. 14). That same year it was taken away by Persian invaders. They were in turn defeated by Heraclius (628), who recovered the Cross. Today, only a portion of it remains to be venerated in the church of the Holy Sepulcher, the rest of it having been taken to Rome at the end of the seventh century.

The icon focuses on the elevation of the Cross by bishop Macarius, who is seen at times holding a sprig of basil. The scene generally takes place in front of a church with seven domes—that of the Holy Sepulcher—in the presence of the people, the empress Helena, sometimes with her son, Constantine, and statesmen who have come to venerate the Cross. The elevation of the Holy Cross serves as a reminder that it reigns over the whole universe which it has redeemed.

> Before thy Cross, we bow down in worship, O Master, and thy holy Resurrection we glorify (Troparion of the feast).

For the Cross, the sign of victory, the protection, glory and honor of all Christians, all things are possible. Liturgical texts as a whole and those of the feast in particular serve as reminders of its foreshadowing in the Old Testament. Consider the tree of Paradise, Noah's ark and Moses, before whom Amalek fled in the Sinai desert.

> The Cross is raised on high and urges all creation to sing the praises of the immaculate Passion of Him who was lifted high upon it. For there it was that He put to death our slayer, and brought the dead to life again: and in his goodness and compassion, He restored our original beauty and counted us worthy to be citizens of heaven (Great Vespers, Lord I Call, tone 6).

The ideas expressed here are the following: Satan is defeated, the dead are raised, a new creation is brought about and we witness the raising of mankind.

> For it was fitting that wood should be healed by wood, and that through the Passion of One who knew not passion should be remitted all the sufferings of him who was condemned because of wood (Great Vespers, Lord I Call, tone 2).

> The four ends of the earth, O Christ our God, are sanctified today by the Exaltation of Thy Cross with its four arms (Matins, Praises, tone 6).

> Hail! life-giving Cross, unconquerable trophy of the true faith, door to Paradise, succour of the faithful, rampart set about the Church. Through thee the curse is utterly destroyed, the power of death is swallowed up, and we are raised from earth to heaven: invincible weapon, adversary of demons, glory of martyrs, true ornament of holy monks, haven of salvation bestowing on the world great mercy (Third Sunday of Lent, Great Vespers, Lord I Call, tone 5).

> Hail! venerable Cross of the Lord which delivers mankind from the curse, from thee shines forth true joy; thou art exalted and thou overthrowest the enemy; thou art our help and our support, the strength of the righteous, the radiance of holy priests; thine image draws us from despair; a sceptre to guide us, a weapon of peace which the Angels bear up with respect, divine glory of Christ which grants to the world the grace of salvation (*Ibid.*).

> Hail! guide of the blind, precious Cross, physician of the sick, resurrection of the dead, raising us up from the pit where we had fallen; through thee the

60. The Burial; fresco, 1191, Church of St George, Kurbinovo, Macedonia.

corruption of the tomb comes to an end, through thee our immortal condition blossoms forth and we mortals become deified; the devil is crushed; and seeing the hands of the pontifs bear thee up, we exalt the One who was lifted up on thee. Bowing before thee, we receive in abundance the grace of salvation (*Ibid.*).

The epistle read on the day of the feast deserves some reflection:

Where is the wise man? Where is the scribe? Where is the debater of this age? Has not God made foolish the wisdom of the world? For since, in the wisdom of God, the world did not know God through wisdom, it pleased God through the folly of what we preach to save those who believe. For Jews demand signs and Greeks seek wisdom, but we preach Christ crucified, a stumbling block to Jews and folly to Gentiles, but to those who are called, both Jews and Greeks, Christ the power of God and the wisdom of God (1 Cor 1:20-24).

The second reading of Great Vespers on the eve of the feast reveals its entire meaning in this light: "Happy is the man who finds wisdom, and the man who gets under-standing...She is a tree of life to those who lay hold of her" (Prov 3:13-18).

61. The Exaltation of the Cross, around which are The Entrance into Jerusalem,
The Transfiguration, The Crucifixion, The Taking Down from the Cross,
The Burial, The Descent into Hell, The Ascension, The Nativity of Christ,
The Baptism of Christ, Pentecost, The Hospitality of Abraham
(the "Old Testament" Trinity); 15th c. icon, from Zdvygen,
Western Ukraine. Lviv Museum, Ukraine (Museum photo).

The first reading, which prefigures Christ's sacrifice, recounts a passage of Exodus in which Moses follows God's command to throw a tree into the bitter waters of Mara, thereby making them drinkable and quenching the thirst of the people thus freed (Ex 15:22-26:1).

The third reading, from Isaiah, points prophetically to the Cross, the new Jerusalem, a sign of shame that becomes a sign of victory and "a joy" (Is 60:11-16).

Though there exist far more texts that praise the Cross than our limited selection would indicate, its resurrectional power is affirmed everywhere:

> When you have lifted up the Son of man, then you will know that I am he (Jn 8:28).
>
> Truly, truly I say to you, before Abraham was, I am (Jn 8:58).
>
> And as Moses lifted up the serpent in the wilderness, so must the Son of man be lifted up, that whoever believes in him may have eternal life (Jn 3:14-15).
>
> Through the Cross all things are fulfilled. Baptism is given through the Cross; the imposition of hands is done through the Cross. And whether we be traveling, at home or wherever, the Cross is a great good, an armor of salvation, an impenetrable shield against demons (St John Chrysostom, *Homily on the epistle to Philemon,* III, 13).
>
> [Already at this period the faithful frequently made the sign of the cross!]
>
> No sooner had the wood of Thy Cross been set up, O Christ our Lord, than the foundations of death were shaken. Hell swallowed Thee eagerly, but it let Thee go with trembling (Matins, Ode 2, tone 2).
>
> A divine ladder enabling us to rise up to heaven... (Matins, Praises, tone 6).
>
> Thou didst ascend the Cross, that with Thyself Thou mightest raise them up that sat in the darkness of death (Bright Thursday, Vespers, Lord I Call, tone 6).
>
> Thy Cross, O Lord, is the Life and the Resurrection of Thy people (Friday of Bright Week, Matins, Praises, tone 6).

In a prefiguration of the New Covenant, the Old Testament recounts the way in which Moses, at God's command, fashioned a bronze serpent, mounted it on a rod, and healed the snakebite victims that gazed upon it. The Cross has the power to chase away demons and to cleanse our sins. The analogy between Amalek and Satan offers another example from the book of Exodus: "Whenever Moses held up his hand, Israel prevailed; and whenever he lowered his hand, Amalek prevailed" (Ex 17:11). If the Cross is not assumed and firmly planted at the heart of our lives, there is no victory over death nor over the death inherent in every sin.

The Cross is ever-present, remaining with us from our baptism to our death. It overflows from inside the churches onto steeples, into houses and onto our own person. It is striking to realize how frequently Orthodox faithful make the sign of the Cross. The power of Life and Resurrection it possesses makes every Christian take the Cross into account. "The word of the Cross is folly to those who are perishing, but to us who are being saved it is the power of God" (1 Cor 1:18).

The first beneficiary of this power, the wise thief, is favorably depicted in the composite icons of the Descent into Hell and in the iconography of the Last Judgment.

> Today our Lord Jesus Christ is hanging upon the Cross and we are celebrating. You must know that the Cross is a feast, a spiritual solemnity. At one time a cross meant disgrace; now, the word means honor. At one time it was the symbol of condemnation, now it is the foundation of salvation. For us the Cross is the source of countless blessings (St John Chrysostom, *First Homily on the Wise Thief,* PG 49, 399).

The Cross was at the center of the life of the first Christians. While they were persecuted and threatened with death, they avoided making the sign of the Cross in public, but they ardently sought its presence in nature. An inscription from Abercius, in the second century, mentions the Christian people bearing the "glorious seal," a cross on their forehead. Likewise, Tertullian described the situation in the second and in the beginning of the third century:

> In all our dealings—when we go in or out, before dressing, before bathing, at the table, when we light our evening lamps, before going to bed, when we sit down to read, in every activity of daily life—we make the sign of the Cross on our foreheads (*De Crono* 3, PL 2,80).

Bearing the mark of this seal (*sphragis* in Greek), the Christians of the early Church were not inconspicuous. St Augustine (354-430) noted that Christians in Africa were recognized by pagans coming out of the amphitheaters by this sign on their foreheads. It seems, however, that the sign of the Cross also had other meanings due to its resemblance to the letter tau (T in Greek). Ezekiel prophesied that a Tau would mark the foreheads of those that had accepted the Messiah. The Hebrew Tau—represented by a "+" or an "x"—is equivalent to the Greek Omega, referring back to God. It refers to a seal mentioned in Revelation, the distinctive sign of the elect (Rev 7:3). Jean Daniélou, whose lead we follow here, declares he is certain that the sign of the Cross borne by the first Christians was for them an expression of the Name of the Lord, meaning the Word, and meant that they had been consecrated to Him (*Les Symboles Chrétiens*, p. 149, Seuil). This is valid, however, only within a Jewish milieu. It would have been impossible for the Greeks to interpret the T in this way; for them this sign stood for the Cross of Christ. Bearing it rendered witness to one's commitment to the dead and resurrected Lord.

62. The Exaltation of the Holy Cross; late 15th c. icon, Russia (Novgorod).
Icon Museum, Recklinghausen, Germany (Museum photo).

63. The Patriarchs and the Wise Thief, detail from The Last Judgment; early 16th c. fresco, Church of St George, Voronetz Monastery, Moldavia, Romania.

In our own age, all too often suffocated by lifeless technology, the Russian poet, Smelev (†1950) revealed in his memoirs:

> Holy Thursday...I bring home a candle that was lit during the reading of the Passion Gospels, gazing fixedly at the quivering flame: it is sacred. In spite of the calmness of the night, I fear that it will go out...The old cook receives it gratefully. She washes her hands, takes the small, holy flame, lights her oil lamp [before the icons—ed.], then we proceed to mark with the sign of the cross the doorways of the kitchen, the cellar and the stable... "The devil has no power over the cross! May Christ save us!" she says, making the sign of the cross with the candle, first over herself, then over the cow.
>
> I sense the presence of Christ in our farm, not only in the stable, but in the cellar and everywhere. The presence of Christ manifested itself in this black cross left by the burning candle! And all that we do is meant for Him! This is what is extraordinary about these days, the days of the Passion, the days of Christ. I fear no longer, for Christ is everywhere (*Leto Gospodnie*, part 2: Pascha).

As the ultimate seal of Christians, the Cross truly seals their New Covenant with God.

> Today is lifted up from the hidden places of the earth the Tree of life on which Christ was nailed, confirming our faith in the Resurrection. And exalted on high by holy hands, it proclaims His Ascension into heaven, whereby our nature, lifted from its fallen state on earth, is made a citizen of heaven (Praises, tone 6).

Ascension

In the Gospel of Luke (ch. 24), every event of Christ's economy that takes place after the discovery of the empty tomb seems to happen in a single day. In fact, this was certainly not the case. The Ascension, along with Pentecost and the Resurrection, is part of the whole of the paschal period which is so aptly illustrated by the composite Russian icon of the Descent into Hell. The feast of the Ascension became progressively detached from the other two and was celebrated universally as early as the fifth century.

The fact that the Gospels are unclear with regard to the event and even differ as to its date is of little consequence. The historical element gives way to the content of the feast, which is a determining factor of salvation history. On this point the Gospels leave no doubt. We must avoid trying to visualize Christ's Ascension as if there were actually a physical body rising up, mysteriously drawn toward heaven. How it actually happened remains a mystery. In biblical terminology, the word "heaven" refers to something supernatural and divine. One thing is certain: Christ joins the Father whose power He shares. In other words, and as we confess, He is seated, in His spiritualized human body, at the right hand of the Father. The icon and the liturgical texts prove to be of precious help in the face of a reality that is not easily formulated:

> Though Thou wast not parted from His uncircumscribable bosom, Thou didst ascend unto Thy beginningless Father, O Christ, and the hosts on high accepted no addition to the thrice-holy praise. But even after Thou becamest man they recognized Thee as the one Son, only-begotten of the Father, O Lord. In the multitude of Thy compassions, have mercy on us (Vespers, Aposticha, tone 1)

> Having come down from Heaven unto the things of earth, O Christ, as God, with Thyself Thou didst resurrect Adam's form which lay prostrate in the nether holds of Hades' vault; in Thine Ascension to the heights Thou didst lead it up unto the Heavens and Thou didst seat it upon the throne of Thy Father, since Thou, the Friend of man, art merciful (Matins of the feast, Kathisma, tone 5).

Thou hast renewed in Thyself Adam's nature, which had gone down into the lower parts of the earth, and Thou didst raise it up above every principality and authority today. For since Thou didst love it, Thou didst seat it together with Thyself, Thou didst suffer with it; and enduring the Passion, though Thou art impassible, Thou didst glorify it. But the Bodiless said: who is this comely man? But He is not only man, but God and man; that which is manifest is twofold (Great Vespers, Litia, tone 1).

Today the hosts on high, beholding our nature in the Heavens, marvel at the strange manner of its ascent, and, being perplexed, they said one to another: Who is this that cometh? And when they saw that it was their own Master, they were commanded to lift up the heavenly gates. With them we ceaselessly praise Thee, Who again shalt come from thence in the flesh, as the Judge of all and Almighty God (Matins, Kathisma, tone 6).

In accordance with the Gospels and the Acts of the Apostles (1:6-12), the icon deals above all with theology. It is not an attempt to situate the event historically. This disregard for chronological accuracy is evident first of all in the presence of the apostle Paul, a presence that evokes the ecclesial fullness established by the Spirit. As in the icon of the Transfiguration, Christ appears enthroned, robed in glory, occupying an elevated space, the ultimate place of theophany. In the lower portion are depicted the apostles gathered around Mary, and an angel on either side saying: "Men of Galilee, why do you stand looking into heaven?" (Acts 1:11). The attitude of praise adopted by the Virgin Mary, standing between them, is in sharp contrast with the excitement of the apostles, who have gathered in this garden represented by rocks and olive trees. The Mother of God represents the Church, fully realized by the presence of the twelve apostles and Christ who is its head. With the scroll of the Gospels in His left hand, to symbolize His connection to the Body of the Church, Christ gives His blessing before sending the Holy Spirit. The Theotokos reminds us of the Incarnation, which affirms Him to be "true God and true man." If the foundation of Christian anthropology is the Incarnation, its fulfillment is the Ascension: the elevation of humanity, henceforth seated in Christ at the right hand of the Father. Christ's Ascension is thus the prelude of the elevation of all those who have clothed themselves in Him.

O all ye people, let us sing a song of victory unto Christ, who is taken up with glory upon the shoulders of the Cherubim, and who hath seated us together with Himself at the right hand of the Father (Matins, Ode 1, tone 5).

Beholding Thy deified flesh on high, O Christ, the Angels beckoned to one another: Truly this is our God (Matins, Ode 9, tone 5).

Thine Angels said unto the Apostles, O Lord: Ye men of Galilee, why stand ye looking up into heaven? This is Christ God, who hath been taken up from

64. The Ascension; early 16th c. icon, Russia. National Gallery, Oslo.
(Photo: Jacques Lathion, National Gallery, Oslo)

65. Christ Pantocrator, enthroned between the Mother of God and
John the Baptist, with the twelve apostles on either side;
16th c. icon, Pangarati Monastery, Moldavia, Romania.

> you into Heaven. He shall come again in the manner ye have seen Him going into heaven (Vespers, Lord I Call, tone 1).

> Let us all sing unto God, who was seen upon Mount Sinai, and who gave the law unto Moses the seer of God, and who ascended from the Mount of Olives in the flesh (Matins, Ode 1, tone 5).

At this point it is important to recall that the One who came to them "during forty days...speaking of the kingdom of God" (Acts 1:3) is the same One whose interventions and revelations are recorded throughout the Old Testament. One must also consider the importance of the number forty (Gen 7:17). It was at that age that Moses was chosen by God as he sojourned forty days on Mount Sinai (Ex 34:28). It represents the number of years the Hebrew people wandered in the desert (Num 32:13) and the days Elijah took to travel to Horeb (1 Kgs 19:8). Jesus, who was presented at the temple forty days after His birth, fasted for forty days in the desert (Mt 4:2). Such symbolism cannot be disregarded. Like the time of waiting before entering the "Promised Land," these forty days are also a time of preparation: the forty days of Lent before Pascha recall the flood in the Old Testament and the time during which Christ was tempted by Satan in the wilderness. It is a time of hope and endurance, therefore, that results in a conversion, a disruption of the established order, a time for new life. These forty days between Christ's Resurrection and His Ascension complete His teaching, confirming the unimaginable in the eyes of His disciples.

On the eve of His Passion, Christ told His followers: "It is to your advantage that I go away, for if I do not go away, the Counselor will not come to you" (Jn 16:7). Although the Ascension marks the end of Christ's visible presence, it also marks the beginning of His invisible, cosmic presence. And it is the Spirit at Pentecost that fully reveals the Risen One, Jesus Christ, the Son of the living God; for "no one can say 'Jesus is Lord' except by the Holy Spirit" (1 Cor 12:3).

The Father, through the power of the Holy Spirit (Acts 2:33), raises the Son whom He glorifies, as He did on the day of the Resurrection. Human reason, which has already been thwarted in its attempt to grasp the Incarnation, is all the more challenged with the thought that Christ is seated, with His human body, at the right hand of the Father. Any explanation lies beyond the limits of human language. The words "descent" and "ascension" refer to a mystical reality. God, who truly is present everywhere, cannot be circumscribed in space as we know it, except in the Incarnation of the Second Person of the Holy Trinity. In Acts (1:4-9), St Luke states that Christ shared a meal with His disciples, who later saw Him go up into heaven. There can be no doubt as to the corporeality of one who consumes food. It is this same Jesus who ascends and is quickly separated from the apostles by a cloud. He does not vanish like a spirit; His human, deified, glorified body, rendered transparent and "trans-spatial" through the energies of the Spirit, is beyond any definition. Fr. Sergius

Bulgakov provided some help when he said that "the ascension into heaven is by no means a removal of Christ into the astronomic space of the galaxies, it is not a removal into another place since 'heaven' is not a place, and certainly not a place other than earth...Heaven is the divine being, beyond the world and creation, it is the Holy Trinity itself in its glory, it is divine wisdom" (from *Du Verbe Incarné*, p. 328, L'Age d'Homme). Although the two natures are inextricably linked, the Ascension does not pertain to Christ's divinity, which is always present within the Trinity, but to His humanity. "As a creature, humanity is incapable of raising itself up to heaven, to divinity; it can only be raised. It is the offering which Christ makes to the Father as High Priest" (*Ibid.* p. 326).

Having assumed human form in order to dwell among us, Christ-Emmanuel descended to the very depths of Hell "to seek the lost sheep," to save and deliver the prisoners from their chains. Ascension and descent, therefore, are unified through the tree of the Cross. The Ascension brings before God the whole of creation which, henceforth, takes part in the life of the Holy Trinity.

> In the greatness of your mercy, O Master, you assumed Adam as he was before his transgression, in his fullness, body, soul and spirit, with all his natural faculties, in order to bring salvation to my entire being, since it is true that "what is not assumed is not saved." And having thus become a "mediator between God and man," you removed all hatred and led back to your Father those who had left Him: you restored that which had been lost, you gave light to those in darkness, you renewed what had been broken and bestowed incorruption on that which had been corrupted (St John of Damascus, *Homily on the Dormition*, I,3. SC 80).

> Even when we were dead through our trespasses, [God] made us alive together with Christ...and raised us up with him in the heavenly places in Christ Jesus (Eph 2:5-6).

> Our nature, which fell of old, is raised up higher than the Angels, and hath been placed on the throne of God in a manner surpassing understanding...(Matins, Ode 8, tone 4).

> Thou who didst descend to the utmost depths of the earth, and who didst save man and exalt him by Thine Ascension, do we magnify (Matins, Ode 9, tone 5).

> Christ ascended whither He once had been (Great Vespers, Lord I Call, tone 6).

> Today, Jesus Christ our Lord has ascended to heaven: may our hearts rise with him! Let us heed the apostle's invitation: "If then you have been raised with Christ, seek the things that are above, where Christ is, seated at the right hand of God. Set your minds on things that are above, not on things that are on earth" (Col 3:1-2). Christ has ascended to heaven but He has

66. The Ascension; fresco, 1183, caves of the St Neophyte Monastery, Cyprus.

not left us; likewise, we are already in heaven with Him; we have received His promise, but it is not yet fulfilled in our bodies. Though He has ascended to the highest heaven, Christ continues to suffer on earth as He bears every test that we endure as members of His body. He attested to this fact Himself when He cried to Saul: "Saul, Saul, why do you persecute me?" (Acts 9:4). And on the day of judgment He will say, "I was hungry and you gave me food" (Mt 25:35) (St Augustine, *Sermon, PL* 2, 494).

The Ascension is of the utmost importance for us because "the Kingdom of God is in the midst of you" (Lk 17:21), meaning within the human heart, where Christ wants to be incarnate, to be enthroned and sit at the right hand of the Father: "If a man loves me, he will keep my word, and my Father will love him, and we will come to him and make our home with him" (Jn 14:23).

Thou didst raise up human nature which was fallen into corruption, O Christ, and in Thine Ascension Thou didst exalt us and glorify us together with Thyself (Matins, Ode 3, tone 5).

And it came to pass that as He was blessing them, He withdrew from them and ascended to heaven. Note that the evangelist does not say: When He had blessed them, when He had completed His blessing, but as He was blessing them, as He continued to bless them. What a marvelous act! The Lord blesses, and without bringing His blessing to an end, still giving His blessing, He ascends to heaven. What does this mean? It means that He did not want to end His blessing, but that He continues ceaselessly to bless the Church and all who believe in Him (Metropolitan Philaret of Moscow (†1867), *Homily on the Ascension*).

The effect that Christ's Ascension had on the Apostles, according to the testimony of the evangelist Luke, may seem surprising: "They returned to Jerusalem filled with great joy." We might have expected them to be dismayed at their separation from their Master and Savior, yet they are full of joy...Why is this? They rejoice because now their faith is made perfect and their minds are open to the understanding of the mysteries of Christ. They believe, and they know that as Christ, by His Resurrection, broke the gates of hell and led the faithful out, so, by His Ascension, He opens the gates of Heaven and leads the faithful in (*Ibid.*).

Pentecost

Although Christ breathed the Spirit upon His disciples for the first time on the very night of the Resurrection (Jn 20:22), they receive it as the Person sent by the Father ten days after the Ascension (Acts 2:1-4). The two accounts agree on the fact that the Spirit is given to them upon the Son's request and according to His promise: "It is to your advantage that I go away, for if I do not go away, the Counselor will not come to you; but if I go, I will send Him to you" (Jn 16:7). There were "men from every nation" (Acts 2:5) who observed with "bewilderment" the effects of the descent of the Spirit upon the apostles, who suddenly began speaking in diverse tongues. By sending the promised Spirit, Christ once again affirms His Resurrection.

> O ye faithful, let us keep and celebrate most radiantly this post-festal and last feast; this is the day of Pentecost, which doth fulfill the appointed time and the promise. For on this day, the fire of the Good Comforter straightway came on earth, as though in the form of tongues, and it enlightened the disciples and proved them heaven's initiates. Behold, the Comforter's light is come and hath illumined the whole world (Orthros, Kathisma 1, tone 4).

Unlike the account in the Acts of the Apostles, which is marked by excitement and exuberance, the icon of Pentecost reflects a serene atmosphere, a static quality that stands in contrast to the dynamism of the different directions each face is turned, expressing their various charisms. Although they have received the same tongues of fire from the one Spirit that unites them, they do indeed manifest a variety of gifts. The way the individuals are positioned corresponds to the scene of the young Christ teaching in the temple.

Although His place is left empty, He is no less mystically present. A fundamental observation is that none of those present is set in a position over the others. The fact that Peter and Paul (the latter once again depicted among the twelve) are seated at the top could suggest a hierarchy. The inverse perspective, however, contradicts such a supposition, creating the impression of equality among them all.

From an ecclesiological perspective, the theological implications of this icon are important. Placing the Theotokos in the empty space between Peter and Paul does not do justice to the truth (although one may be reminded that such icons are found even in Orthodox churches). As she becomes the central figure, she relegates the apostles to a secondary position. This clearly contradicts the liturgical content of the feast. The point is not to deny Mary's presence in the upper room on that day. But to give her such a central position makes of the icon of Pentecost an icon of the Mother of God, whereas it is intended to show the descent of the Spirit upon these men who are thereby being born into new life. The confession: "I believe in the apostolic Church" emphasizes the fundamental role of the apostles, the pillars of the Church, commissioned to proclaim the Good News to the whole world. The old king held captive beneath them symbolizes the cosmos, as he emerges out of a dark cell from which he extends his arms toward the divine light. He is carrying a cloth laden with twelve scrolls that represent the preaching of the apostles, whose vocation is to spread the light they themselves have received.

It would be easier to imagine the apostles' sadness at hearing that Jesus was going to His Father. Had they not left everything to follow Him? What would become of them without Him? Knowing that nothing would ever be as it had once been, Christ promised them the "Comforter," the One who would be with them as well as lead them to Him, who is Himself the "Door" and the "Truth." After the "cloud" of the Old Testament, which was the tangible sign of God's presence among His people, the descent of the Spirit on each believer becomes the divine presence within that person: the same Spirit that was active long before Pentecost, the One that inspired the many prophets, the One through whom the Virgin Mary conceived. He guided the old man Symeon; He inspired John the Baptist and many others. "Receive the Holy Spirit" (Jn 20:23). Jesus used this formula only after His Resurrection. During His earthly ministry, He healed, forgave, gave His flesh for food, but never directly gave the Spirit. As He promised the Samaritan woman: "Everyone who drinks of this water will thirst again, but whoever drinks of the water that I shall give him will never thirst; the water that I shall give him will become in him a spring of water welling up to eternal life" (Jn 4:13-14).

> Christ comes and the Spirit prepares His way. He comes in the flesh, but the Spirit is never separated from Him. Workings of miracles and gifts of healing come from the Holy Spirit. Demons are driven out by the Spirit of God...Remission of sins is given through the gift of the Spirit: "You were

67. Pentecost; 14th c. icon, from Radzouge, Western Ukraine.
Lviv National Museum, Ukraine (Museum photo).

washed, you were sanctified…in the name of the Lord Jesus Christ and in the Holy Spirit of our God" [1 Cor 6:11]. Through the Spirit we become intimate with God: "God has sent the Spirit of His Son into our hearts, crying, 'Abba! Father!'" [Gal 4:6]. Resurrection from the dead is accomplished by the operation of the Spirit: "Thou sendest forth Thy Spirit, and they are created; and Thou renewest the face of the earth" [Ps 103:30] (St Basil, *On the Holy Spirit,* 19:49, op. cit., p. 77).

He that spake in the Prophets and was proclaimed through the Law, even the very God, the Comforter, is made known today unto the servants and witnesses of the Word who aforetime were imperfect (Orthros, Ode 4, tone 7).

Pentecost, which is celebrated fifty days after Pascha, or seven weeks of seven days plus one day, is both a departure from time and an entrance into the age of the Kingdom. It is the ultimate Eighth Day as it fills all things with the Spirit. The fact that one must count the Sundays after Pentecost until the last Sunday before Great Lent, preceding Pascha, shows the extent to which the liturgical cycle revolves around these two inseparable feasts.

Pentecost confirms the paschal message that death is no longer the mere absence of life, but that henceforth it can be transformed into the power of life. The Holy Spirit, the giver of life, sustains each life, helping it to grow and develop to its fullest maturity, progressing from the image of God to His likeness. In contrast with the "Tower of Babel" which this world has become, He reveals the transparency of the Kingdom where languages are abolished, because nothing remains hidden to eyes that are filled with light. Each new birth takes place in the Spirit. The Father raises the Son through the Spirit, while Christ, the image of the Father, filled with the Spirit, recreates humanity by His Resurrection. At the time of the first creation, though He was not yet incarnate, the Word breathed life into Adam (Gen 2-7). Once dead and resurrected, He breathed the Spirit (*pneuma*) upon His disciples (Jn 20:22). His apostles were filled with the Spirit, able to surpass their material and carnal perceptions of things. After their blindness to the divine reality of the One they accompanied had been overcome, there came an indelible conviction, a superhuman endurance that sprang forth from the very light that healed them of their blindness.

The Church that was born at Pentecost grew rapidly. Peter strengthened his brothers through his sermon (Acts 2:14-41) and went immediately to Jerusalem. There he founded the first Church community, which received James as its leader. The Church at Antioch was evangelized by men who came from Jerusalem, and it was further strengthened by Barnabas. Andrew's mission took him through Asia Minor, Greece and the Balkans, while Mark founded the Church of Alexandria in Egypt. Philip journeyed through Asia and southern Russia, while Bartholomew went as far as India and Armenia. Thaddeus and Simon the Zealot proclaimed the Good News in Persia and Mesopotamia, Matthias in

Ethiopia, James in Spain, and John in Ephesus. As for "the least of the apostles," Paul, his epistles sufficiently demonstrate the extent of his travels.

The twelve apostles each received the Holy Spirit, the sure sign of their diversity and equality in the same Spirit that would henceforth enliven the Church. Far from being made of stone or other materials, the latter is made up of men and women who live out their baptism through the confession of Christ's Resurrection and in the hope of their own resurrection, together with their bishops who collectively preserve the faith.

In his book *Orthodox Spirituality*, Fr. Lev Gillet ("A Monk of the Eastern Church") wrote: "The three graces—Baptismal grace, Pentecostal grace, Paschal grace—are but aspects of one and the same divine grace" (Crestwood, NY, SVS Press, 1987; p. 39). The Scriptures, which the liturgical texts imitate in this respect, are replete with analogies between water and the Spirit, alluding to baptismal water, but also to fire:

> I will sprinkle clean water upon you, and you shall be clean from all your uncleanness, and from all your idols I will cleanse you. A new heart I will give you, and a new spirit I will put within you; and I will take out of your flesh the heart of stone and give you a heart of flesh. And I will put my Spirit within you (Ez 36:25-27).

> "If anyone thirst, let him come to me and drink. He who believes in me, as the Scripture has said, 'Out of his heart shall flow rivers of living water.'" Now this He said about the Spirit, which those who believed in Him were to receive; for as yet the Spirit had not been given, because Jesus was not yet glorified (Jn 7:37-39).

> "I came to cast fire upon the earth" (Lk 12:49).

The fire appeared in the form of tongues that came down upon the apostles, while the living water flowed forth from Christ's side on the Cross.

> The Holy Spirit is Light and Life, a living, noetic Fountain, a Spirit of wisdom, a Spirit of understanding. He is a good, an upright Spirit, presiding in power and purging offences. He is Fire, issuing from Fire, speaking, working, distributing the gifts...(Orthros, Praises, tone 4).

The Incarnation unifies human nature, making it one in Christ. The Holy Spirit confirms the plurality of persons on the day of Pentecost, through the bestowing of personal gifts to serve everyone. The Church, far from being a social collective bringing together various individuals, is rather a living organism, the body of Christ, made up of as many different members as there are individuals with a "personal" relationship with the Trinity. The main point is summarized by Vladimir Lossky:

> The Son has become like us by the incarnation; we become like him by deification, by partaking of the divinity in the Holy Spirit who communi-

cates the divinity to *each* human person in a particular way. The redeeming
work of the Son is related to our nature. The deifying work of the Holy
Spirit concerns our persons. But the two are inseparable. One is unthinkable
without the other, for each is the condition of the other, each is present in
the other (V. Lossky, *In the Image and Likeness of God*; Crestwood, NY, SVS
Press, 1985; p. 109).

Undoubtedly, "the Holy Spirit provideth all things; He gusheth forth prophecy; He
perfecteth the priesthood; He hath taught wisdom to the illiterate. He hath shown forth
the fishermen as theologians..." (Great Vespers, Lord I Call, tone 1)

Thus the following prayer that is often repeated in Orthodox worship:

> O Heavenly King, the Comforter, the Spirit of Truth, who art everywhere
> and fillest all things, treasury of blessings and giver of life, come and abide
> in us, and cleanse us from every impurity and save our souls, O Good One.

We are the "Body of Christ" (1 Cor 12:27) through our participation in His nature,
and as unique persons, we are the "temple of the Holy Spirit" (1 Cor 6:19). Yet the union
and the inseparability of the two is evident. The Spirit leads us to the Son whom He
reveals, and to the Father who is contemplated in Jesus.

> Thou hast abundantly poured forth of Thy Spirit upon all flesh, even as
> Thou didst say, and all creation is filled with Thy knowledge, O Lord; for
> Thou, the Son, didst come forth immutably from the Father; and the Spirit
> indivisibly proceedeth (Orthros Canon, Ode 6, tone 7).

The spiritualization of the flesh, for which the Transfiguration represents a fundamental stage, reaches its height first at the Resurrection—when Christ appears through closed
doors, filled with the Spirit whom He breathes upon His disciples—then again at the
Ascension before He takes His place at the right hand of the Father. His victory over
death, which was fulfilled on the Cross, overthrows the barriers and breaks the locks,
shedding light upon all creation. This divine light is none other than the Holy Spirit who
fills all things. Thus, each new Pentecost, every outpouring of the Spirit, presupposes the
Cross, with the death of the old man through an ascetic effort which ultimately leads to
the observing of the commandments, to the "remembrance" of God, and to tears of
repentance, all of which is the fruit of a rediscovered union between our spirit and our
heart. In this sense, Pentecost enables us to commune fully in the power of the Resurrection. By the power of the Spirit, Jesus enters even through doors that are shut and locked.
He moves at will, not only overcoming obstacles but, as the "Door," He opens the "Way"
where there seems to be none, where hope has been lost. The Resurrection is not merely
a fleeting burst of light after which each person resumes his daily living in violence,
darkness and indifference. Only a life in Christ fulfills the presence of the Spirit, making

a "new creation" (2 Cor 5:17), enabling us to discern the presence of the Risen One, to taste of life in the midst of death, and to perceive beneath every mask a true face fashioned "in the image of God."

While the Incarnation establishes the icon's foundation, Pentecost naturally marks its fulfillment, for the light of the Spirit now shines in abundance.

The Dormition of the Mother of God

As the last great feast of the liturgical year, the one the Church wishes to impress on our memory, the Dormition of the Mother of God can usually be seen on the wall of the nave, above the door of Byzantine churches that are covered with frescoes. The feast of the Dormition was probably celebrated already at the end of the second century and was highly regarded in the Byzantine empire at the beginning of the seventh century. Although the apocrypha unanimously situate the death of the Virgin Mary in Jerusalem and her burial in Gethsemane, the Gospels and Acts on this issue are silent. The contrary is unimaginable, since apart from the Gospel of John (whose author was charged with the care of Mary at the foot of the Cross), they were written before her Dormition. St Epiphanius of Cyprus (†403), admitting that nothing is truly known concerning Mary's death, affirmed that this silence was necessary so that "the transcendent grandeur of this marvel might not overwhelm the human mind" (*Panagion,* 78:11, *PG* 42, 716 B). Nevertheless, the most vivid account of the Dormition is given to us at the beginning of the eighth century by St John of Damascus, who claims that this version was transmitted "from father to son from the early ages" (*Homily on the Dormition,* II, 4,3). The icon in its most complete form corresponds to this description.

The icon of the Dormition is constructed around two complementary axes. The horizontal position of the death bed in which the Mother of God is resting, adorned with an *omophorion* and with her eyes closed, contrasts with the vertical movement of Christ, who stands upright in the center. He who is the "Life" bears up the soul of the one who remains lifeless as she awaits the hand that will raise her up. The inversion is striking. It is no longer the Mother that carries her Son, as in the many variations of the icons of the Theotokos (she is never represented alone because she is the handmaid of the Lord, the chosen vessel of the Incarnation, the one who gave Christ to the world). Here the Son bears up His Mother like a new born child. The two axes of the icon imply two levels of interpretation: the Dormition itself, which concerns Mary's death, then her elevation into heaven. This is a mystery beyond all comprehension.

In icons from the beginning of the thirteenth century, the number of people present began to increase. As a reflection of apocryphal accounts already represented in the

68. The Dormition of the Mother of God; late 13th c. icon,
St Catherine Monastery, Mount Sinai, Egypt.

liturgical texts, the apostles emerge, borne on clouds and carried by angels from the ends of the earth to the place of the Dormition. At the top of the icon, the Theotokos is taken up by two angels, like Christ at the Ascension. The gates of heaven are sometimes open to welcome her. Comparing these icons with any that are dated before the early fifteenth century clearly demonstrates a further evolution, however. The beautiful icon of the Dormition done by Theophan the Greek (end of the fourteenth century) still belongs to this earlier style. Later versions would also include Jephoniah, the Jew who tried to profane the body of the King's Mother, who is stretched out on a sumptuous bed covered in royal purple.

The soul of the Theotokos is often depicted in two ways: first, in the arms of the Risen One who is standing at the foot of her bed, then carried up to heaven by the angels. The same method, which represents the telescoping of events, can be found in certain icons of the beheading of John the Baptist. He is often depicted in his bodily wholeness, standing upright, with his disembodied head laying to one side. The posture of the apostles expresses both a deep veneration and the sorrow of children taking leave of their mother. Depending on the number of figures represented, one can recognize Paul of Tarsus and the evangelist John leaning over the Mother of God, Peter with a censer in his hand, and as many as four bishops: James (the first bishop of Jerusalem), Timothy, Dionysius the Areopagite and Hierotheus. The "Sun of righteousness," the New Adam, is surrounded by a mandorla that indicates the celestial realm, beyond the laws of space and our own perception, as He receives the soul of the New Eve. Present in glory and majesty, the Risen One raises His Mother as He will raise all His beloved ones.

> The hosts of angels, present with the fellowship of the apostles, gaze in great fear at her who bore the cause of life, now that she is translated from life to life (Great Vespers, Litia, tone 5).

> What songs filled with awe did all the apostles of the Word then offer thee, O Virgin, as they stood around thy death bed and cried aloud in wonder: 'the Palace of the King withdraws: the Ark of holiness is raised on high. Let the gates be opened wide that the Gate of God may enter into abundant joy, she who asks without ceasing for great mercy upon the world (Vespers, Lord I Call, tone 2).

> The Powers of heaven accompany you, the Principalities bless you, the Thrones sing your praises, the Cherubim rejoice in amazement, the Seraphim glorify the one who was the mother of their own master by nature and in truth unto salvation. You did not go up, like Elijah, "toward heaven," you were not carried, like Paul, "to the third heaven," but you went up to the very throne of your Son where, in joy and inexpressible assurance, you stand beside him (St John of Damascus, *Homily on the Dormition,* I,10).

> It is said that when those carrying the blessed body of the Mother of God began descending the mountain, a Hebrew man, a slave of sin...threw himself as one possessed on this divine abode which the angels themselves feared to approach, and taking hold of the bier with both hands...he tried to overturn it. It is said that he lost both his hands...until he gave in to faith and repentance...and having brought them near this tabernacle, this foundation of life and source of miracles, he found himself whole (*Ibid.,* II,12).

It was the archangel Michael (the name meaning the power of God) who cut off the sinners hands. The account, which is taken from the apocrypha, emphasizes the holiness of the Theotokos, whom God keeps as the apple of His eye.

It is no surprise, therefore, to find that the texts of the feast focus on the two fundamental elements of the Christian life: Resurrection and Transfiguration.

> The Spotless Bride, the Mother of Him in whom the Father was well pleased, she who was foreordained by God to be the dwelling place of His union without confusion, delivers today her blameless soul to her Creator and her God. The spiritual powers receive her with the honors due to God, and she who is truly the Mother of Life departs unto life, the lamp of the Light which no man can approach, the salvation of the faithful and hope of our souls (Great Vespers, Litia, tone 2).

The parallel between the icon of the Descent into Hell and that of the Dormition allows for a transition from a universal to a personal level. Indeed, as Christ descended to raise up the captives, He also brought His Mother into His glory, thereby prefiguring our own resurrection. Over against the hopeless vision that was once held concerning the after-life, in this case the last word does not belong to death, "the last enemy to be destroyed" (1 Cor 15:26); it belongs to life itself.

Unlike the Roman Catholic Church, and in continuity with the Tradition of the undivided Church of the great Councils, Orthodoxy believes that the Virgin Mary died as her Son did, before being raised up to heaven. Although she did not escape the legacy of Adam which made her a mortal creature, she remained the "All Pure One." She simply did not succumb to evil by misusing her free will. She shared her human nature with her Son, who was able fully to assume it in order to save it. Finally, she gave birth while remaining a virgin, because Christ was conceived by the power of the Holy Spirit. The fact that the Orthodox Church has favored the term "Dormition" over "Assumption" is due not to a mere linguistic subtlety but to a specific theological vision.

In praise of the Dormition, St John of Damascus wrote:

> How is the source of life led to life by passing through death? O wonder! She whose child-bearing surpasses nature is now subject to the laws of nature, and her immaculate body is subject to death! One must put away

that which is mortal in order to put on incorruptibility, for the Master himself did not refuse to experience death. For as He died according to the flesh, and destroyed death by His death, upon corruptibility He bestowed incorruptibility and turns the passage of death into the source of resurrection (*Homily on the Dormition,* I,10).

O pure Virgin, thou hast won the honor of victory over nature by bringing forth God; yet like thy Son and Creator, thou hast submitted to the laws of nature in a manner above nature. Therefore, dying thou hast risen to live eternally with thy Son (Matins, Ode 1, tone 1).

But while, according to nature, your all-holy and blessed soul is separated from your holy and immaculate body, and while this body is placed in a tomb according to common law, nevertheless, it does not dwell in death and is not destroyed by corruption (*On the Dormition*).

"As in Adam all die, so also in Christ shall all be made alive" (1 Cor 15:22). The tradition of the Church of Jerusalem claims that Mary's body remained three days in a tomb at Gethsemane. The time is unimportant. The icon bears witness to two things. First of all, the soul of the Mother of God did not descend to Hades. Then, as the "burning bush" was not consumed, and as the "Ark of the Covenant" made of "acacia wood" (Ex 37:1) was discovered to be incorruptible, her soul was not given over to corruption. The liturgy on the feast day gives glory to Mary's body, called to be transfigured, as is every human body.

You have freed us from the shame that befell Eve. She was the mother of clay, you were the mother of light; from her womb came corruptibility, from yours came incorruptibility. She established death in the world, you snatched the world from death. Since the time of Eve, our eyes remained fixed on the earth; you opened them, made them vigilant, reflecting glory. She engendered sorrow, you engendered perfect Joy. She was dust and returned to dust; you brought Life to us and you returned to Life. This same Life you have promised us as a gift beyond death (St Germanus of Constantinople, *Homilies I and II on the Dormition,* PG 98, 347).

Unlike the Ascension, where Christ goes up alone, the Dormition shows Mary being raised up by her Son. Contrary to others whose bodily transfiguration would take place only at the final resurrection, she who is "more honorable than the cherubim and more glorious than the seraphim" experiences this fullness immediately. Mary is not only the Mother of God, but also the most perfect creature in whom humanity is glorified. Henceforth, God sees before Him the human body of the new Eve, the mother of the living, the one in whom "God became man and man became God" (St John of Damascus, *op. cit.*, II, 16), thereby justifying the power of her intercession.

69. The Dormition of the Mother of God; Byzantine icon painted in Venice,
mid-16th c., Hellenic Institute of Venice (Institute photo).

70. The Dormition of the Mother of God; 16th c. fresco, from the
gate of the Pietra Neamt Monastery, Moldavia, Romania.

71. The Dormition of the Mother of God; fresco, 1365 (detail),
Church of St Clement chapel, Ochrid, Macedonia.

> In my Father's house are many rooms; if it were not so, would I have told
> you that I go to prepare a place for you? And when I go and prepare a place
> for you, I will come again and will take you to myself, that where I am you
> may be also. And you know the way where I am going (Jn 14:2-4).

> I am the way, and the truth, and the life; no one comes to the Father but by
> me. If you had known me, you would have known my Father also; hence-
> forth you have known him and have seen him (Jn 14:6-7).

According to the tradition, Thomas was the only one among the apostles to have arrived
after the death of the Theotokos. When he went to the tomb in the garden of Gethsemane,
he found that her body was no longer there, but had been taken up to heaven.

> The Father had foreordained her; then the prophets announced her through
> the Holy Spirit; then the sanctifying virtue of the Spirit visited her, purified
> her and made her holy and, so to speak, watered this earth (St John of
> Damascus, *op. cit.* I, 3).

The Holy Trinity

> In the tomb with the body and in hell with the soul, in paradise with the
> thief and on the throne with the Father and the Spirit, wast Thou, O
> boundless Christ, filling all things (Paschal Hours, tone 8).

> The Father is Light; the Word is Light; and the Holy Spirit is Light, Who
> was sent to the Apostles in the form of fiery tongues; and thus through Him
> all creation is illumined and guided to worship the Holy Trinity (Pentecost,
> Matins, Exapostilarion, tone 3).

Approaching the mystery of the Resurrection necessarily implies a contemplation of the
Holy Trinity, for the Father is revealed through the Son in the Spirit. In other words, as Boris
Bobrinskoy has shown (*Le Mystère de la Trinité,* Paris, Cerf, 1986), the Father sends the Son
(Mk 9:7) who is the image of the Father (Jn 14:9, 11); and at the Son's request, the Father
sends the Spirit (Jn 14:26, 16:7) who in turn raises the Son (1 Cor 12:3).

This continuous descending and ascending movement—from Father to Son, to Spirit,
and from Spirit to Son, to Father—is expressed in a circular form within Rublev's icon of the
Trinity. Here we find a striking summary of the paschal mystery. If the ultimate icon is that
of the "Incarnate Word," what can be said of that of the Holy Trinity, since neither the
Father nor the Spirit can be graphically represented? The answer seems to come from the
liturgy, for which this motif serves as an icon of Pentecost, along with the classic icon of the
apostles gathered in the Upper Room. In any event, those familiar icons that depict the
Father simply betray the truth; since He is not incarnate, He cannot be represented.

Andrei Rublev's icon of the Trinity is a constant source of amazement, beckoning the minds and hearts of the millions of people touched by its inexpressible dynamic quality. It would be incorrect to reduce the persons of the Holy Trinity to these three human-angelic beings that are evidently not part of the human realm. In their respect for the Trinitarian mystery, the Church Fathers favored the example of the sun. Scientists admit that, although they can determine the sun's composition, they do not have a true understanding of it. We all know that it is round, and that it emits rays of light and warmth. These are three of its characteristics, yet it remains only one sun.

This icon of the Holy Trinity has its origin in the biblical narrative of the hospitality of Abraham (Gen 18:1-15). In Greek it is called *philoxenia,* which means "love toward strangers," a term valued in Greece to this day, where hospitality is something of a golden rule. Leonid Ouspensky notes that the angels are arranged in the order of the Nicene Creed: "I believe in one God, the Father, the Son and the Holy Spirit," which is also the order of every Trinitarian invocation in the liturgy: Father, Son and Holy Spirit. Furthermore, the angel in the middle is wearing the stole of the High Priest and the clavus worn by the Kings and Judges of the Old Testament, as a reference to Christ's mission and His teaching in the world. The later Greek term *apostolikon* is more satisfactory; it is often seen in icons, where it is worn by prophets, angels and apostles who have been charged with a mission. Each of the angels, "equal in majesty," is carrying a rod that is half shepherd's crook and half scepter. In the cup is a sacrificial lamb: the paschal lamb that is Christ. The eyes of the two angels are turned toward the Father, in whom everything originates. We ourselves are invited to don white robes and participate in this paschal banquet.

The Genesis account (Gen 18:3-10) is striking in its alternate use of both the singular and the plural, of unity and trinity. One and three at once, these angels are indeed the image of the One, triune God. Love implies a relationship that transcends mere duality, hence the perfection of the number three. Being in communion with someone is being at one, united with them. However, this unity in love does not imply a diminishing of their personal identity. Through His Descent into Hell, Christ gave a face to those who had none. Thus everything in the icon of the Trinity is focused on the face that is the foundation of the person, emphasizing its sacred character and its power of communion. Christ represents personhood in its fullness, being the only human creature to live in full communion with God: "No one comes to the Father but by me" (Jn 14:6). Through communion in Christ, through baptism and the Eucharist, we become a "child of God," a person (*hypostasis*) "in His likeness."

Between individualism and collectivism, between person and community, the Trinity opens a third way, which is the only way out of the inevitable antagonism so clearly demonstrated by the multitude of current domestic, local and international disputes. The Trinity disrupts the closed relationship of the "you-me" construct by introducing a third

72. The Holy Trinity; icon painted in 1411 by Andrei Rublev for the
Trinity-Saint Sergius Monastery. Tretiakov Gallery, Moscow.

73. The Holy Trinity; fresco painted in 1378 by Theophan the Greek,
Church of the Transfiguration on Ilina Street, Novgorod, Russia.

element: one that opens onto the "we" of authentic communion, in which each person can flourish. The "I" is no longer affirmed over against the "you"; it is affirmed, rather, through sharing with others by welcoming whatever is unique in each one.

As shown especially by the vigil service and the eucharistic liturgy, the Byzantine liturgy as a whole is replete with Trinitarian doxology. "The Trinity is, for the Orthodox Church, the unshakable foundation of all religious thought, of all piety, of all spiritual life, of all experience. It is the Trinity that we seek in seeking after God, when we search for the fulless of being, for the end and meaning of existence" (V. Lossky, *Mystical Theology, op.cit.,* p. 65).

The eucharistic liturgy is the perfect icon of the Holy Trinity: the icon of the Father who "brought us from non-existence into being," the icon of the Son who worked among us and continues to act, and the icon of the Holy Spirit who fills all things and changes the bread into the Body of Christ. If "the aim of the Christian life is the acquisition of the Holy Spirit," as St Seraphim of Sarov affirms, it is because the likeness of Christ is achieved through the Spirit. He "transfigures" and "transforms" all things, beginning with the Holy Gifts during the eucharistic celebration. Receiving Him means attaining to the Trinity, which He reveals in its fullness: Father, Son and Spirit. "When the Spirit of Truth comes, He will guide you into all the truth...He will glorify me, for He will take what is mine and declare it to you. All that the Father has is mine; therefore I said that He will take what is mine and declare it to you" (Jn 16:13-15). The Father sends us the Son, who leads us back to the Father through the Spirit, the living water who is the gift of God (Jn 7:37-39).

Man, created in the image of God—after the image of Christ who is Himself the perfect image of the Father (Heb 1:3 and 1 Cor 1:15)—is also called to become a "tri-unity," a person in communion. No longer is he to be an individual alongside other individuals. Rather, he is to become a being who is aware of sharing the nature of Christ, who assumed our humanity. Far from being limited to the here and now, the "being in relation" which we are intended to become requires a breaking down of time and space, to include both the living and the dead. Without any distinction of persons, it becomes possible to keep "in the remembrance of God" both friends and enemies, those who love us and those who offend us. And all of this necessarily takes place on the level of the heart, there where the battle lines are drawn. The icon of the Trinity is a paschal image that ceaselessy beckons us. We must contemplate it at great length if we are to perceive its inner mystery.

6

The New Man

Pascha is the wellspring of the liturgical year that orchestrates the new era, and determines the date of movable feasts. Once transfigured, history takes on a dimension of theophany. The paschal celebrations of Holy Thursday and Holy Friday expound the Nativity before arriving at the descent of the Spirit at Pentecost. Christ's Passion, Death and Resurrection enliven, deify and naturally incorporate the whole of creation into the Trinitarian life of God.

"If any one thirst, let him come to me and drink. He who believes in me, as the scripture has said, 'Out of his heart shall flow rivers of living water'" (Jn 7:37-38). Origen (†254) expressed the presence within each person of a well of living water that had become obstructed through infidelity and insensitivity to the infinite love of God for each of us. It is vital that this well be cleared and allowed to flow. This implies a concerted effort, self-control, a limitation of one's desires and passions, a realization of spiritual reality through the opening of one's spiritual eyes, a *metanoia* of the heart that changes it from one of stone to a compassionate and loving heart of flesh. Love must become the only rule, the only measure, the only warmth to make every being fully open.

Not long before he was delivered up to the wild beasts in the arena, Saint Ignatius of Antioch (†ca. 117) exhorted his brothers one last time: "My earthly desire has been crucified and there burns in me no passion for material things. There is living water in me, which speaks and says inside me, 'Come to the Father'" (*Letter to the Romans,* 7:2; in *Early Christian Fathers,* C. C. Richardson, ed.; Macmillan, New York, 1970; p. 105).

Like champion athletes who subject their bodies to rigorous training, Christians cannot live in apathy. Although encountering Christ is essential, it is not sufficient. One must follow Him, celebrate Pascha with Him, go up to Jerusalem then to Golgotha with Him, and finally receive the baptism by fire through the Spirit. The human person is like iron that turns red in the fire, becoming malleable and transformable in the hands of God.

Time and Space

The Resurrection leads us beyond time. Having become subject to time and to death, the God-man eventually conquered both. He became the victor, as does all of humanity through Him. Creation, which was once contaminated by men, can once again return to God through mankind.

Before the fall, man found nourishment in God who is life, and recognized Him to be the foundation of the life that filled his entire being. By freely choosing to eat of the forbidden fruit, in an act of self-sufficiency that revealed his preference for human nature over the gift of divine kinship, man removed himself from the source of life. He passed from a spiritual to a biological existence, from union with God to a life of independence, contrary to nature. By choosing to eat the perishable fruit, man is cast into a cycle of change and corruption, into a time marked henceforth by death. Once he is subject to death, he struggles to preserve life, trying to escape death. The fall did not simply lead man into a biological form of life. It encompassed the whole of his psychosomatic being which, once turned from its intended state, submitted itself to instincts that led to the realm of the passions. Carnal pleasure for the body is equivalent to avarice for the spirit, all of which leads a person to be disconnected and lacking in harmony; it shatters his original unity.

Already in the fourth century Gregory of Nyssa gave this warning:

> Thus, God cannot be considered responsible for evil, for He is the author of that which is, and not of that which is not; He made sight and not blindness....And this, not by subjecting man to His will and leading him to good by force and against man's will, like an inanimate object. If, when a pure, brilliant light shines...one willingly hides one's eyes, the sun is not responsible for the fact that one does not see (*Large Catechism*, 7, *PG* 45,32).

History reveals that every civilization has concentrated its efforts on seeking stability, harmony and eternity. Thirsting for immortality, human creatures have sought from the beginning of time and by various means to overcome the limits of corruption and death. Since he is created "in the image and likeness of God," it is only natural for man to tend toward his model.

The success of modern medicine in postponing death more and more has led in our day to a particular awareness of degeneration, of a tragic, inescapable void. Must we concur with Sartre in saying that "the fact that we are born is absurd, as is the fact that we die?" We must, if we consider the Resurrection to be an illusion, but not if we believe that "Christ is truly risen!"

The more man is removed from his ultimate aim which is God, the more he is lured by creatures and creation, the greater the tragedy of his uprootedness, his alienation, and his suffering, caused by the disintegration of his being and by ultimate meaninglessness. Relative to man's tragic state of separation from God, biological death, which is in itself already unacceptable, is of little consequence. Man was not created for death and finality, but for immortality and eternity. To consider death strictly as a biological reality renders one insensitive to Christ's death and Resurrection. Communion in His Resurrection, to be sure, does not spare us from biological death. Nonetheless, it bestows incorruption upon our soul, which is the vital principle that leads us from darkness into light.

74. The Descent into Hell; fresco, 1494, Church of
Stavrou tou Agiasmati, Platanistássa, Cyprus.

Time entails corruption, since it changes everything that is subject to it. True growth, which is foreign to possessions and the constraints of fallen time, fully engages us in our deepest being, which is continually progressing toward greater integrity. Reducing growth to economic and technological success causes untold harm; it leads us away from our goal and destroys our relationship with creation which was given to us, not to be wasted and ruined, but that we might use it eucharistically, wisely and harmoniously.

Through His Resurrection, Christ put an end to death, changing it into a necessary passage to immortality. Seen in this perspective, death frees us from the demands and conditions of the fall. Death, the fruit of corruption and "corruptibility," allows us to move beyond time, which in turn abolishes the corruptibility of death. There is one condition, however: that this movement be an entrance into the Kingdom already present in this world. This is what allows Death to open onto eternity. According to St Irenaeus of Lyon:

> This is why God cast [Adam] out of Paradise and sent him far from the tree of life: not because He kept this tree of life from him out of jealousy, as some have dared to maintain, but He acted out of compassion, so that man might not remain in sin forever, so that the sin which weighed him down might not be immortal, so that evil might not be without end and thus without remedy. He kept him from his transgression, therefore, by introducing death...giving him an end through the dissolution of the flesh which would take place in the earth, so that man, having "died to sin" [Rom 6:2], might be "alive to God" (*Adv. Haer.*, III, 23, 6.).

Through His Incarnation, the *Logos* of creation penetrated matter, His own work. The Infinite became incarnate and subject to space; the Eternal entered time. By coming into the world, Christ transformed time and space, effecting a revolution with profound consequences. As God-Man He did not merely assume the corporeal limitations of our condition, He surpassed them. Destined to die by virtue of His Incarnation, whereby He entered into time and space, the crucified Christ bears the suffering and death of every person throughout time and space. Through His Ascension and Resurrection, He leads us beyond the cycle of time, to the never-setting sun. He heals us of the many infirmities that have left their scars on us, just as He Himself retained the mark of the nails and of the spear that pierced His side. Yet within time, it is possible for us, through communion in Christ, to redeem time and bestow upon it an eternal quality. The servant is not above the Master. Leaving the time of "this world" and "passing" into the new age can be done only through death, that is through dying to oneself.

Without the God-man, we are enclosed in space, abused by the elements, constrained by the limitations and conditions of space which isolate us and lead us ultimately to our death within time. Devoid of meaning, time affirms the absurdity of history. Conversely, living the Resurrection "spiritualizes" time and space, rendering them eternal. Once renewed, they are no longer fragmented but whole, open to a profound communion which is the fruit of every authentic encounter. Purged of the evil caused by sin, which itself is the cause of death, time becomes a source of life, a passage to eternity.

Thus the Resurrection contradicts the notion of the wise man Socrates (in Plato's *Theatetus*), who understood that evil would never disappear, since even Hell is filled with God.

Though he is born to die, man is engaged in a constant struggle to postpone death, to hide it and forget it, yet he remains aware of his inevitable defeat. This is true, however, only if we limit ourselves to biological death. From the new Adam, the vanquisher of death and of every individual death, there flows abundant life: He is "the Resurrection and the Life" (Jn 11:25). When it is perceived in the light of the Resurrection, which explains both past and future events, history as such loses its meaning; or rather it takes on a new meaning. For those who are already entering the Kingdom, the Eighth Day encompasses all things in an eternal present.

At our level, time is determined on the basis of lunar and solar cycles. Thus, with a powerful symbolism that all too often goes unrecognized, the Resurrection is celebrated after the spring equinox, on the Sunday after the full moon. Therefore the Great Feasts, and other feasts to a lesser degree, break into the sphere of ongoing time, bestowing on time a new orientation. The first of the fifteen readings for the vesperal liturgy of Holy Saturday ends on the third day of creation (Gen 1:1-13), the day Christ came out of the tomb. The "lights" that were created on the fourth day (Gen 1:14-19) correspond to the new creation and the advent of the Light. In this context, a proper understanding of the numerical symbolism is helpful. The number six, for example, in the book of Revelation, is the sign of evil. The Antichrist bears the mark of the "human number": 666 (Rev 13:17-18). Creation took place over a period of six days, and "God saw everything that He had made, and behold, it was very good" (Gen 1:31). But man desecrated this creation through his idolatry, so that the number six became a symbol of power, of the idolatry that was trampled down by Christ. The number seven, on the other hand, is universally recognized as the image of creation; it appears some forty times in the book of Revelation, as a symbol of the cosmos. It is the sum of the number four, which symbolizes the earth, and the number three, which symbolizes heaven as well as the Trinitarian mystery. Consider also the seven colors of the rainbow. However, in the book of Revelation this number is used most often to denote the end or fulfillment of a particular phase. It signifies first and foremost the "fullness of time," the Sabbath day on which God Himself rested at the end of creation. In this context, the creation of the world corresponds to the number seven, which the Bible uses without distinction to refer to the world both before and after the fall. Within the temporal rhythm of this world, the seventh day is that on

75. Theotokos Hodighitria surrounded by the prophets; 16th c. icon, Panagarati
Monastery, Romania. National Art Museum, Bucharest (Museum photo).

76. The Washing of the Feet; 12th c. fresco,
caves of the St Neophyte Monastery, Cyprus.

which man, after the image of his creator, rests from his work. And yet, this seventh day leads into a new week of exertion and work, until the end of one's life. Having become caught up in a vicious cycle, those of the Old Testament put their hope in a Messiah who would take control of time and definitively abolish it.

Through His Resurrection on the day after the Sabbath, Christ does not abolish time but rather replaces it with the new era of the Eighth Day. He is the Alpha and Omega that leads us beyond time, but He also inverts it: the last day of the week becomes the first. Pascha, the ultimate Eighth Day, marks both a departure from time and the transfiguration of the time by which human existence continues to be measured. Sunday, which represents Pascha, likewise eludes the constraints of time through the eucharistic celebration. Consequently, rather than ignore time, since this is the first day of the new age in the history of salvation, every Christian is reintroduced into time, into the world where he must serve as leaven, as salt and as light. The number eight is eschatological and marks an upward thrust, a disruption of daily life. Entering the Eighth Day enables us better to live out the seven day rhythm in which we are all involved.

The paschal liturgy as a whole constitutes an ode to joy—not the emotional and physical pleasure connected with possessions, but rather the joy of life which is inherent in the Eighth Day (Jn 15:11), the day of transfigured time. For us who remain pilgrims on this earth, that joy includes a measure of sorrow that is evident in the joyful sadness expressed by the faces in the icons of saints. And we might note in passing that the eight tones used consecutively in the Byzantine liturgy are all represented in the services of August 15, the feast of the Dormition, as a way of emphasizing the perfection of the Virgin Mary.

The week following Pascha, referred to as the "week of light" in Slavonic tradition, is known in Greek as the "week of renewal," a clear reference to the "new creation" which culminates in the "new man" created in Christ. The thought of the chasm, the immense gulf, that separates the eternal, limitless God from His human creature, who evolves in time and space, is overwhelming. Through His dual nature, Christ, the lover of man, becomes the bridge between the human and the divine. He renders time eternal and bestows upon space an infinite quality. The more man experiences the Resurrection, the greater his awareness that the only positive outcome to human existence is to be found in the acceptance and the living out of that Resurrection. This is the only antidote to evil and to a death which is henceforth assumed as a "passage" to life. While the life given to us by our parents enables us to meet the challenges of an earthly life subject to the "law of sin," to the passions and to corruption, a new birth in Christ purifies and spiritualizes the "old man," making him able to enter the gates of the Kingdom, to have his life guided by the Spirit into a place where death is no more.

Christ is He "who was and is and is to come" (Rev 4:8), "the same yesterday, today and forever" (Heb 13:8). From these sayings are derived the christocentric understanding of the Old Testament, the coincidence of the mysteries of salvation and of the saints and the eternal youth of those who are truly alive. Those who unite themselves to the body of Christ no longer belong to themselves: "It is no longer I who live, but Christ who lives in me" (Gal 2:20).

In his study, *Deification in Christ* (Crestwood, NY, SVS Press, 1987), the Greek theologian Panayotis Nellas emphasizes the difference between the historical reality and that which should have resulted from being made "in the image of God." Just as God's descent to dwell among men (Incarnation) was followed by man's ascent to dwell in God (Deification), every development and growth requires time. While man was created in the "image" of God, he needs time in order to achieve God's "likeness."

It is not sufficient to claim that the Resurrection enables us to "pass" from a condition of death to life. Such a passage must take place within the Church, through baptism which, far from being a mechanistic ritual devoid of substance, is fulfilled through communion in Christ, through one's neighbor and the Eucharist. The theandric reality which is the Church exists within time and space and evolves in the world by remaining fully rooted in heaven. It is the icon of Christ for the life of the world.

Paul Evdokimov claims that there is no ontological dualism between the Church and the world, between the sacred and the profane. The dualism is a matter of ethics: those of "the new man" and "the old man," of the sacred (redeemed) and the profane (possessed) (see his *The Art of the Icon: A Theology of Beauty*, Oakwood Publications, Redondo Beach, California, 1990). Through the mysteries of Baptism, Chrismation and the Eucharist, "the full union of the created with the uncreated within the sacraments powerfully 'overcomes' the limits of place and time without destroying them, and adds new dimensions to them" *(Deification in Christ, op. cit.,* p. 144). The liturgy, which is the realization of the mystery of salvation, sanctifies time and space, bestowing upon them an infinite and eternal quality, making them into a means of access from earth to heaven, from the visible to the invisible, from the created to the uncreated. All this is founded on the divine-human body of the Risen One. At the very heart of the mystical Body of the Church, each person understands himself or herself to be a contemporary of those deified members who have lived in every place and time.

Space and time are therefore characteristics of the Incarnation which, insofar as it is the foundation of the icon, makes the latter an essential means of encountering God in the context of prayer. Through its use of matter, the icon sanctifies the present world, though in a way unlike the Eucharist in which the bread, "the fruit of man's labor and his food," becomes the body of Christ, true God and true man. As seen through the eyes of faith, the icon sanctifies the space in which it is contained; it enables the light to shine forth as the fire of the Spirit which quickens the human heart. As the meeting place of history and eschatology, the icon transfigures time. On the one hand, it confirms the events of salvation and renders the depicted persons present. On the other hand, it anticipates the future and incorporates it into the present, thereby transforming the various dimensions of time into eternity, that is, into an eternal present.

In his search for truth, man has directed his greatest efforts toward expanding his knowledge. The end of this century has been marked by an avalanche of knowledge as never before seen in history, a flood of technology, an acceleration of change in every domain. Though he is over-informed and subject to his own inventions, man nevertheless emerges with a greater need for meaning than ever before. Time and time again we must proclaim the fact that truth is not some "thing" but rather someone, a person, the God-man Jesus Christ. He is "the way, the truth and the life" (Jn 14:6). As "the way," He alone can lead us to the "truth" in all its fullness, for no one comes to the Father but by Him, and He alone represents the fullness of humanity.

All things are from Christ and all things tend toward Him. His Resurrection gives new meaning to history; or, more accurately, it reveals its meaning. History, thus transformed, is no longer directed toward death but toward transfiguration.

All of history is rooted in the Resurrection which opens our lives onto the future by transfiguring the past. In an age when all things seem possible, any Christian seeking deification must take history into account. Together with the prayer that follows the consecration of the Holy Gifts, the eucharistic prayer of oblation expresses the proper attitude: "Thou it was who brought us from non-existence into being, and when we had fallen away didst raise us up again, and didst not cease to do all things until Thou hadst brought us up to heaven, and hadst endowed us with Thy heavenly Kingdom which is to come...Thine own of Thine own, we offer unto Thee, on behalf of all and for all" (Liturgy of St John Chrysostom). This fusion of time is suggested in the Deisis icon, which represents every time and space, the whole of human history, until the Parousia. Yet, while there does exist between the present life and the life to come a definite continuity, determined by the intensity of our life in Christ, there is also a radical change, since at the time of the Parousia, faith will give way to a vision of God (1 Jn 3:2).

As we have observed, the Risen One is not bound by the laws of time and space. He is able to come and go from several places simultaneously. Closed doors do not keep Him out. His appearance in various forms explains why his followers were unable to recognize Him immediately and serves as an indication for us that, being everywhere present, He reveals Himself henceforth to the poor, the oppressed and to all mankind: "'Lord, when

77. Deisis; exterior fresco, 1547, southern facade of the Church of
St George, Voronetz Monastery, Moldavia, Romania.

did we see thee hungry and feed thee, or thirsty and give thee drink? And when did we see thee a stranger and welcome thee, or naked and clothe thee? And when did we see thee sick or in prison and visit thee?' And the King will answer them, 'Truly, I say to you, as you did it to one of the least of my brethren, you did it to me'" (Mt 25:37-40). This significant transference leads us to encounter Christ in each and every person, beyond every mask, beyond all of our "craziness" and pathology.

St Augustine of Hippo wrote about "two different and opposed cities...where one lives according to men, and the other, according to God...However, if man lives according to man and not according to God, he is like the devil" (*The City of God*, 14:6). Man cannot serve two masters at once. Whoever does not make sacrifice to God, who does not sing His glory, sacrifices to idols of his own invention. A fallen man who turns away from the Christ who came to raise him up remains subject to history and to every temptation from which the Gospel invites him to free himself. Entering into history takes place within a body which is bound to life and death. To be nourished by a world contaminated by death perpetuates one's state of corruptibility. However, "if any one is in Christ, he is a new creation; the old has passed away, behold, the new has come" (2 Cor 5:17).

A Face of Light

> God became incarnate so that man may contemplate his face through every face. Perfect prayer seeks the presence of Christ and recognizes it in every human being. The unique image of Christ is the icon, but they are innumerable, and this means that every human face is also the icon of Christ. A prayerful attitude discovers it. (P. Evdokimov, *The Struggle With God,* Paulist Press, Glen Rock, New Jersey, 1966; p. 178)

> Every representation of the human face tends toward the image of Christ, deriving this ability from the power of His coming to earth, from the power of God made man (Monk G. Krug, *Carnets d'un peintre d'icônes,* L'Age d'Homme, p. 39).

Having been created "in the image" of God, man is able, within a transfigured time, to fulfill his destiny and achieve the divine "likeness." Just as Christ is the image of the Father, man becomes the image of Christ through the Holy Spirit, for "the Word became flesh so that we might receive the Spirit" (St Athanasius of Alexandria). The icon simply reveals man in his restored humanity, with the purified countenance of the Eighth Day, according to the divine likeness. Every face is intended to reflect God and has as its vocation to become an icon. Accordingly, during the liturgy the deacon or priest censes each of the faithful as well as the icons.

The apostle Paul appeals to the Christians of Colossea: "If then you have been raised with Christ, seek the things that are above, where Christ is, seated at the right hand of God. Set your minds on things that are above, not on things that are on earth. For you have died, and your life is hid with Christ in God. When Christ who is our life appears, then you also will appear with him in glory" (Col 3:1-4). Christ shall return in the full manifestation of His divinity: "Our God comes, He does not keep silence" (Ps 50:3), no longer to be judged as in the Incarnation, but as supreme Judge, through whom "the righteous will shine like the sun" (Mt 13:43).

To say that God is light and that man is made in the image of God means that, from the time of conception, every human being possesses a divine potential, one ready to be developed and to grow until he reaches the full stature of a "child of God" (Jn 1:12). "For this is the will of God, your sanctification" (1 Thess 4:3), which is none other than salvation and seeking the light. This is why the whole meaning of the resplendent light of the Resurrection is to be found in the promise of the coming Spirit, who alone transmits the life-giving effect of the Resurrection. The ancient Greeks understood the sun to be the heart of the world (*kardia cosmou*); but our sun is Christ, the light that illumines and warms the heart of every human being.

78. Christ Pantocrator; 15th c. icon from a Deisis, Novgorod School.
National Gallery, Oslo. (Photo: Jacques Lathion, National Gallery, Oslo)

79. The Entrance of the Righteous into Paradise; fresco, 1547 (detail),
Church of St George, Voronetz Monastery, Moldavia, Romania.

The fall of man consisted in seeking after his own image rather than that of God. This narcissistic and egocentric tendency is what turns man into a "diabolical" being, meaning separated from others and no longer a person in communion, modeled after the Holy Trinity. Conversely, a "stavrophoric" person ("who bears a cross") becomes "pneumato-phoric" (bearer of the Holy Spirit). Once stripped of the self and of every defense, his eyes are no longer turned inward. Far from resembling Narcissus and far from every idolatry, he becomes fundamentally oriented toward God and in God. Once he is restored to his role of priestly kingship, he gives himself as a free will offering. He is a liturgical being who, having become an icon, the vessel of the Word revealed in the divine light, participates in the transformation of this world into an icon.

Every human face is like a part of a whole which constitutes the face of Christ. "Adam" is the collective name given to all of humanity. Our faces which became withered in the first Adam were renewed in the new Adam, as he assumed a human face. "All of human

80. The Last Judgment (at the bottom from the center toward the left,
The Entrance of the Righteous into Paradise); fresco, 1547.
Church of St George, Voronetz Monastery, Moldavia, Romania.

nature, from the origins to the very end, is therefore a single image of the One who is" (St Gregory of Nyssa in *The Creation of Man*, XVI). The unity of Christ leads those who follow Him to live beyond every division, be it racial, national, cultural, social or otherwise. While Christ effects a new creation by assuming human nature, the Holy Spirit is given to human persons who in turn become gods: "The work of Christ and the work of the Holy Spirit are therefore inseparable. Christ creates the unity of His mystical body through the Holy Spirit; the Holy Spirit communicates Himself to human persons through Christ" (V. Lossky, *Mystical Theology, op. cit.,* p. 167).

St Basil (†379) claimed that man's origin "situates him above the light, above heaven, above the stars, above all things." Unlike the firmament which was created by His divine word, "God deigned to fashion our body with His own hands," without the work of "the Powers that serve him" (*On the Origin of Man*, II, 2). It is hardly believable, yet God summons us: "Be holy, for I am holy" (1 Pet 1:16). St Paul's invitation to a "mature manhood, to the measure of the stature of the fullness of Christ" (Eph 4:13), corresponds to the deification on which the Fathers comment at length. Man recovers his "likeness" to

God in the spiritual body of Christ. "All of us are made in the image of God. However, to be 'after his likeness' belongs only to those who, through abundant love, have bound God to their freedom" (St Diadochus of Photike, *Gnostic Chapters*, 4). The true saints are spiritual athletes who see everything in a new light, who perceive the intimate nature of things and of beings, and who sense the deepest meaning of life. As Paul Evdokimov aptly noted: "the 'ontological tenderness' of the great spiritual saints (St Isaac the Syrian and St Macarius of Egypt) toward all creatures, including reptiles and even demons, goes hand in hand with an iconographic way of contemplating the world, seeking in it the transparency of divine thought" (*The Art of the Icon, op. cit.,* p. 58). As reflections of the presence of the Spirit within them, saints such as Seraphim of Sarov have become beacons to other faithful. Nevertheless, just as Christ's divinity went unrecognized by His contemporaries—the vision of His Transfiguration was granted only to His three closest disciples—the holiness of many who are already filled with the Spirit in this life, such as St Silouan the Athonite, has remained and still remains unknown to many.

In *The Way of a Pilgrim*, a small work that conveys with such joy the essence of the Russian spiritual tradition, the anonymous author reveals that, as he walked toward Irkoutsk, he would continually recite the "prayer of the heart." Then, he says, "all that was around me appeared beautiful to me: the trees, the grass, the birds, the earth, the air, the light, everything seemed to be telling me that they existed for the sake of man, that they bore witness to God's love for man; all things were in prayer, all things were singing God's glory. In this way I understood what the *Philokalia* called 'knowing the language of creation,' and I saw how it was possible to converse with God's creatures."

There is nothing in the icon to distinguish Christ from the saints other than the cruciform halo, and at times the mandorla, which depict Him in His glory. As for the departed, the liturgy again leaves no ambiguity: "Give rest with the righteous to Thy servants, O our Savior, and make them dwell in Thy courts, as it is written, in Thy goodness passing over all their transgressions" (Saturday of the departed, Orthros, Evloghitaria, tone 5).

When we are faced with the temptation of reducing our inner life to the level of intellect and emotions, as if the true spiritual life which is union with God were no more than deception, we need to hear the word: "And this is eternal life, that they know thee the only true God" (Jn 17:3). This knowledge, or enlightenment, is the purpose of life. Light and truth constitute an inseparable pair, for we cannot find the way without light. Christ is the "Light" and the "Way," but in his freedom, man chooses between light, which requires a sustained effort, and darkness. St Symeon the New Theologian expressed the heart of the problem in these terms: "He who is blind to the One is completely blind to all things. But he who sees the One is able to contemplate the whole. He ceases to contemplate the whole so as to enter into a contemplation of the whole, yet he remains apart from that which he contemplates. Thus, when he is within the One, he sees the whole. And when he is within the whole, he sees none of it. He who sees the One sees himself and sees everything and everyone through the One. Hidden within the One, he sees nothing of all that is in the world" (see "Chapitres Théologiques et Pratiques," 35 [1:51-52] in *Philocalie des Pères Neptiques*, Bellefontaine, 1984, p. 111).

Thanks to recent developments in physiology and psychology in particular, the interaction of body and spirit is no longer in question. Every thought, whether positive or negative, influences the movement of the body, and vice versa. "Anyone who wants to look at sunlight naturally wipes his eyes clear first, in order to make, at any rate, some approximation to the purity of that on which he looks; and a person wishing to see a city or country goes to the place in order so to do" (St Athanasius, *On the Incarnation*, 57, p. 97). God dwells within a purified heart, and there He goes in search of beauty. And since we become that which we frequent, "the soul which draws near to the light also becomes light" (St Gregory of Nyssa, *Homily V on the Song of Songs*).

"Seen from above, a saint is already clothed in light, but seen from below, he never ceases to struggle" (see P. Evdokimov, *The Struggle With God, op. cit.,* p. 216). This light that is hidden away in the hearts of many will flow forth at the final resurrection.

Like a rising tide, the affirmation of the Resurrection during the paschal liturgy bursts into an overflowing joy that affects one's whole being: Christos anesti, Christus surrexit, Christos voskresse, Hristos a inviat, Al Massiah kam, Christ is risen!

The Transfiguration of the Flesh and of the Cosmos

At a time when assurance is giving way to doubt, when relativism shows signs of supplanting every notion of truth, and while godless humanism explores every fruitless avenue at man's expense, the true icon proclaims a vision of man and of the cosmos as intended for deification. Mere appearances are difficult to overcome in trying to perceive the light of the Resurrection. Every day we are confronted with the dramatic consequences of the fall which, due to its spiritual nature, eludes any scientific analysis. We are also liable to forget that Christ, the cosmic new Adam, in whom we are all called to transfiguration and spiritualization, died on the cross in order to destroy evil, suffering and particularly death, the "last enemy" (Cor 15:26). Like Joshua who prefigured Him, Jesus leads us in and through His Death and Resurrection to the heart of the Promised Land.

The apostle Peter writes: "According to his promise we wait for new heavens and a new earth" (2 Pet 3:13). This proclamation of new heavens and a new earth is present already in the prophecy of Amos (9:13ff) and is interpreted in Revelation: "Then I saw a new heaven and a new earth...and I heard a loud voice from the throne saying, 'Behold the

81. The Last Judgment and The Dormition of the Mother of God; mid-14th c.
fresco, Church of the Pantocrator, Decani Monastery, Serbia.

dwelling of God is with men. He will dwell with them, and they shall be His people, and God Himself shall be with them; He will wipe away every tear from their eyes, and death shall be no more, neither shall there be mourning nor crying nor pain any more, for the former things have passed away.' And he who sat upon the throne said: 'Behold, I make all things new'" (Rev 21:1-5).

We are faced with the same question the Virgin Mary asked of the angel Gabriel, who had come to foretell her giving birth to the Son of the Most High: "How shall this be?" (Lk 1:35). It would be presumptuous to try and answer such a question. What we know from the apostle Paul is that "the whole creation has been groaning in travail" and that "creation waits with eager longing for the revealing of the sons of God" (Rom 8:22, 18). The connection between human destiny and cosmic destiny could not be more clearly stated.

Persons who live in Christ, the New Adam, bear the world within themseves as they become members of the universal body of the Risen One, the glorified, human-divine body that is One of the Holy Trinity. Christ bears up the whole world in His resurrected body, which is not dematerialized, but rather spiritualized. As God-man and the ultimate perfection of man, His flesh is the sure sign of a metamorphosis through which the Spirit fills all things and the senses perceive the realm of divinity. Christ is the seed of the recreated universe.

"Today Christ on Mount Tabor has changed the darkened nature of Adam, and filling it with brightness He has made it godlike" (Feast of the Transfiguration, Vespers, Aposticha, tone 2). The transfiguration to which man is called involves both body and soul. "Through the two hands of the Father, namely the Son and the Spirit, it is man and not a part of man that is made into the image and likeness of God" (Irenaeus of Lyon, *Adv. Haer.*, V, 6, 1). Man is both body and soul, which make up the whole person, and therefore he is made in the image of God, not only in his soul but in his body as well, as St Gregory Palamas so adamantly maintains. As an incarnate spirit, man takes part in the world of matter and in that of spirit; he is a microcosm uniting within himself both the heavenly and earthly creations. Thus, when the soul becomes united to God, the body becomes a medium for the Spirit. For a Christian, there must be a reunification of the fundamental ontological composite of soul and body.

"Now all is filled with light: heaven and earth and the lower regions" (Paschal Canon, Ode 3). This light which has just dawned in the Nativity of Christ is present also in the Transfiguration, in the Descent into Hell, as well as in the Ascension, when all of creation is filled with His presence. This illumination is a summary of salvation history, since the Ascension includes eschatology and Christ will return at the Parousia.

The Resurrection stands in direct opposition to the notion of corruption. The gates of Hell have been shattered forever. Even though nothingness and death, the forces of evil that have already been defeated, remain present for a time, creation has been freed and has found its essential meaning and its deepest unity. Matter, which was darkened by sin, has found its translucence there where man has found a face: in Christ. The paschal summoning to rejoice echoes throughout the universe. Not a place remains in which the light of the Resurrection does not shine, though it can only be perceived through transfigured eyes.

In its faithfulness to the Tradition, the icon reveals the epiphany of form, its truest fulfillment, because it opens one's heart to the knowledge of things invisible, to the ultimate end or purpose of things and of beings. The icon raises questions about an art form that is founded on the close connection between matter and the human person. Authentic art tends to look beyond perceivable reality in order to express what is essential. In this sense it includes an eschatological dimension. Any artist with a metaphysical view of the world is able to convey its beauty and rhythm which are necessary for the transfiguration of matter.

When Dostoievsky declared that "beauty will save the world," he was referring to a spiritual, inner beauty. This is the beauty an artist must promote, rather than the illusive and seductive beauty, confused with aesthetics, which has no ontological foundation and remains foreign to goodness and truth. Far from bringing creation back to the creator, as would befit his vocation, an artist who is bound by such "demonic beauty" is shaping golden calves and sacrificing to idols. Conversely, authentic art serves beauty without creating false art. Insofar as it speaks to the very depth of one's being, it leads one naturally to speak of "holiness." The latter implies harmony, a rejection of every sort of disintegration caused by sin which pollutes and distorts the soul. Because the Resurrection stands as the only event to give meaning to man's struggle, art that is infused with resurrectional life bears witness to the harmony of a restored cosmos. A heart that is touched by this theophanic beauty is naturally drawn to contemplating its mystery. "It was for the new man that human nature was created at the beginning, and for him mind and desire were prepared. Our reason we have received in order that we may know Christ, our desire in order that we might hasten to Him. We have memory in order that we may carry Him in us, since He Himself is the archetype for those who are created. It was not the old Adam who was the model for the new, but the new Adam for the old" (*The Life in Christ*, VI, *op. cit.*, p. 190).

The history of mankind reveals a close connection between art and the altar, between worship and culture. The fact that this relationship has been forgotten lies behind the impoverishment of contemporary artistic productions, in spite of their current proliferation. This does not mean that art must be subject to the requirements of worship, as was once the case. It means that art must remain free from bias, always reverting back to Good, to the love that is expressed in all of creation, and to the harmony that was restored through Christ's Resurrection which, in a single inspired movement, does away with evil and ugliness.

Man may achieve the fullness of his stature only insofar as he fulfills his destiny, which is *theosis* or the acquisition of the Spirit. The result would be a more human world in that more and more men and women would live in Christ, relentlessly seeking Him with their whole being, as many often do without yet knowing Him.

"If anyone destroys God's temple, God will destroy him. For God's temple is holy, and that temple you are" (1 Cor 3:17). This is a far cry from the Platonic play on words: *soma-sema* (body-tomb) which sees the body as a prison rather than a vessel for the Spirit.

The human struggle for integrity leads us back to the icon. In a world filled with eroticism, where the flesh is idolized and seduces the misguided senses, where the body is reduced to a mere object of pleasure, the icon bears witness to "personhood," to spiritualized flesh and to a body whose senses are focused upon the Spirit. The violation of one's heart which accompanies the violation of one's body—even if it is in thought alone—stands in contrast to the icon which is *communion*. Ultimately, our predatory attitude on every level must be converted into the only authentic relationship, which is precisely that of communion. In his participation in both the spiritual and the material world, man must remain ever aware of the divine-humanity which is neither an escape into the purely spiritual realm, nor a capitulation to the seduction of the tangible world, but rather a spiritualization of matter. The increasing dehumanization of persons and of society stems from a lack of awareness of this divine-humanity.

As human persons become consubstantial and interdependent in Christ, we are called to true life modeled after the communion shared by the persons of the Holy Trinity. In the life in Christ there is neither individual salvation nor autonomy. To recognize Him as the head of the body of which we are all members involves a dynamic of inter-relationship, nourished by a common source, such that the suffering, the fall or the exaltation of one member concerns every other. Unity among persons can be achieved only in Christ. His Resurrection gives us the strength to forgive our enemies, to reach out to those who do not return our friendship, and to love with a selfless love. The hate, the contempt and the indifference so often witnessed today are the product of a profound loss of meaning which tends toward objectification and depersonalization.

If anyone were to submit the earth today to a medical exam, they would be horrified to discover to what extent it has been damaged, poisoned, scorched and dessicated. How blind must we be not to recognize that the condition of the earth reflects the very condition of our own mind and heart? The Aztecs, who were wiser than we are, claimed

82. St Silouan of Mount Athos; 20th c. icon.

that the earth becomes what mankind becomes. Profaning nature goes together with reducing the human person to a mere individual, profaning that which is most sacred within that person.

In his prophetic work, *Save Creation* (Paris: Desclée, 1989, p. 19), Patriarch Ignatius IV of Antioch gave this warning: "If nature is not being transfigured, it is being disfigured.

Today we are threatened both by barbarism and by suicide of the species." It is impossible to refer to the transfiguration of the new creation without taking into account the preservation of our natural environment. Every attack on nature reveals our predatory disposition and impedes the transfiguration toward which we strive. To deny or ignore our divine vocation leads to the most severe personal and social upheavals; it serves to divide rather than unite, and frustrates our most noble efforts. Rejection of God leads inevitably to allegiance to the "Beast." In his fallen and misguided state, man is capable only of exploiting the earth as a predator since, in his desperate quest for possessions and pleasure, he has lost any discernment of the "Truth," who is the Risen One. On the other hand, those who have been raised up, and who bear Christ within themselves, make out of their relationship with creation a perpetual Eucharist.

In continuity with the Old Testament passage in which "the Lord said to Abram, 'Go from your country and your kindred and your father's house to the land I will show you'" (Gen 12:1), Jesus encourages His disciples to seek detachment. Following Him implies a reversal of our values. It means going in a direction other than the way of the world, which advocates the acquisition of every kind of possession: money, power, possessions and property, with every sort of passion they entail: ambition, greed, envy and hard-heartedness. In a world where wealth is idolized, Jesus warns against laying up treasures for oneself (Mt 6:19). Instead, He preaches dispossession, abnegation and sharing: "Blessed are you poor, for yours is the kingdom of God" (Lk 6:20). It is well worth reading the passage of the temptation in the desert (Mt 4:1-11), in which the Prince of this world appeals to a possessive instinct which Jesus strongly condemns. If we realize that every form of greed stems fundamentally from a mental condition, it becomes easier to understand the efforts of the great ascetics, which consist in focusing their minds on their repentant hearts.

In the same way that our disorders, loss of inner harmony and personal disintegration can lead to similar conditions in the world around us, those who are truly "in Christ" can shape and nourish science, culture and humanity as a whole. The audience for whom the following words of Dostoievsky's were intended seems to be growing day by day:

> You who deny God and Christ have not even considered that without Christ, everything in the world would be impure and corrupt. You judge Christ and you dismiss God; but what sort of example do you yourselves offer? You are petty, debauched, greedy and arrogant! By eliminating Christ, you remove from humanity the epitome of beauty and goodness, you make Him inaccessible. For Christ came precisely for this reason: that humanity might know and recognize that a true human spirit can appear in this heavenly condition, in the flesh and not merely in a dream or in theory—that it is indeed both natural and possible. Christ's disciples proclaimed His radiant flesh to be divine. Through the cruelest of tortures they confessed the

blessing of bearing this flesh within themselves, of imitating His perfection, and of believing in Christ in the flesh (see *Carnets des Démons*, Belov An VI, 281, 155).

In the Orthodox Church, the fifth Sunday of Great Lent is dedicated to St Mary of Egypt, a woman who put an end to her life of debauchery in order to become once again a temple of the Spirit. Christ does not prefer evil-doers and prostitutes; He is a friend to all those who put away the old man of flesh and turn toward Him, those who are ready to start anew through the spiritualization of their senses, their bodies and their minds. We are brought to life when we truly believe in the Resurrection. From that moment, instead of leading to death, Christ's coming into the world leads to immortality. Then, "as countless candles are lit from a single flame, so the bodies of the members of Christ shall become what Christ Himself is" (Pseudo-Macarius, *Homily 15,* 38, PG 34, 602).

"First-born from among the dead" (Col 1:18), Jesus confirmed the resurrection in His response to the Sadducees who had come to question Him (Mk 12:18-27). Like Job who exclaimed: "from my flesh I shall see God" (Job 19:26), the early Church was grounded in its faith in the resurrection of the dead. To become convinced of this, one need only take a close look at the inscriptions in catacombs, all of which express joy and the assurance of eternal life. Not long before his martyrdom, St Ignatius of Antioch wrote to the Romans: "That is whom I am looking for—the One who died for us. That is whom I want—the One who rose for us" (*Letter to the Romans*, 6). In his novel, *The Brothers Karamazov*, Dostoievsky creates a dialogue between Alyosha and the children who are questioning him about the coming resurrection:

> "Karamazov!" cried Kolya, "can it be true what's taught us in religion, that we shall all rise again from the dead and shall live and shall see each other again, all, Ilusha too?"

> "Certainly we shall rise again, certainly we shall see each other and tell each other with joy and gladness all that has happened!" Alyosha answered, half laughing, half enthusiastic" (Epilogue, chapter 3, p. 940).

Once again, let us look to the liturgical texts to determine what is the faith of the Church:

> "Christ is risen, releasing from bondage Adam the first-formed man and destroying the power of hell. Be of good courage, all ye dead, for death is slain and hell is despoiled; the crucified and risen Christ is King. He has given incorruption to our flesh; He raises us and grants us resurrection; He counts worthy of His joy and glory all those who, with unwavering faith, have trusted fervently in Him" (Saturday of the Departed, Praises, tone 8).

Both the good and the evil alike will be raised in their bodies at the end of time, when the nations are to be judged. To use René Habachi's felicitous expression, we will have "the body of our soul" (see *Le Transgresseur*, Paris/Brussels: DDB, p. 277). What will happen, then, to those who have denied Christ or through neglect have failed to draw near to Christ during their lifetime? This is a crucial question if there ever was one!

Father Sophrony, the spiritual son of St Silouan of Mount Athos, once asserted that at the time of Christ's return in glory, tears would be shed by all men. The gift of tears, in fact, is one for which all great Spirit-bearers pray, for Christ awaits our conversion as the response to His boundless love.

> I look for the resurrection of the dead and the life of the world to come (Nicene Creed).

> But we would not have you ignorant, brethren, concerning those who have fallen asleep, that you may not grieve as others do who have no hope. For since we believe that Jesus died and rose again, even so, through Jesus, God will bring with him those who have fallen asleep (1 Thess 4:13-14).

> Of old Thou didst create me from nothingness and honoured me with Thy divine image; but when I disobeyed Thy commandment, Thou didst return me to the earth whence I was taken: lead me back again to Thy likeness, refashioning my ancient beauty (Saturday of the Departed, Orthros, Evloghitaria, tone 5).

> The second coming of Christ is not only terrifying for us (for He comes as Judge) but also glorious, for He comes in His Glory; and His glory is, at the same time, the glorification of the world and the fulfillment of all creation. The glorified condition of Christ's resurrected body will be communicated to the whole of creation; a new heaven and new earth will appear, a transfigured earth, resurrected with Christ and His humanity (S. Bulgakov, *The Orthodox Church*; New York, SVS Press, 1988; p. 183).

If immortality is of any significance to us, then we ought to be fascinated by the resurrection. This faith in the resurrection of the flesh and in eternal life precludes the very idea of a cycle of rebirth, such as in the Hindu teaching on reincarnation. We believe, nevertheless, that the notion of the mystical body of Christ extends far beyond the limits we usually ascribe to it, and that it is possible for righteous men and women of other traditions to encounter Christ in other ways. Let us not set limits on the Incarnation and on the love of God. The Church is certainly more vast than we imagine and many are those who have been baptized in the Spirit.

The Church, the Body of Christ, is undoubtedly the source of living water for those who come to quench their thirst. "In this union without confusion, within Christ, of the created and uncreated, creation becomes one with the Lord's flesh, it is mysteriously united and transfigured, becoming and living as the Body of Christ" (P. Nellas, *op. cit.*).

83. The Last Judgment and the Mother of God enthroned between two archangels;
fresco, 1643, from the wall of the old refectory, Bachkovo Monastery, Bulgaria.

Fashioned after the "spiritualized" flesh of man, the flesh of the world also becomes an icon, a presence and a "passage." As Patriarch Athenagoras, of blessed memory, would say: "The Resurrection is not the resuscitation of a body, it is the beginning of the transfiguration of the world" (see O. Clément, *Dialogues avec le Patriarche Athénagoras,* Paris: Fayard, 1976, p. 141).

84. The Last Judgment; 16th c. icon, from the village of Polana.
National Museum, Krakow (Museum photo).

7

On the "Risen Ones"

Can a person be Christian without Christ, without experiencing Him on a personal level? A Christian is precisely one who discovers the image of a face becoming engraved within the depths of his being, the face of the Risen One which underlies each face of the descendants of the New Adam. It is not enough to say that we will one day rise again. If we are truly Christian, we have already been raised. As the anonymous author of the Epistle to Diognetus (second century) states: "Christians cannot be distinguished from the rest of the human race by country or language or customs...It is true that they are 'in the flesh,' but they do not live 'according to the flesh.' They busy themselves on earth, but their citizenship is in heaven. They obey the established laws, but in their own lives they go far beyond what the laws require. They love all men, and by all men are persecuted. They are unknown, and still they are condemned...They are reviled, and yet they bless...To put it simply: What the soul is in the body, that Christians are in the world. The soul is dispersed through all the members of the body, and Christians are scattered through all the cities of the world" (*Letter to Diognetus,* 5, 6; in *Early Christian Fathers, op. cit.;* p. 216ff). This is a magnificent portrait of a Christian, one which God-bearing Fathers such as St Isaac the Syrian and St John Chrysostom were able to elaborate upon so aptly and powerfully:

> Consider that all men, be they Jews, unbelievers or murderers, are equal in goodness and honor, and that each one, by nature, is your brother, though he may have unwittingly strayed far from the truth (St Isaac the Syrian, *Ascetical Discourses* 23).

> Christ left us here below that we might spread the light...that we might be the leaven...that we might be the adults among children, that we might be spiritual amidst those who are carnal, and seeds that will bear much fruit. Actions are more profitable than words. Were we to act as true Christians, there would be no more pagans (St John Chrysostom, *Homily on the First Epistle to Timothy,* 10, 3).

One might conclude that the progressive secularization of our society stems from the unfaithfulness of Christians. "You are the salt of the earth; but if the salt has lost its taste, how shall its saltness be restored?" (Mt 5:13). The purity of one's faith determines the purity of one's life: *lex credendi, lex vivendi!* But when an image expresses the faith, it

85. The Descent into Hell; mid-16th c. Byzantine icon.
Hellenic Institute of Venice (Institute photo).

86. The Ladder of Divine Ascent; 16th c. fresco (detail), northern wall of the
Church of the Resurrection, Sucevitza Monastery, Moldavia, Romania.

cannot settle for approximations, defective and distorted elements, or anything that contradicts the truth. If these images do not convey a presence and do not express transcendence, they promote indifference and may even bear the seeds of atheism, because they have obscured the features of the Risen One.

St Paul is unambiguous: "For me to live is Christ" (Phil 1:21). As for us, we become "resurrected" when we unite our lives to Christ, when He is reflected in us and His activity is carried out through us. In other words, within the condition of being resurrected, there can be no vanity or feeling of superiority. Just the opposite is true: every step we take toward the light leads to an ever-greater awareness of our own darkness, weakness and insufficiency. This is neither a superiority nor an inferiority complex, but rather the ever-renewed confidence placed in the One who raises us up. Being resurrected means becoming aware of a progressive internal transformation, aware that our life is directed toward a specific goal and built upon an unshakable foundation. It means bearing witness to the fact that God is present in every part of the cosmos and that every tragedy becomes meaningful. Finally, it means rejecting every form of compromise over the mortal conditions that surround us. It is an uncomfortable position, to say the least, but the true life to which creation is called is achieved through the cosmic battle waged within the human heart.

Man's rejection of God has placed him in a state of illness from which he cannot recover so long as he refuses to recognize his mortality. Because the fundamental connection between death and sin is so often forgotten, we must be reminded that death is the enemy we must defeat, and that Christ died precisely for this purpose. Then the flow of our spiritual life can resume its course and our bodies will live again: "Death shall be no more" (Rev 21:4). The icon of the Descent into Hell substantiates this truth and leads us towards the future. As a passage, Pascha implies the foundation of a new way of life in which it is better to give than to receive. The values of the fallen world give way to a new perception of reality, thanks to a resurrectional vision which is that of the icon with its inverted perspective. Adherence to Christ, in a transparent and pure relationship of communion, means adherence to the light and to all that He is as light. We must therefore struggle against everything within us that keeps us apart from Him. Spiritual blindness keeps us from seeing that the light of the Risen One has already penetrated the entire cosmos.

"As you did to one of the least of these my brethren, you did it to me" (Mt 25:40). These words of Christ at the Last Judgment make love the ultimate criterion for a spiritual life. Hence Paul's insistence: "For as many of you as were baptized into Christ have put on Christ. There is neither Jew nor Greek, there is neither slave nor free, there is neither male nor female; for you are all one in Christ Jesus" (Gal 3:27-28). "You have put off the old nature with its practices and have put on the new nature, which is being renewed in knowledge after the image of the creator" (Col 3:9-10). This presence of Christ in every hungering and suffering person (Mt 25:35ff) challenges us more than any other. "He who loves his brother abides in the light, and in it there is no cause for stumbling. But he who hates his brother is in the darkness" (1 Jn 2:10-11). Love for one's neighbor is a criterion for truly belonging to Christ, who exhorts us not to judge (Mt 7:1). St Isaac the Syrian wrote that a man with a pure heart sees neither impurity nor stain in others since they invariably appear to him to be good (*Ascetical Treatise,* 85). Although things can be profaned, they are never themselves profane, for the creator Spirit of God fills all things. The sweet odor of those who bear Christ calms wild beasts and pacifies those who are in the thralldom of evil. Henceforth, one may better understand why every revolution that is not a spiritual one, meaning a *metanoia,* is only a reversal of roles where the oppressed become the oppressors.

While Christianity sees in man a fallen being, it also calls him to deification. This apposition of fallenness and ultimate exaltation is clearly reflected in the sacred texts:

> He has trampled down death by death (Paschal troparion).

> He humbled himself and became obedient unto death, even death on a cross. Therefore God has highly exalted Him and bestowed on Him the name which is above every name (Phil 2:8-9).

> I am an image of Thine ineffable glory, even though I bear the marks of sin. Take pity on Thy creature, O Master, and cleanse me in Thy loving-kindness. Grant me the fatherland for which I long, making me once more a citizen of Paradise (Saturday of the Departed, Orthros).

In our struggle against self-deification and greed, we are called to deification through death and resurrection. "The gate is narrow and the way is hard, that leads to life" (Mt 7:14). However, the way of Christ entails the purification of images and of every thought that darkens the soul, an uprooting of the passions to which we are bound and the abandonment of our garments of skin (Gen 3:21). Having become responsible for ourselves, we are constantly challenged with a choice between this world and the next. The Beatitudes encourage an emptying of the self. By leaving the world to go into the desert, the holy monks of Egypt were merely following Christ's invitation to become detached from the world. In the desert this became a necessity on every level. The kingdom of the Prince of this world, though it has already been conquered, remains manifest for a time, wielding power and deception in every form. Choosing Christ entails being misunderstood, rejected and subjected to losses every day, even in the midst of Christian communities. Just as Christ's body remains stigmatized by the marks of the spear and the nails yet is now exempt from wounds and from death, so His faithful disciples, though they may suffer physically and mentally, already mystically participate in the Resurrection. This paschal hymn thus becomes the cry of every heart that knows pain and suffers in silence, gazing upon the icon of the Savior: "Yesterday was I buried with Thee; today Thou dost raise me up, O Thou who art resurrected, though I was crucified with Thee." Because we are raised with Christ, we find the strength to die with Him.

> In Him also you were circumcised with a circumcision made without hands, by putting off the body of flesh in the circumcision of Christ; and you were buried with Him in baptism, in which you were also raised with Him through faith in the working of God, who raised Him from the dead (Col 2:11-12).

> The cup of blessing which we bless, is it not a participation in the blood of Christ? The bread which we break, is it not a participation in the body of Christ? Because there is one bread, we who are many are one body, for we all partake of the one bread (1 Cor 10:16-17).

Our true countenance emerges through our life in Christ. Having become, through grace, of one nature with the Risen One, every Christian is called to become His icon. Restored to his proper place in the world as priest, king and prophet, the Christian sees before him a boundless openness. Putting on Christ means becoming transformed by the Spirit into a state of transparency. It is a subtle transformation that most often eludes those who live "according to the flesh," and are thus incapable of perceiving the spiritual realm. Hence the disdain often shown those who are humble, gentle and guileless.

The Orthodox Church's extreme sensitivity to the Resurrection is coupled with a similar awareness of hell, which is powerfully illustrated by Christ's descent. The word of Christ that was once revealed to St Silouan of Mount Athos (†1938) makes evident the indissoluble link between humiliation and exaltation: "Keep your mind in hell and despair not!" As for St Seraphim of Sarov, who is so highly venerated today, there is a tendency to overlook the forty years of his monastic life which were lived out under the sign of the cross, in ordinary daily living, and to remember only the last eight years which were filled with light.

> If any man would come after me, let him deny himself, and take up his cross and follow me (Mk 8:34).

> What is the characteristic mark of those who eat the bread and drink the cup of the Lord? Ever to remember the One who died for us and was resurrected. What characterizes those who make such remembrance? "That they live no longer for themselves but for Him who for their sake died and was raised" (2 Cor 5:15) (Basil the Great, *Moralia*).

Do Christians have anything left to "say" to today's world? First and foremost, they must "be." In the present era of secularization, latent anti-Christianity and rising spiritualities of

87. The Ladder of Divine Ascent; 1603, refectory of the
Dionysiou Monastery, Mount Athos.

88. The Descent into Hell; two-sided icon painted in 1572 by
Longinus, Decani Monastery, Serbia.

all sorts, the Christian life is becoming the best witness to the Resurrection. It both questions and provides answers, thereby defeating every conformity and concession to the spirit of the times.

Undoubtedly, Christian art of the last few decades poses some questions. Art itself has become a new religion. Proliferating museums have become the new temples of the modern age. Meanwhile, quarrels among Christians continue to obscure the truth they are called to proclaim.

In accordance with the radical demands of the Gospel, a Christian always accepts to be out of step with the world. This is what explains the contrition of heart and the interior tension caused by the persistent rift between the human will and human action. A humble person never believes himself to be saved. Two gaping chasms are to be found on either side of the path to the Kingdom: heresy and idolatry. Heresy through words, images and actions; idolatry of every kind that our consumer society tends only to aggravate. The father of monks, Anthony the Great, claimed that "he who wishes to live in solitude in the desert is delivered from three conflicts: hearing, speach and sight; there is only one conflict for him and that is with fornication" (*Sayings of the Desert Fathers, op. cit.,* p. 174). "Blessed are the pure in heart, for they shall see God!" To achieve such blessedness, we must live with the "remembrance" of the Risen One. Christianity involves a state of tension, very unlike the "relaxation" of oriental meditations; it is a tension that takes as its model the person of Christ outstretched on the cross. This tension exists between today and tomorrow, between the old and the new, between the world and what is not of the world; it involves being in time and beyond time, in contemplation yet present to one's neighbor, being detached yet caring for the matters of this world, awaiting Christ yet contributing to culture. The Resurrection, the Ascension and Pentecost all condition our behavior. If God entered into time so as to lead us out from it, it is not in order to remove us from history, because we must not forget either the Incarnation or human reality. On the contrary, God has opened our existence to eternity, which penetrates and transfigures time. As for the Logos of creation, He is the same in the Incarnation, in the Resurrection and at the Parousia: "I am the Alpha and the Omega, the beginning and the end" (Rev 21:6).

Christ is all things for us, as St Ambrose of Milan emphasizes: "If you wish to heal your wound, He is a physician. If you have a burning fever, He is a fountain. If you are in need of help, He is strength. If you fear death, He is life. If you are fleeing darkness, He is light. If you are hungry, He is food" (*De Virginitate* 16, 99). And with the relevance that characterizes every spiritual reality, the anonymous author of the Odes of Solomon adds: "The Lord is our mirror: open your eyes and fix them upon Him, and come to know your own face!" (Ode 13).

Long before His Passion and Resurrection, Jesus said to Martha: "I am the resurrection and the life; he who believes in me, though he die, yet shall he live, and whoever lives and believes in me shall never die. Do you believe this?" (Jn 11:25-26). Everything is given, faith alone enables us to receive it. If the liturgical texts denounce Arius as the bearer of the most perverse notions, it is because in denying the identity of nature between Father and Son, he likewise denied the dual nature of the Son, thereby depriving us of any possibility for deification. The same is true for Nestorius, who challenged the notion that the Son was at once "fully man and fully God."

Islam is a religion of absolute transcendence where man moves toward a merciful yet impersonal God, who always remains distant. Christianity, on the other hand, bears witness to the same path, but in reverse: it is God who moves toward man, entering into a relationship with him. Through communion in Christ, God penetrates to the heart of our existence, in order to spiritualize our entire being. "Apart from me you can do nothing" (Jn 15:5).

A hymn to Christ offered by a tormented man is particularly moving. Consider the following excerpt from a letter written by Dostoievsky to Natalie von Vizine upon his release from prison in 1854:

> "I will say this about myself, that I am a child of this century, a child of unbelief and doubt to this very day, as I will be, I am sure, until my death. Dreadful suffering has been my lot because of my desire for faith—which is all the greater within my soul, the more arguments I find against it. Nevertheless, at times God grants me moments of perfect peace. In those times I love and find that others love me, and it is during such moments that I have made for myself a Creed according to which all things are clear and sacred. This Creed is simple; here it is: to believe that there is nothing more beautiful, more profound, more sympathetic, more reasonable, more manly or more perfect than Christ, and not only that there is nothing, but—and I say this out of a jealous love—that there can be nothing. Beyond that, if anyone were to prove to me that Christ is outside of the truth and that the truth is in fact outside of Christ, I would prefer to remain with Christ than with the truth!" (in P. Pascal, *Dostoievski,* Paris/Brussels: DDB, 1969, p. 114).

At this, the dawn of the third millennium, it is imperative that we move beyond the moral aspect of sin. Moralizing is poison to the Christian message, which is woven out of love and freedom, and not out of constraints and legalism. The Christ of the Gospels is constantly pointing a finger at the Pharisees who, nonetheless, had a highly developed moral sense. Likewise, it is important to distinguish between a religious life and a spiritual life. The first does not necessarily include the second. The spiritual life has true love as its foundation, meaning the love for one's enemies. It implies that one pray for them and wish them well from the heart: "He who abides in love abides in God and God abides in

89. The Crucifixion; mid-14th c. fresco, Church of St Nicholas, Kakopetriá, Cyprus.

him;" "You are my friends if you do what I command you;" "This I command you, to love one another" (Jn 15).

Man shares his possessions more easily than he shares of himself. He is able to give much without ever giving himself. Out of their destitution, the poor can share only their "being." From the perspective of the Gospels, the rich evolve on the level of possessions, always tormented by the more or less conscious fear of losing what they have. The poor in spirit await everything from God; having conquered fear, they are free relative to others. A growing sensitivity to the Resurrection enables a person to surpass fear and to overcome the obstacles of the kind which Christ's temptation in the desert helps put into perspective: obstacles such as giving in to passions, to the spirit of domination and to self-worship. Over against the defeatism into which we risk falling at times, we must reaffirm that Christ is our life. He alone has conquered death. He came to renew us, to restore us to our original dignity, and to free us from fear and alienation. Rather than falling into a rigid conservatism, which in our day is a common defense against anxiety, we need to put on a robe of light, the apparel of those who live without fear, since they have already conquered death and the multiple anxieties associated with it.

90. Partial view of the refectory frescoes, 1603, Dionysiou Monastery, Mount Athos.

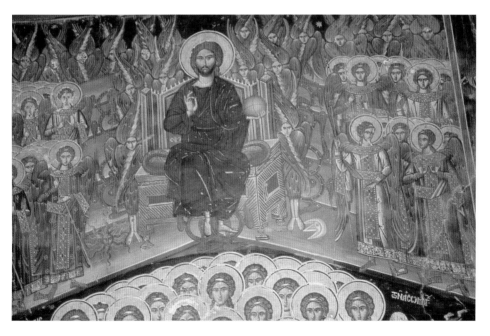

91. The Assembly of Angels around Christ; fresco, 1603 (detail),
refectory of the Dionysiou Monastery, Mount Athos.

Just prior to his exile in 403, St John Chrysostom wrote:

> Tell me, what do we have to fear?... I mock the threats of this world; I disdain
> its favors. I do not fear poverty, I do not desire wealth; I am not afraid of
> death; I wish to live only for your benefit...Do you not understand this word
> of the Lord: "When two or three are gathered together in my name, I am
> there, in the midst of them?" And where so many people are united by the
> bonds of love, will the Lord not be present with them? I have His word;
> should I trust in my own strength? I have His word; He is my support, my
> safety, my haven of peace. Should the world know total upheaval, I never-
> theless have this one Word: I can read it; it is my protection, my safety.
> Which text? "I am with you always until the end of the age." Christ is with
> me: what then shall I fear? (*First Homily Before Exile,* 1-2).

Let us remind this Faustian age, so infatuated with technology, that stands in awe of
scientific discoveries while forgetting its original maker—let us remind it that those who
succumb to self-worship and perceive themselves to be the measure of all things merely
open the door to arbitrary judgments, to deviant ideologies and to horrendous genocides.
From the distant second century, our contemporary in Christ, St Irenaeus of Lyon,
proclaimed: "The glory of God is a living person, and the life of the person is given by the
vision of God" (*Adv. Haer.,* IV, 20, 7). St Paul insists: "Be sure of this, that no fornicator
or impure person, or one who is covetous (that is, an idolater), has any inheritance in the
kingdom of Christ and of God" (Eph 5:5). While the fall was caused by an idolatry
consisting of earthly nourishment, salvation is begun through fasting, for "there is a death
which leads to life, and a life which leads to death" (St Leo the Great, *Sermon 71*, the *First
on the Resurrection, PL* 54, 388). As for the *logoi spermatikoi*, the seeds of truth, they are
present in each of the sciences. It is up to us to draw them out. This is possible, because
the measure of all things is the incarnate God, the resurrected Christ. The absolute
overthrows the relativism of a society limited to the strictly human; the infinite bursts
through our finite condition; eternity breaks down the barriers of time; meaning takes the
place of nonsense; and all things are filled with the light which is Christ. To assume
current humanist ideologies effectively obliterates the divine aspect of the God-man,
through whom, since the time of the Ascension, we find ourselves seated at the right hand
of the Father.

Without doubt the Risen One disturbs us, as do His disciples. This is why the words
which Dostoievsky's Grand Inquisitor addressed to Christ continue to resound throughout the ages:

> Why then, art Thou come to hinder us? For Thou hast come to hinder us,
> and Thou knowest that. But dost Thou know what will be tomorrow? I
> know not who Thou art and care not to know whether it is Thou or only a

semblance of Him, but tomorrow I shall condemn Thee and burn Thee at the stake as the worst of heretics. And the very people who have today kissed Thy feet, tomorrow at the faintest sign from me will rush to heap up the embers of Thy fire (*The Brothers Karamazov*, Book V, chap. 5, p. 297).

The fact that the ultimate paschal icon is that of the Descent into Hell can only inspire our reflection and move our hearts. The tragedy of the Crucifixion, with the tears of the apostles and disciples on earth, is inseparable from the destruction of the gates of Hades, with the advent of a brilliant light at the heart of darkness and the joy of the dead who were finally set free. "God our Savior...desires all men to be saved and to come to the knowledge of the truth" (1 Tim 2:5). Today, Christ continues His descent into the hell of the human condition, invisibly penetrating it with the light of the Transfiguration. The Risen One shows us the path to follow, as He invites us to recognize His tarnished image in every person, however vile and depraved they may be. The eyes of the oppressed become His eyes, the outstretched hand of the poor becomes His hand. The Wise Thief, before his conversion, was an outlaw, while Mary Magdalen was a known prostitute. Christ is mysteriously present wherever a human being is suffering; from the heart of the Beatitudes, as in the icon, He extends His hand to each one.

In his novel, *Les Sept Jours* [*The Seven Days*], Vladimir Maximov attributes these poignant words to an atheist woman:

> "It is not bread but His soul that the Other shared, that is why there was enough for everyone. It is easy to distribute what is not one's own, but try giving of what is yours. It is far from easy. Goussev does not seek justice in endless debates: he does his work, he likes his job. After his death, his work will remain. And after me? What will remain after me? Nothing but empty words. Hurry, Lachkov, hurry while you still have breath in you!"

As Jesus walked with the two disciples on the road to Emmaus, their eyes were kept from recognizing Him (Lk 24:16). Their hearts which had been cold began to burn within them as the life came to them. "The Life walked with them; but it had not yet entered their hearts. If you wish to have life, therefore, do what they did, and you will discover your Lord: they offered him their hospitality. Welcome the stranger and you will discover your Savior" (St Augustine of Hippo, *Homily 235, 2-4. PL* 38, 1117ff). The frequent appearances of Christ after His Resurrection, during which He was not immediately recognized by His followers, underscore the reality of His presence in every person we encounter. May we discover Him wherever He seems absent or rejected!

The night of Pascha brings with it an outpouring of joy. But what is left when the candles are put out and life resumes its routine, marked by struggles and temptations? Does the feast mark nothing more than an intrusion into ordinary time? Is the Resurrection merely a sedative given to Christians who want to forget the harsh realities of this world? No, Christ is risen! We no longer believe simply because of the testimony of others, we have our own conviction, grounded in our communion with the Risen One. Pascha is the Feast of feasts which leads the disciples into the joy of their master. We celebrate the Resurrection every time we find joy in our hearts, in spite of the pain that lingers there. By virtue of the Resurrection we pass beyond the limits of human history. Yet as it loses its grip on us, history—in the light of the Resurrection—comes to find its true meaning.

"I have earnestly desired to eat this passover with you before I suffer" (Lk 22:15). The Risen One has come and is knocking at the door: "Behold, I stand at the door and knock; if any one hears my voice and opens the door, I will come in to him and eat with him, and he with me" (Rev 3:20). To recall the image of St Silouan of Mount Athos, the door to human life is the heart, set ablaze as it draws near the fire.

> One day during vespers I was standing, praying before the icon of the Savior, looking at His image: "O Lord, Jesus Christ, have mercy upon me, a sinner!" With these words I saw, in place of the icon, the Living Lord Jesus, and the grace of the Holy Spirit filled my soul and my body. And I knew in the Holy Spirit that Jesus Christ is God, and I was taken with a desire to suffer for Him.
>
> Ever since that moment, my soul burns with the love of God. I am no longer drawn to earthly things. God is my joy and my strength, my wisdom and my wealth (*Écrits spirituels,* Bellefontaine, 1976, p. 75).

Any iconographer worthy of his calling can only approach the depicted subject in an attitude of fervent prayer, with tears and repentance. The "Jesus Prayer" ("Lord, Jesus Christ, Son of God, have mercy upon me") consists in leading one's mind down into the heart, in unifying one's being, thereby developing the image of Christ within the inner person and allowing it to fill one's entire life. A true iconographer does not sketch works for others to admire. Rather, in a humble gesture, having as his guide the Tradition which makes of the Church Fathers the true creators of icons, he lends his hands to the action of the Spirit. In the manner of a priest, he offers to the the world the image of the One who became incarnate and assumed our countenance in order to restore it to its initial beauty.

The Church is the assembly of those who bear witness to the Resurrection. It is the sacrament of the presence of Christ, represented in the icon and made manifest in the liturgy. As such, the Church grows and develops by virtue of a continually renewed Pentecost. The icon prepares our mind and heart for the very essence of the liturgy: the eucharistic celebration, the focus of the Christian mystery through the presence of the Risen One (In this regard, the meal at Emmaus inevitably comes to mind). Through the bread and wine the whole of human and cosmic reality is penetrated and enlivened by the

92. The Descent into Hell, The Ascension, The Dormition; fresco, 1495 (detail),
Church of St Mamas, Louvarás, Cyprus.

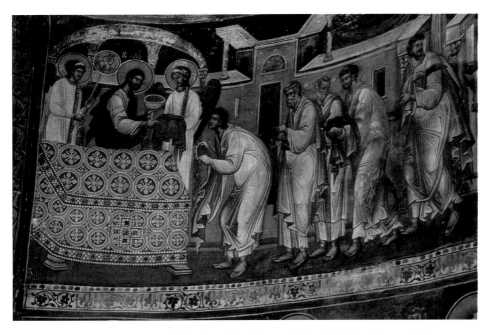

93. The Communion of the Apostles; fresco, 1313-1314 (detail), apse of the
Church of the Mother of God, Studenica Monastery, Serbia.

presence of Christ. As the very image of the Eucharist, the icon renders divinity itself present at the heart of matter. Material substances thereby become an image of the Kingdom that is to come yet is already invisibly present among us.

If Christ is our Pascha, we celebrate this Pascha every time we conform our lives to the Beatitudes and clothe ourselves with Christ. We are then resurrected, to dwell in communion with heaven and earth; we become citizens of the Eighth Day and of the New Creation which is the Kingdom of God. This transformation is neither cosmetic nor superficial; it is ontological: "In my Kingdom, I shall be God, and you shall be gods with me!" (Holy Thursday, Matins, Ode 4).

Conclusion

> "Christ died and lived again, that he might be Lord of both of the dead and of the living" (Rom 14:9).

"My joy, Christ is risen!" declared St Seraphim of Sarov as he greeted his visitors. What good are culture and science and technological advancements without faith in the Resurrection? Yet even that is not enough, because the demons themselves believe in it. We must go further and confess Christ's Resurrection with a pure heart. We must commune intensely with it, every day of our life. "O Christ, great and all holy Pascha! O Wisdom, Word and Power of God! Grant us to partake of Thee more fully in the never ending day of Thy Kingdom!" (Liturgy of St John Chrysostom, Prayer after communion).

In this book we have attempted to show the way in which the mystery of salvation is condensed and reflected in the Resurrection of Christ. We have noted the theological and symbolic depth of the icon, the coherence of the liturgical cycle, and the convergence of iconography with the liturgical texts. We now have a better understanding of the way in which a decadent icon betrays the truth, caricatures the mystery of salvation, and paves the way for atheism. History has demonstrated that heresy in images often precedes heresy in words.

The icon, together with the Orthodox liturgy whose content it explains and extends, demands that we return to the sources of the undivided Church. Over and above theological arguments, the icon enables us to refocus our life, to make a firm confession of Christ's Resurrection and of our own resurrection to come. "Let the heavens be glad, and let the earth rejoice. Let the whole world, visible and invisible, keep the feast. For Christ is risen, our eternal joy!" (Paschal Matins, Ode 1).

Let us leave the final words to the liturgical texts themselves, by quoting from the second part of the homily of St John Chrysostom read during the matins of Pascha:

> The table is full-laden; feast ye all sumptuously.
> The calf is fatted; let no one go hungry away.
> Enjoy ye all the feast of faith, receive ye all the riches of loving-kindness.
> Let no one bewail his poverty, for the universal kingdom has been revealed.
> Let no one weep for his iniquities, for pardon has shone forth from the grave.
> Let no one fear death, for the Savior's death has set us free.
> He that was held prisoner of death has annihilated death.
> By descending into Hell, he made Hell captive.
> He embittered it when it tasted of His flesh.
> As Isaiah prophesied, crying out:

94. Christ Raising Adam; fresco, 1315-1321 (detail), funeral chapel of the
Church of the Holy-Savior-in-Chora, Kahrié Djami, Constantinople.

Hell was embittered, when it encountered Thee in the lower regions.
It was embittered, for it was mocked.
It was embittered, for it was overthrown.
It was embittered, for it was fettered in chains.
It took a body, and met God face to face.
It took earth, and encountered Heaven.
It took that which was seen, and fell upon the unseen.
O Death, where is thy sting?
O Hell, where is thy victory?
Christ is risen, and thou art overthrown.
Christ is risen, and the demons have fallen.
Christ is risen, and the angels rejoice.
Christ is risen, and life reigns.
Christ is risen, and not one dead remains in the grave.
For Christ, being risen from the dead, has become the first-fruits of those who have
fallen asleep.
To Him be glory and dominion unto ages of ages! Amen.

"Truly He is risen!"

List of Illustrations

Cover: The Descent into Hell; contemporary icon, painted in Russia.

1. The Visible and Invisible Church; 16th c. fresco, Church of the Resurrection, Sucevitza Monastery, Moldavia, Romania.

2. The Virgin of the Sign surrounded by angels and the righteous; fresco, 1535, Church of the Dormition of the Mother of God, Humor Monastery, Moldavia, Romania.

3. Christ Pantocrator; 18th c. fresco, Church of the Xeropotamou Monastery, Mount Athos, Greece.

4. The Creation of the Heavens; 12th c. mosaic, Monreale Cathedral, Sicily.

5. The Creation of Adam and the Animals; 12th c. mosaic, Monreale Cathedral, Sicily.

6. The Prophet Elijah; icon, first half of the 13th c., Church of St John Lampadistis Monastery, Kalopanayotis. Byzantine Museum of Nicosia, Cyprus.

7. The Raising of the Son of the Widow of Nain; 14th c. fresco, Church of the Pantocrator, Decani Monastery, Serbia.

8. The Raising of Lazarus; late 15th c.-early 16th c. icon, two-sided tablet, from the Cathedral of St Sophia of Novgorod. History and Architecture Museum, Novgorod.

9. The Apostle Paul; late 13th c. icon, Panagia Chrisaliniotissas Church. Byzantine Museum of Nicosia, Cyprus.

10. The Descent into Hell; 1191 fresco (detail), St George Church, Kurbinovo, Macedonia.

11. Christ Pantocrator together with the Mother of God and John the Baptist, with the twelve apostles on either side. Byzantine icon, 1545. Bishopric Museumof Roman, Romania.

12. St Macarius the Egyptian; fresco painted in 1378 by Theophan the Greek, Church of the Transfiguration of Ilina Street, Novgorod, Russia.

13. St John the Baptist; 15th c. icon, element of a Deisis, Novgorod School. National Gallery, Oslo.

14. Theotokos Orans (Virgin of the Sign); 18th c. icon, Russia. Private collection, France (Photo: Victor Bakchine).

15. Mandylion ("acheiropoieic image," that is not made with human hands); scenes around the border of the icon: 1) King Abgar sends a messenger to Christ, 2) who makes an impression of his face on a napkin 3) before offering it to the messenger 4)who takes it to the king; 16th c. icon, Sts Cosmos and Damien Church of Lokov-Venecia. National Slovenian Gallery, Bratislava.

16. Christ Enthroned; early 17th c. icon, from an iconostasis of Petesti, region fo Arges, Romania. National Art Museum, Bucharest.

17. Christ separating the wheat from the tares (parable); 19th c. fresco, Church of the Pantocrator, Decani Monastery, Serbia.

18. The Parable of the Wise and Foolish Virgins; fresco, 1335-50, Church of the Decani Monastery, Serbia.

19. The Descent into Hell; 12th c. (?) fresco, Karanlik Kilise, Cappadocia.

20. The Descent into Hell; mid-11th c. fresco, Church of St Nicholas, Kakopetria, Cyprus.

21. The Descent into Hell; late 15th c. icon, from the iconostasis of the Church of the Dormition of Volotovo, near Novgorod. History and Architecture Museum, Novgorod.

22. The Descent into Hell and the Last Judgment; fresco, 1315-21, funeral chapel of the Church of the Holy-Savior-in-Chora, Kahrié Djami, Constantinople.

23. The Descent into Hell; icon, ca. 1680, from the iconostasis of the Cotroceni Monastery, near Bucharest, Romania. National Art Museum, Bucharest (Museum photo).

24. The Myrrhbearing Women at the Tomb; 20th c. icon, private collection, Switzerland.

25. The Myrrhbearing Women at the Tomb; fresco, 1637 (?), from the nave of the Church of the Nativity, side wall, Arbanassi, Bulgaria.

26. The Descent into Hell; composite icon, early 19th c., Russia. Private collection.

27. The Descent into Hell; composite icon, center portion of a portable triptych, 17th c., Abou Nidal collection, Lebanon. (Photo: U. Held. Reproduced with permission of the Archeology and History Institute of the University of Lausanne)

28. The Descent into Hell; composite icon, early 19th c., Russia. Private collection (Photo: Victor Bakchine).

29. The Appearance to the Mother of God and to Mary Magdalen; icon painted in 1546 by Theophan the Cretan, Stavronikita Monastery, Mount Athos.

30. The Appearance to Mary Magdalen (Raboni); fresco, 1335-1350, Church of the Pantocrator, Decani Monastery, Serbia.

31. The Doubt of Thomas; late 15th c., early 16th c. icon, two-sided tablet, from the Church of St Sophia, Novgorod. Architecture and History Museum, Novgorod.

32. The Doubt of Thomas; early 16th c. Russian icon (Novgorod). Icon Museum, Recklinghausen, Germany (Museum photo).

33. Icon of the Twelve Great Feasts with the Descent into Hell in the center; 18th c., Russia. Private collection, Switzerland. (Photo: Elsa Bloch-Diener Gallery, Berne.)

34. The Nativity of the Virgin Mary; 20th c. icon, painted in Russia.

35. The Presentation of Mary in the Temple; mid-18th c. icon, from an iconostasis and a workshop in Valachia, Romania. National Museum, Bucharest.

36. The Annunciation, known as *Oustiog*; late 12th c. icon, Novgorod. Tretiakov Gallery, Moscow.

37. The Annunciation; icon, ca. 1560, from the iconostasis of the Cathedral of the Nativity of the Mother of God, Antoniev Monastery, Novgorod. Architecture and History Museum, Novgorod.

38. The Archangel Gabriel; detail from a fresco, 1388-1391, Church of the Cozia Monastery, Transylvania, Romania.

39. The Double Annunciation, at the well and in the house; late 15th c. fresco, Church of the Holy Cross, Pelénderi, Cyprus.

40. The Nativity of Christ; 20th c. icon, inspired by that of the Rublev School (early 15th c., Russia).

41. The Nativity of Christ; 16th c. icon, painted by Longinus, Decani Monastery, Serbia.

42. The Nativity of Christ; early 16th c. icon, Moscow School. National Gallery, Oslo. (Photo: Jacques Lathion, National Gallery, Oslo)

43. The Meeting or Presentation in the Temple; mid-16th c. icon, Moldavia, Romania. (Photo: National Art Museum, Bucharest)

44. The Baptism of Christ; fresco, 1637 (?), side wall of the nave of the Church of the Nativity, Arbanassi, Bulgaria.

45. The Baptism of Christ; 15th c. icon, St Thekla Chapel, Greek Patriarchate, Jerusalem.

70. The Dormition of the Mother of God; 16th c. fresco, from the gate of the Pietra Neamt Monastery, Moldavia, Romania.

71. The Dormition of the Mother of God; fresco, 1365 (detail), Church of St Clement chapel, Ochrid, Macedonia.

72. The Holy Trinity; icon painted in 1411 by Andrei Rublev for the Trinity-Saint Sergius Monastery. Tretiakov Gallery, Moscow.

73. The Holy Trinity; fresco painted in 1378 by Theophan the Greek, Church of the Transfiguration of Ilina Street, Novgorod, Russia.

74. The Descent into Hell; fresco, 1494, Church of Stavrou tou Agiasmati, Platanistássa, Cyprus.

75. Theotokos Hodighitria surrounded by the prophets; 16th c. icon, Pangarati Monastery, Romania. National Art Museum, Bucharest (Museum photo).

76. The Washing of the Feet; 12th c. fresco, caves of the St Neophyte Monastery, Cyprus.

77. Deisis; exterior fresco, 1547, southern facade of the Church of St George, Voronetz Monastery, Moldavia, Romania.

78. Christ Pantocrator; 15th c. icon from a Deisis, Novgorod School. National Gallery, Oslo. (Photo: Jacques Lathion, National Gallery, Oslo)

79. The Entrance of the Righteous into Paradise; fresco, 1547 (detail), Church of St George, Voronetz Monastery, Moldavia, Romania.

80. The Last Judgment (at the bottom, from the center toward the left, The Entrance of the Righteous into Paradise); fresco, 1547, Church of St George, Voronetz Monastery, Moldavia, Romania.

81. The Last Judgment and The Dormition of the Mother of God; mid-14th c. fresco, Church of the Pantocrator, Decani Monastery, Serbia.

82. St Silouan of Athos; 20th c. icon.

83. The Last Judgment and the Mother of God enthroned between two archangels; fresco, 1643, from the wall of the old refectory, Bachkovo Monastery, Bulgaria.

84. The Last Judgment; 16th c. icon, from the village of Polana. National Museum, Krakow (Museum photo).

85. The Descent into Hell; mid-16th c. Byzantine icon. Hellenic Institute of Venice (Institute photo).

86. The Ladder of Divine Ascent; 16th c. fresco (detail), northern wall of the Church of the Resurrection, Sucevitza Monastery, Moldavia, Romania.

87. The Ladder of Divine Ascent; fresco, 1603, refectory of the Dionysiou Monastery, Mount Athos.

88. The Descent into Hell; two-sided icon painted in 1572 by Longinus, Decani Monastery, Serbia.

89. The Crucifixion; mid-14th c. fresco, Church of St Nicholas, Kakopetriá, Cyprus.

90. Partial view of the refectory frescoes, 1603, Dionysiou Monastery, Mount Athos.

91. The Assembly of Angels around Christ; fresco, 1603 (detail), refectory of the Dionysiou Monastery, Mount Athos.

92. The Descent into Hell, The Ascension, The Dormition; fresco, 1495 (detail), Church of St Mamas, Louvarás, Cyprus.

93. The Communion of the Apostles; fresco, 1313-1314 (detail), apse of the Church of the Mother of God, Studenica Monastery, Serbia.

94. Christ Raising Adam; fresco, 1315-1321 (detail), funeral chapel of the Church of the Holy-Savior-in-Chora, Kahrié Djami, Constantinople.

Glossary

Acheiropoieic: Image of the Savior "not made with human hands." It is the image of Christ that was miraculously imprinted on a cloth to be sent to King Abgar of Edessa and then moved to Constantinople in the tenth century.

Anastasis: From the Greek, *raising up.* In the paschal icon of the Descent into Hell, which bears the Greek inscription *Anastasis,* the risen Christ raises Adam and, through him, all of humanity.

Apocrypha: Texts included among the books of Scripture which have not been universally recognized as canonical (i.e., not accepted as authoritative by some Christian denominations).

Apophthegmata: Sayings, words of Life spoken by one of the Desert Fathers.

Archetype: Original pattern or model.

Arianism: This heresy, which was condemned by the 1st Ecumenical Council of Nicaea in 325, was elaborated by a priest from Alexandria, Arius, who professed a fundamental difference between God and Christ. He denied Christ's divinity and considered rather as the supreme creature chosen by God to effect the salvation of the world.

Axus mundi: Latin expression meaning the *axis of the world.*

Canons (for icons): Rules and teachings of the Orthodox Church that define the form and content of the icon as well as its veneration.

Christophoric: From the Greek meaning *bearer of Christ.*

Church Fathers: Particular writers and teachers among the Christians of the early centuries of the Church recognized as proponents and defenders of the true faith, unparalleled witnesses of the teachings of Christ. By referring to them in this way, the Church affirms the importance of their teachings for our understanding of and faithfulness to the Gospel.

Deisis: Which means *Intercession.* Christ enthroned with the Theotokos on his right, representing the New Testament Church, and John the Baptist on his left, representing the Old Testament Church. This prayer of the Church for the world is the central theme of the iconostasis.

Ecclesia Domestica: Latin meaning *house church.* "For where two or three of you are gathered in my name, there am I in the midst of them" (Mt 18:20).

Ecumenical Councils: Among its many councils, the Orthodox Church calls *ecumenical* (gathering the people of the whole empire) only seven which have defined with the greatest authority the faith of the Church and the mystery of Christ. The first was that of Nicaea, in 325, while the last was the second Nicaean council held in 787.

Eschatology: Pertaining to the end times. Christians know they will rise with Christ at his Second Coming in the *Parousia*, but if they live in Christ they have already been raised: the Kingdom is within them. In this sense, eschatology is already realized.

Forerunner: name designating St John the Baptist who preceded and announced Christ's coming.

Gladsome Light: Vesperal hymn in praise of Christ, marking the setting of the sun and the lighting of lamps.

Hades: Greek name for the god of hell in Greek mythology. The people of Israel imagined a vast underground realm where the souls of the dead remained. It is called *Sheol* in the Old Testament. The term is often used in the New Testament to refer to the realm of death which Christ conquered.

Hesychasm: From the Greek *hesychia,* meaning rest, silence, tranquillity. From the fourth century on the hesychasts were hermits in search of unceasing prayer. This movement grew well beyond the confines of monasteries toward the end of the thirteenth century under the influence of the *Philocalia,* a well known work that is to this day recommended to anyone wishing to progress in the spiritual life. The unceasing prayer of the hesychasts is now known as the *Jesus Prayer* or *Prayer of the Heart,* usually rendered: "Lord, Jesus Christ, Son of God, have mercy upon me a sinner."

Heterodox: Who does not confess the faith of the Orthodox Church.

Hieratic: From the Greek: *pertaining to sacred things.* Attitudes and ritual movements which draw one's attention to a transcendent reality.

Hypostasis: An important word in Orthodox theology used to designate the *person.* When we say that Christians are called to *be,* we mean that they must become *persons* (hypostases). This implies a life of *communion,* in relation to God and to others (the living and the dead), modeled after the Holy Trinity.

Iconoclast: Enemy and destroyer of icons.

Iconophile: From the Greek meaning *lover of images.* He who takes the part of holy icons.

Julian Calendar: This calendar, which was established by Julius Caesar and runs thirteen days behind the astronomical calendar, was replaced by the Gregorian (civil) calendar. While the *new calendar* has been adopted by part of the orthodox community, the *old calendar* is still widely used in liturgical practice.

Kenosis: From the Greek meaning *to empty oneself.* Saint Paul uses this word to express Christ's ultimate condescension: "He emptied himself, taking the form of a servant, being born in the likeness of men. And being found in human form he humbled himself and became obedient unto death, even death on a cross" (Phil 2:7-8).

Kontakion: Liturgical hymn sung at nearly all the daily offices.

Lex orandi, lex credendi: "The rule of worship is the rule of faith." That which we express in our worship is what we believe.

Litia: Intercessory prayer said during Vespers on the eve of feast days.

Liturgical texts: There are many liturgical books in addition to the text for the Divine Liturgy, the principal ones being.
the *Horologion*: *Orthros* (Matins and Praises), the Hours (First, Third, Sixth and Ninth), Vespers and Compline.
the *Menaion*: Twelve volumes containing the daily services for fixed feasts and saints' days.
the *Lenten Triodion*: For the period prior to Pascha.
the *Pentecostarion*: For service from Pascha to Pentecost.
the *Euchologion*: A collection of prayers for various occasions which includes the *Psalter*, Old Testament readings and passages from the Gospels and the Epistles.

Matins: Morning service. In parish practice, the Matins of feasts are often celebrated immediately after Vespers on the previous night. This is known as the *Vigil* service.

Metanoia: From the Greek meaning *turning about,* a change heart, a conversion and repentance.

Microcosm: From the Greek meaning *little world.* Man sums up the universe within himself.

Microtheos: From the Greek *little god.* This term can be used to describe man created *in the image of God.*

Monophysite: Designation of Christians who did not accept the fourth ecumenical council (Chalcedon, 451) that referred to Christ as one *person* or *hypostasis in two natures*—human and divine. Christ is indeed fully man and fully God.

Myrrhbearing Women: Holy women who, on the day after the Sabbath, carried spices to the Tomb to anoint Christ's body.

Mystical body: The assembly of faithful, both living and dead, who abide in Christ.

Nestorianism: This heresy was condemned by the third ecumenical council (Ephesus, 431). It had been put forth by the Patriarch of Constantinople, Nestorius, who saw in Christ separate elements, human and divine, thus denying the unity of his person.

Ode: Old Testament canticle included in the service of Matins.

Ontological: pertaining to being, to essence.

Orthodox: From the Greek *Orthos* (right) and *Doxa* (faith and worship). That which agrees with the faith of the Church, particularly as expressed in the seven ecumenical councils.

Orthros: Greek name for the service of Matins with the Praises.

Parousia: From the Greek meaning *presence.* The second coming of Christ which the Church actively awaits.

Paschal Canon: Collection of eight *Odes* sung at Pascha and during the following week, also known as the *Week of Renewal* or *Bright Week*.

Philanthropos: From the Greek meaning *lover of man.* The Orthodox Liturgy often refers to Christ as the "Lover of mankind."

Philokalia: From the Greek meaning *lover of beauty.* Composed between the fourth and the fourteenth centuries, these fundamental and incomparably rich texts convey the spirituality of the Orthodox tradition.

Pneumatophoric: From the Greek meaning *bearer of the Spirit.*

Praises: Readings from the service of Matins including Psalms 148-150. It also refers to the stichera sung at this time.

Staretz: From the Russian meaning the *elder*. A monk or hermit of the Eastern Church who has become known as a spiritual father.

Stichera: Composed hymns sung at "Lord I call…" and at the Praises, interspersed with Psalm verses. The name is also applied to the verses of the Litya, the Aposticha (at Vespers) and to the verses following the Gospel reading at Matins.

Theophoric: From the Greek meaning *bearer of God.*

Theotokos: From the Greek meaning *she who gave birth to God.* As the bearer of Christ who is both fully man and fully God, the Virgin Mary was confessed to be the "Mother of God" by the third ecumenical council (Ephesus 431).

Troparion: Liturgical composition intended to convey the theme of a given feast.

Wise thief: One of the two crucified with Jesus. Full of remorse, he spoke these words: "Remeber me when you come into your kingdom." To which Christ answered: "Truly, I say to you, today you will be with me in Paradise" (Lk 23:42-3).
Thus the cross becomes the means for his entrance into paradise.

Index

Page references in bold indicate illlustrations.

Other Titles on Iconography from
ST VLADIMIR'S SEMINARY PRESS

The Meaning of Icons

Leonid Ouspensky and Vladimir Lossky

This revised edition of the classic work on iconography speaks of the techniques, language and interpretation of icons in the context of theology and faith. Wide use of Scripture, liturgical texts and patristic sources illumine the commentary and analysis of the main types of icons. Lavishly illustrated, this edition contains more than four times the number of color plates of the original volume. 160 pages of text with drawings, 13 black and white and 51 color plates.

> *"In the nearly 40 years since the publication of the first German edition of this book, it has lost virtually none of its value for researchers, collectors, and in general anyone interested in iconography."*
> Konrad Onasch, *Thologische Literaturzeitung*

9 x 12 in., 244 pp.
Paper 0-913836-99-0 $39.95
Hard 0-913836-77-X $49.95

The Theology of the Icon

Leonid Ouspensky

The most comprehensive introduction available to the history and theology of the icon. It surveys the development of the sacred art of the Christian East from its beginnings in catacomb art through the iconoclastic controversies of the eighth and ninth centuries to the development of early Russian iconography and the state of iconographic art today.

> *"...every student of icons and of the Orthodox Church, and indeed anyone interested in sacred art should take time to read [The Theology of the Icon]."*
> John Yiannias, *Religious Studies Review*

2 volume set:Vol. I: 200 pp., 23 b/w plates.
              Vol. II: 328 pp. 25 b/w plates, 4-panel color fold-out.
Set 0-88141-124-8 $26.95

The Icon
A Window on the Kingdom
Michel Quenot

There has been a recent "rediscovery" of icons by Western Christians, and an increasing awareness that the icon is not merely a work of art, but also an aspect of divine revelation. To achieve a full understanding of the icon, one must comprehend its organic unity: artistic, spiritual theological. Already published in eight languages, this brief yet highly descriptive history of iconography includes discussion of the canons governing iconography, its theological and biblical foundations, and iconographic themes. 25 color photos and 34 illustration.

"This book is a welcome addition to the middle-of-the-range literature on icons. It is generously illustrated."
John Baggley, *Sobornost*

0-88141-098-5   176 pp. $16.95

Doors of Perception
Icons and their Significance
John Baggley and Richard Temple

This perceptive introduction to icons offers an entry to the understanding of the significance and the spirituality of icons. Among the topics covered are historical background, biblical language, the visual language of icons and their interpretation. Will be welcomed by art lovers and all who are interested in understanding more about icons. 19 color plates.

"I would vote this book as probably the best introduction to icons that we have at present."
Roman Lewicki, J.J., *VJTR*

0-88141-071-3   160 pp. $15.95

Iconostasis
Pavel Florensky

Born in 1882, Fr. Pavel Florensky was a brilliant philosopher, theologian, scientist, and art historian who, in 1911, became an Orthodox priest. By the time of the 1917 Bolshevik revolution, Fr. Pavel had become a leading voice in Russia's great movement in religious philosophy. in 1922 he was arrested on false charges, tried, imprisoned, and in 1937, was murdered by KGB directive. *Iconostasis* is Fr. Pavel's final theological work. Composed in 1922, it explores in highly original terms the significance of the icon: its philosophic depth, its spiritual history, its empirical technique. Fr. Pavel also sketches a new history of both Western religious art and the Orthodox icon.

0-88141-117-5   168 pp. $9.95

On the Divine Images

St. John of Damascus

St. John of Damascus wrote these three treatises *Against Those Who Attack the Divine Images*, in response to the iconoclastic heresy of the eighth century, which violently rejected Christian veneration of images. He reminds us that the use of images is a necessary safeguard to the doctrine of the Incarnation of Christ.

"[This] book accomplishes its most important purpose, to make available for class-room use a significant text in an inexpensive edition."
Robert L. Wilken, *Religious Studies Review*

0-913836-62-1   106 pp. $8.95

On the Holy Icons

St. Theodore the Studite

Written in the midst of the iconoclastic controversy of the eighth and ninth centuries, these essays affirm the Incarnation and its meaning for icon veneration and life in Christ, focusing on the relation between the image and the prototype.

"This is a welcome book. A convenient and inexpensive version of a patristic text of seminal importance in the history of Byzantine theology during a period crucial to the formation of the Byzantine synthesis."
R. Taft, S.J., *Orientalia Christiana Periodica*

0-913836-76-1   115 pp. $8.95

ST VLADIMIR'S SEMINARY PRESS

575 Scarsdale Rd., Crestwood, NY 10707
1-800-204-2665